Antonio Rosmini, Henry Parry Liddon

Of the Five Wounds of the Holy Church

Antonio Rosmini, Henry Parry Liddon

Of the Five Wounds of the Holy Church

ISBN/EAN: 9783337003531

Printed in Europe, USA, Canada, Australia, Japan

Cover: Foto ©Lupo / pixelio.de

More available books at **www.hansebooks.com**

Works by the same Author.

Large Type. 24mo. 1s.
PRAYERS FOR A YOUNG SCHOOLBOY. By the late E. B. PUSEY, D.D. With a Preface by H. P. LIDDON, D.D.

Cheap Edition, Revised. Small 8vo. 2s. 6d.; or in Paper Cover, 1s. 6d.
SOME ELEMENTS OF RELIGION. Lent Lectures.
The Crown 8vo (Fourth) Edition, 5s., may still be had.

Sixth Edition, Revised. Crown 8vo. 5s.
SERMONS PREACHED BEFORE THE UNIVERSITY OF OXFORD. First Series, 1859-1868.

Third Edition. Crown 8vo. 5s.
SERMONS PREACHED BEFORE THE UNIVERSITY OF OXFORD. Second Series, 1868-1882.

Second Edition, with new Preface, 1882. Crown 8vo. 2s. 6d.
THOUGHTS ON PRESENT CHURCH TROUBLES. Occurring in Four Sermons preached in St. Paul's Cathedral in December 1880. With a Preface.

Ninth Edition, Revised. Crown 8vo. 5s.
THE DIVINITY OF OUR LORD AND SAVIOUR JESUS CHRIST: Eight Lectures preached before the University of Oxford, in the Year 1866, on the Foundation of the late Rev. JOHN BAMPTON, M.A., Canon of Salisbury.

DIE GOTTHEIT UNSERES HERRN UND HEILANDES JESU CHRISTI. Acht Vorlesungen gehalten von H. P. LIDDON, Domherr und Professor an der Universität Oxford. Autorisirte Uebersetzung der 7. Auflage. Mit einem Vorwort von Ph. Fr. Mader, deutscher Pfarrer in Nizza. Basel Bahnmaier's Verlag (C. Dethoff. 1883).

Second Edition. 8vo. 2s. 6d.
WALTER KERR HAMILTON, BISHOP OF SALISBURY. A Sketch.

Crown 8vo. 3s. 6d.
REPORT OF PROCEEDINGS AT THE REUNION CONFERENCE, held at Bonn, September 1874. With a Preface by H. P. LIDDON.

WORKS BY THE REV. DR. LIDDON—Continued.

Crown 8vo. 3s. 6d.

REPORT OF PROCEEDINGS AT THE RE-UNION CONFERENCE OF 1875, with Preface by H. P. LIDDON. [London: B. M. PICKERING.]

Fourth Edition. With Portrait. Large Type. 24mo. 2s. 6d.

A MANUAL FOR THE SICK; with other Devotions. By LANCELOT ANDREWES, D.D., sometime Lord Bishop of Winchester.

The Recovery of St. Thomas. A Sermon preached in St. Paul's Cathedral on the Second Sunday after Easter, April 23, 1882. With a Prefatory Note on the late Mr. Darwin. Second Edition. 8vo. 1s.

Phœbe in London: A Sermon preached at the Parish Church of Kensington on the Second Sunday after Trinity, June 10, 1877, for the Parochial Mission Women Association. 8vo. 1s.

Bishop Wilberforce: A Sermon preached at the Parish Church of Graffham, Sussex, on its Reopening after Restoration, Nov. 2, 1875. 8vo. 1s.

Love and Knowledge: A Sermon preached in King's College Chapel, at its Inauguration on the Twenty-second Sunday after Trinity, 1873. 8vo. 1s.

The One Salvation: A Sermon preached in St. Paul's Cathedral on the Fifth Sunday after Easter, 1873, at the Anniversary Service of the Bishop of London's Fund. 8vo. 1s.

The Moral Groundwork of Clerical Training: A Sermon preached at the Anniversary Festival of Cuddesden College on Tuesday, June 10, 1873. 8vo. 1s.

St. Paul's and London: A Sermon preached at St. Paul's Cathedral on the Fourth Sunday after Epiphany, 1871. 8vo. 6d.

The Day of Work: A Sermon preached in St. Paul's Cathedral on Sunday, August 6, 1871, being the Morrow of the Funeral of the Very Rev. H. L. Mansel, D.D., Dean of St. Paul's. 8vo. 1s.

The Purchas Judgment: A Letter of Acknowledgment to the Right Hon. Sir J. D. Coleridge, one of the Lords of her Majesty's Most Honourable Privy Council; together with a Letter to the Writer by the Rev. E. B. Pusey,. D.D., Eastertide, 1871. 8vo. 1s.

The Purchas Judgment: A Letter to the Right Hon. and Right Rev. the Lord Bishop of London by the two Senior Canons of St. Paul's Cathedral, June 1, 1871. 8vo. 1s.

Pauperism and the Love of God: A Sermon preached at St. Paul's, Knightsbridge, on the Second Sunday after Trinity, 1870, for the Convalescent Hospital at Ascot. 8vo. 1s.

The Model of our New Life: A Sermon preached at the Special Evening Service in St. Paul's Cathedral on Easter Day, 1870. 8vo. 3d.

The Work and Prospects of Theological Colleges: A Sermon preached at the Cuddesden Anniversary Festival, on June 10, 1868. 8vo. 1s.

OF THE FIVE WOUNDS
OF THE HOLY CHURCH

Of
The Five Wounds of the Holy Church

BY

(ANTONIO ROSMINI)

EDITED WITH AN INTRODUCTION BY

H. P. LIDDON, D.D.

CANON RESIDENTIARY OF ST. PAUL'S

RIVINGTONS
WATERLOO PLACE, LONDON
MDCCCLXXXIII

TO THE HONOURED NAME

OF

ALEXANDER PENROSE FORBES,

LATE LORD BISHOP OF BRECHIN,

THIS

ENGLISH EDITION OF THE "CINQUE PIAGHE,"

PUBLISHED, AFTER A LAPSE OF YEARS,

IN OBEDIENCE TO HIS WISHES,

IS

REVERENTLY AND AFFECTIONATELY

DEDICATED.

PREFACE.

THE author of the subjoined treatise, Antonio Rosmini-Serbati, was born at Rovereto in the Italian Tyrol, on Lady Day, 1797. His father and mother were both people of good family, and considerable fortune. Antonio was the second of their four children : his elder sister became a nun, and his youngest brother died in infancy. His parents were educated and devout members of the Church; and the atmosphere of his home must have fostered the intellectual and devotional tendencies which made him what he became in later years. The boy studied first at the gymnasium of Rovereto, and then for two years at home, under a tutor, P. Orsi, whose instructions in philosophy had a considerable although apparently an indirect and unintended influence on his later life. When eighteen or nineteen years of age, he determined to take Holy Orders. His parents at first met this resolution on the part of their eldest son with a determined opposition. But his love for God and for his fellow-men seemed to impel him to the one calling in life which afforded the highest opportunities for its practical exercise ; and in 1817, at the age of twenty, he began his theological studies at Padua. His father died in 1820, leaving him the bulk of his property ; he was ordained priest in 1821, and then, after a short visit to Rome, he settled down at his old home in Rovereto.

Rosmini's boyhood happened on a time when Italy was yet reeling under the effects of the First French Revolution; when old institutions had largely crumbled before the irruption of the armies of the Directory, and old beliefs were still more rudely assailed or undermined by the invasion of infidel thought. Rosmini's mind fully opened just as the religious reaction was making itself felt; and he shared the aspirations of the best young men of that day in desiring to do something towards restoring Religion to its true place in human life. After his ordination, he spent six years in his ancestral home, laying out his time between severe study, and prayer, and exercising his ministry among the poor of the surrounding villages. During these years, he worked hard at philosophy, mainly with a view to its bearing on Christian Apologetics; but he also conceived and shaped the idea of a religious institute, which should promote holiness and learning among the members and teachers of the Church. At first it was to be lay; then lay and clerical. In 1826 he removed to Milan, where he began to publish; while, under the influence of Loewenbruck, he set himself to the task of organizing his projected order. Thence, in February, 1828, he retired to Domodossola, the pretty Piedmontese town, which the traveller remembers at the Italian foot of the Simplon Pass. Here in the cold winter months he took up his abode in a ruined house on the top of the adjacent Calvary, where he led a life of great austerity; abstaining from animal food, often from food altogether, sleeping on leaves or on the dry ground, and devoting his energies to reading, thinking, and writing. Here he wrote a large part of his *Nuovo Saggio sull Origine delle Idee*, and constructed the Rule of his Institute. But his health soon broke down under the strain and exposure; and

x   Editor's Preface.

after a visit to his home at Rovereto, he made his way to Rome, where he remained from November, 1828, until March, 1830, in order to secure the encouragement and sanction of Pius VIII. for his new Institute, and to publish his *New Essay*, to the great satisfaction of the educated part of the religious public.

In May, 1830, he returned to Domodossola, and, although with weakened health, he betook himself to his life of privation and solitude on the Calvary. The welcome monotony of this was, however, broken in upon by an invitation to found a house of his order at Trent; and between 1830 and 1834, he spent his time between that city and Domodossola, in efforts to weld his Institute into coherence and shape, and to promote sanctification and learning among its members. It was during this period of his life in 1832, that he composed the *Five Wounds of the Holy Church*. The anxieties which had led him to attempt the formation of a new Institute and to discover a philosophical basis, or setting, for Divine Revelation, took, as a third and highly practical form, the production of this treatise, designed to point ut what Rosmini conceived to be the five chief mischiefs which beset the Church of his day and country. These evils her highest authorities were thus implored to consider and remedy. To the same date belong his *Principles of Moral Science*, and part of his unpublished work on Supernatural Anthropology.

In 1834 he undertook for a year the partial charge of St. Mark's in Rovereto : but he resigned it in 1835. He had undertaken it with reluctance, and he returned with pleasure to the undisturbed care of his Institute. But his popularity at Rovereto was viewed with displeasure by the Austrian Government, which saw in him at once an Ultramontane ecclesiastic and an Italian patriot. Austrian influences led to his resignation of his cure ; and Austrian prejudice followed him on his resuming his earlier occupations. He was forbidden to connect his house at Trent in the Austrian territory, with the "foreign" house at Domodossola ; and at last the house at Trent had to be broken up. In order to escape from these perplexities, Rosmini, in 1837, fixed his home at Stresa, on the Lago Maggiore ; and thus he entered upon the most productive period of his career. In 1839, Pope Gregory XVI. formally approved of his Institute ; and it rapidly attained to considerable importance. From this period until 1846, were the most tranquil years of Rosmini's life; the only disturbing incident was a controversy with Gioberti, who attacked Rosmini's philosophy with vehemence. Rosmini used the opportunity to show that in thought and speculation, no less than in his practical efforts, he had kept in view the interests of the Christian Religion and Church ; and Gioberti, in after years, admitted that he had been mistaken in the motives of his hostility.

With 1846, a new period in Rosmini's life began. In that year Pius IX. became Pope ; and the first years of his reign led Italy and the world to believe that a brighter era had commenced both for the Papacy and for Italy. It seemed, for a moment, as if some of the hopes of Rosmini's life were about to be realized, by the union of all Italians in a confederacy of States under the presidency of the Pope. But this result could not be practically realized without a preliminary struggle with Austria. And Pius IX. was a pastor first and afterwards a politician. In an Allocution of April 29, 1848, he announced publicly that, as the common father of the flock of Christ, he could not take part in a war against Austria. Rosmini could not but submit; but he still hoped to gain his end, by some confederation of States, of which the Pope would be *ex-officio* president, while the direction of affairs would rest with the federal congress. Meanwhile the Pope became more and more inclined to separate himself from the political aspirations of the Italian people, while the Romans were asking for a constitution and for some kind of self-government. Rosmini published, in 1848, his *Constitution according to Social Justice*, in the hope of giving a religious turn to the popular movement, and of retaining their due share of power for the clergy and the upper classes under liberalized institutions. This work had no practical results. In 1846, he had given to the world the *Five Wounds*, which had been written in 1832.[1] He thought that with the accession of Pius IX. new opportunities were opening before the Church of Italy : but that, in order to take advantage of them, she must reform herself in

[1] The title of the book is, "Delle Cinque Piaghe della Santa Chiesa, trattato dedicato al clero cattolico, con appendice di alcune lettere sulla elezione de vescovi a clero e popolo di Antonio Rosmini. Bastia, 1849."

accordance with Primitive rules, and must study the conditions under which the spiritual society founded by our Lord can best influence the modern world.

The most important episode in Rosmini's life was the embassy to Rome, with which he was charged by the Piedmontese Government. The object of the Government in sending him was to secure the countenance and aid of the Pope, while carrying on its war against Austria. Rosmini accepted the mission, but, at first, owing to some misunderstanding, with a mistaken conception of the work in hand. The Government wanted at the time an armed alliance with Rome and the other Italian States, against Austria; while Rosmini was dreaming of a permanent confederacy of States under the Pope as president. For a moment, indeed, the Government, under the influence of Gioberti, seemed to accept the programme of Rosmini, who accordingly started on this mission. He was received at Rome with great consideration, and even promised a Cardinal's hat. But the prospect soon changed. No instructions, such as had been promised, reached Rosmini from Turin for some weeks; and when they came, he was ordered to abandon his favourite scheme, and to advocate an armed alliance. Deserted by his own Government, and opposed by the Papal minister Rossi, Rosmini resigned his mission; which had, however, strengthened the Pope in his resolve to take no part in the war against Austria or in the general policy which found favour at Turin. This determination of the Pope probably precipitated a political crisis. Rossi was brutally assassinated. An effort was made to compel the Pope to appoint a liberal ministry. Rosmini, whose real mind was imperfectly understood, was marked out by the popular voice as its representative, and the Pope conferred on him the presidency of the new cabinet, with the department of Public Instruction. Rosmini declined: he would not accept a post which had been offered to him by the Pope under pressure; and he may well have doubted his capacity for grappling with the sterner duties of political life.

Events, however, were moving fast. In a few days the Pope was a fugitive from his capital; and Rosmini followed him to Gaeta. But the opportunity for distinguished public service had passed. Those about the Pope had no difficulty in persuading him that his misfortunes were traceable to his encouragement of schemes with which Rosmini's name was identified. Rosmini left Gaeta, and devoted himself to his religious publications at Naples. His enemies, both at the Papal court and at Naples, were bent upon his ruin. Rosmini was a Consulter of the Congregation of the Index; but not until three months had passed was he informed of the meeting of the Congregation in which his two books on the *Constitution according to Social Justice* and the *Five Wounds of the Church* were prohibited. He had entered Rome to receive the promise of a place in the Sacred College; he left central Italy for his northern home in utter discredit. The last seven years of his life were spent at Stresa, in developing his Institute of Charity, and in completing his philosophical publications. A final effort was made to accomplish his ruin: and it was hoped that his other works might be condemned as easily as those on the *Constitution* and the *Five Wounds*. But the Pope insisted on his having fair play, and all Rosmini's publications were submitted to the Congregation of the Index. Instead of meeting hurriedly with a practically foregone conclusion, the Congregation now extended its labours over nearly four years; and in

1854, it declared that all the works of Rosmini were free from censure. Rosmini only lived a year after this triumphant acquittal; he died in the peace of Christ on July 1, 1855.

Rosmini's philosophy has been recently recommended to the English public by an able writer,[1] and his Institute is well represented among the Roman Catholics of this country. That his book on the *Five Wounds of the Church* should not have been translated into English is to be accounted for, partly by the excessive redundancy of even good Italian prose which unfits it for an idiomatic English rendering, but still more from the impression that the characteristic ideas which it represents were likely to be transient, and were not calculated to affect the future of the Church in Italy. However, the late Bishop of Brechin, Dr. Forbes, was anxious for a translation of the work into English. It would "show English Churchmen what, speaking from personal knowledge " some ten years ago, " he believed some of the best Italian minds to be still thinking ; " and it was " by no means without bearings, although indirect," upon our own circumstances.

[1] "The Philosophical System of Antonio Rosmini-Serbati," by Thomas Davidson. London, Kegan Paul, 1882.

The title of the book is more mystical than its contents would lead us to expect; and may require a word of explanation for at least some English readers. It was probably suggested to the writer by his sojourn on the hill of the Calvary near Domodossola. It presupposes an analogy which naturally results from the well-known language of St. Paul,[1] between our Lord's natural Body, crucified through weakness, and His Mystical Body, the Church, pierced by the sins and errors of men in the ages of Christian history. The five main evils of the contemporary Italian Church correspond, in Rosmini's view, to the Five Wounds of the Hands, Feet, and Side of the Divine Redeemer. These Wounds, according to Rosmini, are a legacy of feudalism. Beginning with the Wound in the Left Hand of the Crucified, he sees in it the lack of sympathy between the clergy and people in the act of Public Worship, which is due, not merely to the use of a dead language in the Church Services, but to the want of adequate Christian teaching. This is to be accounted for by the Wound in the Right Hand,—the insufficient education of the clergy: and this again was both

[1] 1 Cor. xii. 12, 27; Eph. i. 23; Col. i. 24.

caused and perpetuated by the great Wound in the Side, which pierced the Heart of the Divine Sufferer, and which consisted in the divisions among the Bishops, separating them from one another, and also from their clergy and people, in forgetfulness of their true union in the Body of Christ. Such divisions were to be referred to the nomination of the Bishops by the Civil Power, which often had the effect of making them worldly schemers and politicians, more or less intent on selfish interests. It formed the Wound of the Right Foot. But the claim to nominate was itself traceable to the feudal period, when the freehold tenures of the Church were treated as fiefs by an over-lord, or suzerain, who saw in the chief pastors of the flock of Christ only a particular variety of vassals or dependants. In the modern results of this estimate Rosmini notes the Wound of the Left Foot.

It is unnecessary to point out why this half-religious, half-political study would not have been allowed to pass unchallenged. Its plain speaking on the subject of public worship in Italy, could only be welcome to those—a minority in all communions—who care more for real improvement, and for that preliminary recognition of shortcomings which promotes it, than for any lower or selfish objects which are often to be secured by a policy of *quieta non movere*. It was easy to suggest that to criticize the education of the clergy was to be disrespectful to their order, and that to hint at disunion in the Episcopate was disloyal to the Church. Then the Civil Power had its own quarrel with an author, who could refer ecclesiastical shortcomings to the State's exercise of rights which did not originally belong to it. The persecution to which Rosmini was exposed at Naples was at any rate in part traceable to the resentment of the still existing Bourbon Government at his language on the subject of nominations to the Episcopate by the Civil Power ; and his theory of the feudal origin of rights secured by Concordats which modern Liberalism in France or elsewhere knows so well how to use against the Church, was not calculated to procure acceptance for his views in very different quarters.

Not that an English Churchman will find in Rosmini an author whom he can accompany without hesitation. Rosmini is an unfaltering believer in the Papal Supremacy ; with him the Pope rules, not only in the sphere of outer

Editor's Preface. xxi

conduct and discipline, but in the court of conscience and in the processes of secret thought. It is not merely that he received great kindness from successive Pontiffs, from Pius VIII., from Gregory XVI., and at the beginning, and still more particularly at the close of their intercourse, from Pius IX.; it is that he is, from first to last, a conscientious Ultramontane, who seriously holds the Papal Government to be an integral, or rather the most important portion of the Divine Organization of the Church. The passages in which this conviction is stated or implied are of course left in their integrity, but the conviction governs the general mind of the writer and, as we must think, distorts his view of Christian history. Thus he can only account for the separation of the Eastern and Western Churches by the increasing temporal grandeur of the See of Constantinople. He does not stop to reflect that the Roman Chair gained or suffered in the same way but on a larger scale, and that the Eastern Church was really alienated by Western pretensions which were unknown to the first ages of the faith. Indeed, while he urges that the temporal grandeur which gathered round the Bishops of the Middle Ages was a source of weakness to the Church, by introducing motives for conflicting action among her pastors, he never applies this principle to Rome; he has not a word of criticism for such a Pontificate as that of Julius II.; nay, he sees a providential purpose in the temporal power of the Papacy which is apparently undiscoverable in the worldly aggrandisement of other sees. In like manner, he has not a suspicion that the position of Gregory VII. and of Pascal II., when nobly struggling with the Empire, rested on a radically insecure basis; it does not occur to him that the fabric of the Papal claims was largely indebted for its existence to the false Decretals. The deposing power, he admits, was novel, at least in its exercise by Gregory, but then it had, he thinks, always been latent in the idea or constitution of the Papacy, and was only produced when it was needed to chastise the misconduct of a Christian sovereign. He seems for a moment to be on the point of condemning Leo X. for conceding to Francis I., in the Concordat of Bologna, the very right of nomination to Bishoprics against which earlier Pontiffs had struggled so earnestly; but he finds an excuse for the Pope in the hard necessities of the times. Again, he has no eye either for the causes or the effects of the Reformation. Some of his references to the worldliness and cowardice of certain English Bishops in the Tudor period may be accurate. But so vast a system as that of the mediæval Church would never have been shattered as it was in the sixteenth century unless there had been deep-seated and widespread corruption both in belief and practice, and a corresponding alienation of the higher conscience of the people from the hierarchy. The Papal jurisdiction was theologically and historically vulnerable; but it might have lasted on in England if it had not been long associated with memories of ambition and avarice which Englishmen could not forget. Looking at the whole subject from beyond the Alps, and by the light of the traditional teaching of the Roman Church on the subject, Rosmini sees no difference between the English Church, still preserving the means of full communion with our Lord Jesus Christ, through an apostolical ministry and real sacraments, and those other bodies which have issued from the Reformation with the loss of both, and, as we see to our sorrow, day by day, with the prospect of gradual forfeiture of those portions of the Christian faith, which they had at first been enabled to preserve. For Rosmini, all who are not in communion with the Roman See, are equally cut off from Christ. His language about Gallicanism is especially significant. Looking only or chiefly at its bearing upon the question of nominations to the Episcopate, and ignoring all in Christian antiquity to which writers like Bossuet could appeal in its behalf, Rosmini even makes it largely responsible for the misfortunes of the Church of France at the date of the Revolution. As if no Ultramontane clergy had ever been closely associated with a corrupt or despotic court! As if Pius VII., great as were his virtues and his misfortunes, did not sanction concessions, which, had they been only the work of statesmen, or of a national clergy, would have been condemned with an unsparing severity!

Rosmini, then, is an Ultramontane. His mental attitude towards the Papacy was part of his earliest religious creed, and he never had occasion to examine the grounds on which it rested. But is he therefore a writer from whom English Churchmen have nothing to learn? The present treatise, it is hoped, will answer that question; it is instructive and suggestive in more ways than one. If we set aside what we must deem the exaggerated phraseology, the mistaken historical and moral estimates which belong to its Ultramontanism, we shall find ourselves in communion with a sincere and beautiful mind, which those who come after us will not improbably deem one of God's greatest gifts to Western Christendom in the present century. It would indeed be interesting to follow him in his speculations on the nature of ideas, and their mode of existence; but, although it is as a mental philosopher, to whom Locke, Berkeley, Reid, Kant, and Fichte are familiar friends, that he is best known to Europe, we must confine ourselves to the little treatise in which he probably expresses his deepest thoughts respecting the condition and dangers of the Church of Christ in his native land. And surely one lesson which may be learned from our author is that a keen sense of evils besetting that portion of our Lord's kingdom in which a man's lot is cast is quite compatible with a loyal temper, and with the patience and hopefulness which belong to it. Rosmini is deeply sensible that the Church of Christ in Southern Europe might do more than she does for the moral and spiritual well-being of man. He is no merely academical disputant; he feels himself face to face with real evils, and he suggests, at least, some very practical remedies. It may be true that in the Churches of the Roman obedience there are other and even graver mischiefs to which no reference is made in this treatise on the *Five Wounds*. But the points on which Rosmini touches are sufficiently delicate. He longs for an intelligent union of the clergy and people in public worship, for a well-trained clergy, for an Episcopate united in heart and soul, for a restoration of the primitive method of electing Bishops, for the emancipation of Church property from the trammels of feudal tenure. In his language on the subject of nominations to the Episcopate by civil governments, he traverses, however cautiously and respectfully, Papal decisions as embodied in concordats. But it never occurs to him that such language is disloyal. Indeed, after keeping his essay in his desk for fourteen years, he only gives it to the world on the accession of a Pope who will, as he hopes and believes, more or less sympathize with its plea.

The "wound" which Rosmini feels most deeply,

and on which he insists at the greatest length, still exists, if indeed it has not widened. In England and the United States the Roman Church appoints its Bishops, without intervention on the part of the State, although not, as Rosmini would allow, in the primitive way of election by clergy and people. But generally the Civil Governments cling to what they regard as a right secured by Concordats, while, from a religious point of view, they have become less and less fit to exercise it. If the nomination of the French Bishops by the most Christian king was indeed open to such serious objection, what is to be said of their nomination by the representative men of the Third Republic?[1] Yet is it likely that the French Government will surrender this means of controlling the Church, so long as the Church retains a sou of the pittance which was left her at the Revolution in exchange for her old endowments?

But, perhaps, the most useful way of studying this treatise will be to consider, not so much its direct bearing on certain portions of the system of the Church of Rome, as whether it does or does

[1] Cf. the striking passage in D'Haussonville, " L'Église Romaine et le Premier Empire," tom. ii. pp. 216, 217.

not suggest anything analogous in the Church of England. We have outlived that old conception of loyalty to the English Church—the foe of the humility which precedes improvement—which held it treason to confess shortcomings at home or to admit excellence abroad : the danger rather is that in our reaction against this unthinking optimism we should become forgetful of the great blessings which God has given us.

So far as the English Church is concerned, the Reformation has done much to heal the Wound of the Left Hand ; and, as in the first days of the Faith, our public worship is conducted, and our sacraments administered, in "a tongue understanded of the people." But is this Wound so entirely stanched, that the poor and uninstructed among us bring their hearts and understandings fully to the work of joining in public worship ?

Again, are our clergy so educated in the mysteries of the Kingdom of Heaven—as distinct from the little packet of earthly knowledge which, in our well-nigh secularized universities, is considered necessary for the future squire or lawyer—as to be able wisely to guide the steps of the living heavenward, and to administer true comfort in the hour of death? And if the universities are failing us, is the effort to establish, and raise the standard of theological colleges sufficiently general and hearty to secure to the Church of England a highly-educated and devoted clergy in the troublous days which are probably before us?

Once more, may we not ask whether our Bishops are so entirely at harmony with each other, and so united in heart and will with the clergy and the faithful of their dioceses, as to enable us to say that there is nothing in the Church of England which corresponds to the Wound in the Side of the Church in Italy? That they are nominated to their sees by the Minister of the day is notorious, and, where no capitular body exists, without any check, however shadowy, on the part of the Church. Are they always selected with a view to the spiritual interests of the body over which they are to preside, and without any reference to political sympathies, or to personal bias?

We may indeed gratefully recognize the fact that, in some well-known instances, appointments have of late years been made to the English Episcopate, at variance with the political interests of the minister who has recommended them, and solely with a view to what was believed to be the highest good of the Church of Christ. So far Rosmini's anticipations and arguments on the subject are contradicted by our happier experience; but this conscientious use of Crown patronage is of comparatively recent growth in English history, and it may be rash to assume that the days of Sir Robert Walpole or of some later Ministers will never return.

At the same time, it may be doubted whether, as a Church, we are as yet in a condition to make good use of this privilege if it should be restored to us. Certainly so long as the mischievous fiction is maintained, that every Englishman is, as such, a member of the Church of England, an election by popular vote to the Episcopate would be probably as disastrous in itself and in its results, as is that of an incumbent in those few parishes where every ratepayer has a vote in the election. And even if the electors were to be only Churchmen and communicants, would much be gained by transferring to them the election of their Bishops until they are instructed sufficiently to realize what their Creed really means, and what are the awful privileges and risks of membership in the Holy Body ? Can the disestablished Church of Ireland be said to have done so much for its Episcopate by its recent elections, as did the Crown in the years preceding the Disestablishment ? And are there no English dioceses in which it may be conjectured, that as yet nothing better would come of an election by clergy and people than in an average diocese in Ireland ? Rosmini would have the Bishops elected, as in primitive days, by a Church of serious believers, animated by a warm desire to advance Christ's Kingdom and Glory, and duly instructed in the distinctive principles of their Creed.

Rosmini's opposition to feudalism is probably exaggerated, and if the representatives of religion are to urge her claims in the great council of the nation, they may as well do so in the capacity of feudal barons as in that of the elected delegates of mixed popular constituencies. But is it certain that while sitting among the nobles of the land, the pastors of the Church will always preserve a keen unworldly temper, which is alive to the dangers of a great social position, and fearless in its advocacy of the cause and Kingdom of Jesus Christ?

And must not we of the Church of England feel

the justice of our author's remarks respecting the idea of Church property, changed from that of a common fund held in trust for the support of the clergy and the relief of the poor, to that of a number of separate estates absolutely appropriated by the holders of single benefices ? If the last chapter of the book is open to some obvious objections, at any rate it supplies matter for very serious reflection.

It remains to say that the translation is due to an accomplished friend, who has not thought it necessary or desirable to follow the idiom or even the words of the original very closely. Metaphors and epithets are omitted, and sentences and paragraphs are condensed, where the true sense of the Italian has seemed to permit, or the spirit of English prose to require, such liberties. Whether they should be taken or not in any circumstances is, in the Editor's opinion, an open question ; but at least there is no room for misunderstanding, if the character of a translation is thus notified to the reader. In comparing it with the original the Editor has been assisted by one of our best Italian scholars, and he hopes that Rosmini's sense is fairly represented; certainly it is in no case intentionally obscured. Quotations from the

Bible, and in some cases even from Greek councils and writers, have been left in their Latin dress, as characteristic of the author. The editions of the work which have been used are those printed at Bastia in 1849, and at Lugano in 1863; and it is of course possible that these may contain errors which the author's MSS. will hereafter furnish means for correcting. For the headings of each page, which necessarily involve to a certain extent a running interpretation of Rosmini's meaning, the present Editor is alone responsible. For the materials which have furnished the earlier portion of this preface, the writer is indebted to the introduction prefixed to the *Philosophical System of Antonio Rosmini-Serbati*, by Mr. Thomas Davidson, and to *Della Vita di Antonio Rosmini-Serbati Memorie di Francesco Paoli*, Paravia, Roma, etc., 1880. He has also pleasure in referring to the first volume of the copious and interesting *Life of Antonio Rosmini-Serbati, founder of the Institute of Charity*, by G. S. Macwalter, London, Kegan Paul, 1883, which, through the courtesy of the author and publisher, he has been allowed to examine before its publication.

H. P. L.

CHRIST CHURCH,
Eastertide, 1883.

CONTENTS.

	PAGE
AUTHOR'S PREFACE	xxxvii

CHAPTER I.

OF THE WOUND IN THE LEFT HAND OF THE HOLY CHURCH, WHICH IS THE DIVISION BETWEEN THE PEOPLE AND THE CLERGY IN PUBLIC WORSHIP 1

CHAPTER II.

OF THE WOUND IN THE RIGHT HAND OF THE HOLY CHURCH, WHICH IS THE INSUFFICIENT EDUCATION OF THE CLERGY 27

CHAPTER III.

OF THE WOUND IN THE SIDE OF THE HOLY CHURCH, WHICH IS THE DISUNION OF THE BISHOPS 78

CHAPTER IV.

OF THE WOUND IN THE RIGHT FOOT OF THE HOLY CHURCH, WHICH IS THAT THE NOMINATION OF BISHOPS IS GIVEN UP TO THE LAY POWER 133

CHAPTER V.

OF THE WOUND IN THE LEFT FOOT OF THE HOLY CHURCH, WHICH IS THE SERVITUS (OR ENFORCED INFRINGEMENT OF THE FULL RIGHTS) OF ECCLESIASTICAL PROPERTY ... 299

APPENDIX.

ON THE ELECTION OF BISHOPS BY CLERGY AND PEOPLE:

LETTER I. 351

LETTER II. 355

AUTHOR'S PREFACE.

A few Necessary Remarks by way of Preface.

I. I WAS staying in a country house near Padua, when I began to write this book, in order to relieve my own troubled mind, and possibly also to comfort others.

Not without some hesitation, however. For the question occurred to me: Can it be fitting that a man without any jurisdiction should treat of the woes of the Holy Church? Is there not a certain audacity even in dwelling upon, still more in writing about them, inasmuch as the care of the Church of God belongs of right to her Pastors? And may not some disrespect towards those Pastors be implied in thus displaying her wounds, as though her Pastors discerned them not, or at all events were unable to find a remedy?

But to this I replied mentally that it cannot

be wrong even for a layman to ponder over the woes of the Church, if he be moved so to do solely by an earnest zeal for her welfare, and for the glory of God. And on examining myself, I felt as sure as a man can feel of his own motives, that this alone was the source of all that I was thinking about. I also reflected that whatever these meditations are worth, there is no cause for concealing them ; while if they are faulty, the Pastors of the Church will reject them. I write with no intention of deciding any question, but merely with the design of giving expression to my thoughts and submitting them to the Pastors of the Church, especially to the Sovereign Pontiff, whose revered utterances will always be for me the true and safe rule with which to compare, and whereby to correct, all my opinions. The Pastors of the Church are absorbed and burdened with many matters, so that they have little time for quiet thought, and therefore they are wont to desire that other men should set before them such reflections as might avail them in the government, whether of the Church Universal, or of their own especial branches of it. Moreover, I called to mind how in all ages of the Church there have been found holy persons, such as St. Jerome, St. Bernard, St. Catherine, and many more, who, without wielding episcopal authority, spoke and wrote with striking freedom and decision of the evils besetting the Church in their times, of the urgent necessity for curing them, and of the mode of effecting it. Not that I would liken myself to such great names for one moment; but I felt that their example proved that the investigation I was led to make could not in itself be wrong, any more than was the fact of calling the attention of the heads of the Church to those things which distract and harass the Bride of Jesus Christ.

II. Thus reassured, and daring to entertain the thoughts which crowded on my mind concerning the present state of the Church, to commit them to writing, and to mention them to others, there arose within me a further doubt as to the prudence, and even as to the honesty, of publishing such thoughts. I called to mind that all who in our times have written on these subjects, purposing and professing to occupy a *via media* between the two extremes, instead of pleasing both powers, the Church and the State, have equally displeased both. This proved the great difficulty of treating such subjects so as to give general satisfaction. Hence I asked myself whether in writing my reflections I should not probably offend and clash with both those powers, instead of gratifying them.

But to this I replied that, if I acted conscientiously, no one ought to blame me even although I were mistaken. I was in no way seeking the favour of men, nor any temporal advantage whatsoever. Thus, even supposing both parties found fault with me, I should find a reward in the testimony of my conscience, and in the expectation of that Judgment from which there is no appeal.

III. On the other hand, I asked myself, in what respects I might possibly offend men on both sides?

On the side of the State, I could only see one thing which might give offence. I could not consent to leave the nomination of Bishops in the hands of the secular authority. But while disapproving of this prerogative, I am deeply convinced that it is not more [1] prejudicial to the Church than

[1 Ital. *meno*. But either this is a lapse for *più*, or the words *chiesa* and *stato* have been transposed.]—ED.

Author's Preface. xli

to the State, and that to believe the contrary is a serious political error. The proofs which I hold of this seeming paradox, and which I have set forth in this book, are such, that I would appeal to any statesman who knows how to fathom a question, and who by a mental effort can overcome ordinary prejudice; who can see the far-off consequences of a political principle; who can calculate and combine all the concurrent causes by which alone it is possible to predict and to measure the total result of any State maxim whatever. This being premised, I think that I show no less desire for the weal of the State than for that of the Church, in maintaining my opinion, and that therefore sovereign princes cannot reasonably demur to what I say, but should on the contrary approve of it. At the worst, those who disagree with me can but urge that I know little of politics; but would that be a just cause for making war upon me? It has been said that in politics, as elsewhere, you must judge by the intention.

IV. On the side of the Church, I found nothing in the contents of my book likely to offend, unless it be what I have said with respect to the excess of pontifical reservations in elections. But this abuse does not belong specially to the present times; it is historical. And all men of sound sense will agree with me that there is no reason to fear a frank confession of such patent abuses, when it is required by the thread of the treatise, since thereby it is plainly shown that my object is not to advance the cause or works of men but the cause and Truth of God. Moreover, I do not feel that I ought to refrain from writing, for fear of displeasing persons who are more well-intentioned than far-sighted, while I have good reason to believe that what I write is not displeasing to the Holy See, to whose judgment I would always submit everything. I have ever found the mind of the Holy See noble, dignified, and, above all, in harmony with truth and justice. Now I have treated of no abuses but those which have been recognized and dealt with as such by the Supreme Pontiffs themselves. Among other things, I called to mind that remarkable Congregation of Cardinals, Bishops, and Abbots, to which, A.D. 1537, Paul III. committed, under oath, the charge of seeking out and freely exhibiting to himself every abuse and departure from the right way which had crept even into the Roman Court. It would be impossible to name more venerable personages than those who were thus assembled. They comprised four Cardinals—Contarini, Caraffa, Sadolet, and Pole; three of the most learned Bishops—Federigo Fregoso of Salerno, Girolamo Alessandro of Brindisi, and Giovammatteo Giberti of Verona. To these were added Cortesi, Abbot of San Giorgio at Venice, and Badia, Master of the Sacred Palace, who were both made Cardinals subsequently.[1] These men, so remarkable for their learning, their prudence, and their integrity, that their very names are sufficient, faithfully fulfilled the Pope's commission. Among the abuses which they pointed out to him, they did not fail to include those connected with reversions and reserves, together with other defects in the collation to benefices. Neither did they fail with keen penetration to discover and point out the deep roots of such abuses; especially one which so often leads, not only the State, but the ministers

[[1] Cf. "*Consilium delectorum Cardinalium et aliorum Prælatorum, de emendanda Ecclesia, S. D. N. D. Paulo iii. ipso jubente conscriptum et exhibitum.* MDxxxvii. *Imprimebatur anno* MDxxxviii."—ED.]

of the Church to stray from the right path in the use of their power. And this I have also indicated as "the refined adulation of men of the law." Assuredly nothing can be more frank or effective than the language used on this topic by those learned men in the memorial presented by them to the Pope. They say, " Your Holiness, being taught of the Holy Spirit, Who, as Augustine says, speaks to the heart without sound of words, knows well what has been the beginning of these evils. It is that certain of your predecessors, 'having itching ears,'[1] as the Apostle Paul says, heaped to themselves teachers after their own lusts, not in order to learn what was right to do, but rather, through the study and astuteness of those men, to find excuses for doing what they would. Not to dwell on the fact that adulation clings to all great people, as the shadow follows the body, and that the ears of princes have rarely heard the truth, it thus came to pass that doctors were forthcoming who taught that the Pope was lord of all benefices, and consequently, since a lord may sell that which is his without injustice, that the Pope cannot be guilty of simony. And, moreover, that

[1] 2 Tim. iv. 3.

Author's Preface. xlv

the will of the Pope, whatever it be, is the rule whereby his proceedings and actions are to be guided. Thus, without doubt, it followed that whatever the Pope might wish, was lawful. From this fountain, O Holy Father, even as from the Trojan horse, there have burst forth upon the Church of God so many abuses and such grievous ills, that now we see her oppressed with them almost without hope of deliverance, and the evil report of them (may your Holiness believe us who know!) has spread abroad even to the infidels, who chiefly for this cause deride the Christian religion. Thus through us—through us, we say—the Name of Christ is blasphemed among the Gentiles."[1]

[1] In translating this passage we have followed the Latin, which is as follows :—

"Ex quoniam Sanctitas tua Spiritu Dei erudita, Qui ut inquit Augustinus, loquitur in cordibus nullo verborum strepitu, probe noverat principium horum malorum inde fuisse, quod nonnulli Pontifices tui prædecessores prurientes auribus, ut inquit apostolus Paulus, coacervaverunt sibi magistros ad desideria sua, non ut ab eis discerent quod facere deberent, sed ut eorum studio et calliditate inveniretur ratio, qua liceret id quod liberet; inde effectum est, præterquam quod principatum omnem sequitur adulatio, ut umbra corpus, difficillimusque semper fuit aditus veritatis ad aures Principum, quod confestim prodirent Doctores, qui docerent Pontificem esse dominum beneficiorum omnium; ac ideo, cum dominus jure vendat id quod suum est, necessario sequi in Pontificem non posse cadere Simoniam ; itaque voluntas Pontificis, qualiscunque ea fuerit, sit regula qua ejus operationes ac actiones dirigantur : ex

Having weighed all these considerations, I put aside all my doubts, and with a clear mind and free hand I sat down to write this little treatise, praying God to use it to His glory, and to the good of His Church.

CORRETTOLA,
    November 18, 1832.

quo procul dubio effici, ut quicquid libeat, id etiam liceat. Ex hoc fonte, Sancte Pater, tanquam ex equo Trojano, irrupere in Ecclesiam Dei tot abusus et tam gravissimi morbi, quibus nunc conspicimus eam ad desperationem fere salutis laborasse, vel manasse harum rerum famam ad infideles usque (credat Sanctitas vestra scientibus), qui ob hanc præcipue causam, Christianam religionem derident adeo, ut per nos, per nos inquimus, nomen Christi blasphemetur inter gentes."—ED.]

OF THE FIVE WOUNDS
OF THE HOLY CHURCH.

CHAPTER I.

Of the Wound in the Left Hand of the Holy Church, which is the Division between the People and the Clergy in Public Worship.[1]

V. THE Author of the Gospel is the Maker of Man. Jesus Christ came to save the whole man.[2] Man is a being composed of body and spirit. Therefore the law of grace and love must penetrate and possess itself both of man's mind and of his body. It must be so set before the world as to attain this end. It must so combine ideas

---

[1] By "division," I do not mean a separation in communion and in spirit, which can never be wanting in the Church of Jesus Christ; but only the lack of that practical union which exists between the clergy and people when the latter fully understand the rites and prayers recited and performed by the former in their sacred duties.

[2] St. John iii. 2-6.

with actions, thus appealing no less to intellect than to feeling, that the whole man, yea, the very dry bones of humanity may be touched by their Creator's will and live through Him.

VI. It was not enough that the Gospel should take possession of the individual man. The glad message was destined to save all mankind. Not only was it to act upon the several elements of man's nature; its Divine action was to accompany our nature unfailingly in all its developments, and to support it in all the stages of its history. Thus instead of man's ruin being precipitated by his natural gravitation towards evil, a kindly law of progressive improvement would govern his onward course. In short, the Gospel was to mingle itself with and display itself in single lives, and thence to pass into the communities formed out of them. Having saved the individual man, it was to renew and save every association of men; the family, the nation, humankind at large. It was to impose wholesome laws on all these associations of men, ruling them in the Name of the God of peace. For associations are the work of man; and it is natural that the Divine law which rules man himself, should also control his handiwork.

VII. The Apostles, who were sent forth by

their Divine Master to teach and baptize all
nations, and who were trained by His Word and
His example, presented themselves to the world as
commissioned to do this great work, and showed
that they were endowed with that fulness of the
Spirit which was required for such a mission.

They did not pretend to found a school of
philosophy. Had this been all that was put
forward, men would not have thronged to listen
to the Apostles, although in their school nothing
but truth was taught. So it had happened
in the case of all the philosophical sects of
Greece. They were not more followed because of
the larger proportion of truth which they taught,
or the lesser proportion of lies which they upheld.
All the tongues together would have given forth
nothing but ideas, doubtless under various forms
of expression, but still only ideas. Whereas human
nature craved for something more, something to
be actually done for it. And the Apostles did
not, as the philosophers, pour out upon the human
race mere words: they announced acts. Had it
been otherwise, no gift of tongues would have
ensured the successful issue of their undertaking.
So that while they revealed luminous truths
and profound mysteries to the passive side of
man's understanding, and supplied by their own

CHAP. I. lives heroic examples for imitation, they simultaneously gave to the active element in man's nature a powerful impulse, a new direction, and a new life. Let it here be borne in mind that when I speak of the works by which the company of Evangelists accompanied and completed the efficacy of their words, I do not only allude to the miracles which they worked on external nature, and by which they proved the divinity of their mission. The powers with which they showed themselves to be furnished, and by which they bent the laws of nature in obedience to and in witness of the truth which they announced, could do no more than convince men that their doctrine was true. But the truth of their doctrine could be proved in other ways, and men might be convinced without being satisfied. For, as I said, while human nature aspires to find truth in the sphere of ideas, and cannot rest without attaining thereto, it has also a no less urgent and pressing need which causes it to aspire continually to find happiness in something real. And to this it gravitates by a law of its nature.

VIII. Were, then, these works, with which the Apostles reinforced the sublime words which they addressed to the human race, the virtues which they themselves put in practice?

Assuredly virtue is an essential need of mankind. For without moral dignity man is despicable in his own eyes, and as such, he cannot be happy. And the Apostles set before the eyes of corrupt mankind a new spectacle. In their own lives they practised all the virtues which they had seen in their Divine Master and had learned of Him.

But what could this effect? The natural need of virtue in man was stifled, suffocated, by idolatry, by the artificial need of evildoing. Nor could the virtues of the Apostles draw forth a whisper of approbation from the depths of human nature, since those depths had become an abyss, guarded by human perversity, as by a fierce Cerberus, lest any ray of light should penetrate them. On the contrary, their virtues did but serve to kindle against the Apostles of the Lord the cruelty and ferocity of the sons of men, who shed their blood with savage eagerness. Men had forgotten the very outward semblance of virtue, or they recognized it only as an object of hatred. A few were yet impressed by its beauty, and were reached by some ray of its Divine attractions. But they were without moral strength; and an unattainable perfection of obedience to the commands of Christ could only aggravate their own despair of reaching it. Thus they were thrown back

6 New virtues taught by the Apostles

CHAP. I. into that degradation which results from despair, and leads to the deadly torpor wherein depraved human nature ceases to make any effort, and gives itself up to open vice. Especially was this the case, because, in the lives of these new messengers, there appeared a class of virtues altogether new to the world. They were supernatural. And these supernatural virtues could not only not be appreciated, they could not even be justified without a Wisdom which began by calling mere madness that which the human understanding had hitherto esteemed as most precious, most advantageous, most surely matter for self-congratulation.

IX. Thus the doctrines of the Gospel, whether at first or in their development, could not be rendered sufficiently powerful and effective to penetrate and control humanity either by the wonderful miracles or by the exemplary virtue which accompanied them. For the miracles could only bear witness to the truth of theories,[1] which, if unaided, must be barren and ineffective; and the

---

[1] [It is right perhaps to observe that the depreciatory sense which often attaches to the word "theory" in English, as meaning speculation, *in opposition to* action or practice, is not characteristic of the foreign use of the word, according to which it stands for doctrine or speculation without, or not yet issuing in, practice or action. The English use of the word is a product of the English character.—ED.]

value of the good examples could not and would not be appreciated by men sunk in vice. At best they would receive a scanty and profitless admiration from some few, as prodigies worked by rare beings, whom ordinary mortals could not imitate. Whence, then, was that hidden force by which the Apostolic words became more than mere words, and by which they so far exceeded those of all the masters of human wisdom? Whence did they derive that saving power which grappled with man within the last defences of the soul and there triumphed over him? What further special agencies did the Apostles produce in order to save man as a whole—his intellectual as well as his practical nature—and to subject the entire world to a Cross?

In order to know these agencies with which the messengers of Christ were charged to accompany their oral promulgation of His commandments, we must go back to the text of the commission which they received. What were the words of Jesus Christ?—" Go ye therefore and teach all nations, baptizing them in the Name of the Father, and of the Son, and of the Holy Ghost."[1] Never had any human teacher spoken thus to his disciples. In this commission was

[1] St. Matt. xxviii. 19.

combined that which the Apostles were to do with respect to the passive part of human nature, as well as with respect to its active side. As regards the understanding, which is passive in so far that its duty is to receive the truth, it was said, "Teach all nations." At the same time an order was given for the regeneration of the will, which comprehends all human activity, nay, man himself, in the words, " baptizing them in the Name of the Father, and of the Son, and of the Holy Ghost." Thus was instituted a sacrament, which is the door to all other means of grace, through which the unseen restorative power of the One Triune God was to renew the face of the earth, by promoting the resurrection of human nature, long dead in sin and ruined for eternity.

X. The wonderful works, the mysterious rites, by means of which the Apostles reformed the world, were the sacraments; and among these the greatest—that sacrament which originated in the Sacrifice of the Lamb, Who before His death had fed them with His own Flesh, saying, "This do in remembrance of Me."[1] Certainly these sacraments were words, that is to say signs, but such words as the schools of Greek sages knew not. They were not such words as only struck

---
[1] St. Luke xxii. 19 ; 1 Cor. xi. 24, 25.

upon the bodily ear, or only instructed the understanding; they revealed to the awakened heart of man the immortal beauty of truth, the royal rewards of virtue; they discovered God Himself to the spirit of man—that God Who had hidden Himself that He might not be contaminated by the touch of impurity. In short, they were words and signs, but from God; words which created a new soul within the old, a new life, new heavens and a new earth. That which the Apostles added to their preaching was the Catholic worship, which chiefly consists in sacrifice, sacraments, and the prayers thereto pertaining.

XI. The doctrines which they spread abroad by preaching were so many abstract assertions;[1] but the practical force, the force of action, arose from that worship, whereby man could attain the grace of the Almighty.[2] It was not uncommon to confuse the two words *moral* and *practical*, and to use them in the same sense, speaking indiscriminately of *moral philosophy* and *practical philosophy*. Hence it arose that the philosopher who taught moral precepts, held himself thereby to be a virtuous man; and his disciples considered themselves as free from vice and possessed of all virtue, inasmuch as they listened

[1] [Ital., *teorie*.—ED.]   [2] [Cf. however, Ar. Eth. i. 3, 6, etc.—ED.]

Chap. I. to definitions of vice and virtue. Fatal human pride! the devil's exaltation of intellect, which imagines itself to contain all good, and which is ignorant that knowledge is but a slender and elementary principle of good; and that that which is truly and perfectly good belongs to genuine action, to effective will, and not to a merely intellectual process! And yet this pride of intellect has been until now the perpetual snare of mankind. It began on the day in which it was said to man, "Your eyes shall be opened, and ye shall be as gods."[1]

XII. Meanwhile, when the Maker of man undertook man's reformation, He was not content with presenting *moral* precepts to the intellect, He also gave to man's will the *practical* strength to fulfil them. And if He attached this strength to external rites, it was to show that He gave it *gratis* to man, and could attach to it whatsoever conditions He would. If, moreover, He willed that these rites should be so many sacraments, that is signs, it was because they were adapted to the nature of the being for whose salvation they were instituted, that is to say, of an intelligent being, to whom life and salvation were most fitly conveyed by signs and words.[2]

[1] Gen. iii. 5. [2] [St. Aug. De Doct. Christianâ, iii. 11, § 13. Ed.]

XIII. That grace which strengthens the will is communicated by means of the understanding; and it is through a sign apprehended by the understanding that the Christian feels the presence of God; and by this feeling lives, and is vigorous in action. When the Apostles and their successors added holy prayers, usages, outward symbols, and stately rites to the sacraments instituted by Christ Himself, in order that the public worship offered to the Redeemer of men might be more worthy of an Incarnate God, and more fit for the assembling together of those who believed in His Word, they were but following the example of their Divine Master. Nothing was introduced into His temple without a meaning; everything spoke and set forth high and Divine truths. Nothing could be mute and dark that was done in those solemn assemblies, since their purpose was to adore and pray to Him Who enlightens the understanding of His intelligent creatures; and in them the Supreme Intelligence, while receiving a reasonable worship, Himself blessed, penetrated, and kindled the natures He had created. And those usages, those *sacramentals* which the Church, in accordance with the power given to her, has added to that part of her worship which Christ Himself instituted, as being the foundation of all Catholic worship, not only have their special meanings like the sacraments; they also share in the life-giving strength conveyed by the sacraments to the spirit of man, and diffuse over his heart a healing virtue, which rekindles within him the will to do that which is right.

XIV. We may remark another fact respecting that Christian worship which was introduced at the same time with Christian teaching. That worship, to which God had annexed His grace, in order to render men able to practise the moral lessons inculcated on them, was not merely a spectacle set before the eyes of the people. The people were not to be only lookers-on without any active part or share in the devotional scene. Undoubtedly believers in Christ might have been taught solely by seeing that which was done in church, as simple spectators of a sacred representation; and God, sole Disposer of His own gifts, had He so willed it, might have made the mere view of the services offered Him by His priests, to be a quickening means of grace. But in His wonderful adaptation of all things to His creature man, He would not do this; He willed rather that the people gathered together in His temple should contribute a considerable part to His worship. Sometimes they are the subjects of the Divine action, as when the sacraments and ministerial benedictions are administered to them; sometimes they are united with the clergy, not only in thought, but in will and effort. Thus it is whenever the congregation joins in the prayers, when it answers to the salutations or invitations of the priest, when it returns the salutation of peace, when it makes its offerings, and when it takes a direct part in the rite which is administered, as in Holy Matrimony. In short, the clergy of the Catholic Church at one time represent God while speaking to and acting upon the people in His Name. At another they are identified with the people; and as belonging to the Head of mankind, united with His [mystical] Body, they speak to God, awaiting His mysterious operations of moral healing and refreshing. Thus the sublime worship of the Holy Church is only one, rising up from clergy and people, who, with well-ordered harmony and united intention, promote together the same sacred work.

XV. All the faithful in the Church, clergy and people, represent and form that beautiful unity of which Christ spoke when He said, "Where two or three are gathered together in My Name, there am I in the midst of them;"[1]

[1] St. Matt. xviii. 20.

CHAP. I. and again, addressing the Father, "The glory which Thou gavest Me I have given them; that they may be one, even as We are One."[1] This ineffable unity of spirit, spoken of by Christ Himself in words so sublime, so often repeated, has its foundation in the "clearness of intellectual light" which Christ gave to His Church in order that the faithful might be one with Him, cleaving to the same truth, or rather to Him Who is Truth. Now in order to attain a perfect consent in those petitions which they meet together to present before God, it is necessary that all should understand what they say in the prayers which they join in offering at the Throne of the Most High. Thus we may almost say that this perfect unanimity of feeling and affections is a condition of Christian worship imposed by Christ Himself, in order to its being acceptable to Him, and to His being found in the midst of His worshippers. It is worthy of note, too, how forcibly Christ expresses this condition or law which should distinguish the true Christian's prayer from that of the Jew, which consisted in a material worship, and an unrealized[2] faith. Our Lord is not content with saying that His faithful

[1] St. John xvii. 22.
[2] [Ital., *implicita*, cf. Heb. ix. 6-10.—ED.]

if the service be not understood.

people must pray, united to each other, and with a consenting will; He says expressly that they are to be united "in *all things* whatsoever they should ask."[1] So careful is Christ for the unity of His people! not only for a union of bodies, but for a union of minds and hearts; a union by means of which all Christians of every rank are gathered together like one man before their Saviour's altars, even as Holy Scripture says of Israel that it fought "as one man."[2] And when can we now say that the Christian people are consenting in all things, and perfectly one, unless it be when, assembled together in the Lord's House, they join with one accord in the sacred ordinances; each one knowing what is done, and what he has to do; all sharing the same interests; all, in short, taking not merely an outward part in Divine service, but also possessing a full and perfect comprehension of the sacred mysteries, of the prayers, symbols, and rites of which the Divine service is composed? Therefore it is essential that the people should understand the language of the Church in her public worship, that they should be duly instructed in what is said and done in the holy sacrifice, in the administration of the sacraments, and in all other ordinances of

[1] [St. Matt. xviii. 19, Vulg.—ED.]
[2] [Judg. vi. 16, xx. 1, 8.—ED.]

CHAP. I. the Church. And for this reason, the fact that the people are all but separated and cut off from an intelligent share in the Church's worship, is the first of those open, gaping wounds in the mystical Body of Jesus Christ whence its life-blood oozes forth.

XVI. The causes of this unhappy separation are manifold; but, among these, two appear to be pre-eminent.

In the symbols which were instituted by Christ, and in the rites added thereto by the Church, we find expressed and as it were represented all that is taught either by the dogma or by the moral law of the Gospel, in a language common to all nations, that is the language of signs, which sets forth truth by means of visible representations. But before this natural and universal language can be fully understood by him to whom it is addressed, he must have within himself a full knowledge of those truths, which are thus to be kept ever present to his soul. And consequently the less our Christian people are instructed by the preaching of the gospel, the less will they understand and receive of the high truths set forth in Christian worship. For this cause our Lord appointed that they should be instructed in the truth before an external worship was given to them; bidding His Apostles first to "teach all nations," and then "baptize them." The first cause, then, of the wall of division raised between the people and the ministers of Christ's Church is to be found in the lack of a full and living teaching; and this evil is fostered by a foolish prejudice held to by some that the people should be kept in a state of ignorance, or that they are not capable of appreciating the more sublime truths of the Christian Faith.

XVII. I say advisedly, a *full* and *living* teaching; since, so far as the fact of teaching goes, there is perhaps more now than of old. Every one learns catechisms; and catechisms contain those dogmatic formulas, those final, simple, exact expressions of truth, to which the Christian doctrine has been reduced by the united labours and careful thought of the learned of many ages, assisted by the Holy Spirit present at the Councils of the Church and speaking in her as dispersed throughout the world. Such precision and exactness in doctrinal formulas is assuredly a gain. The words convey truth, wholly and only. A safe path is traced, by means of which teachers may impart to the faithful, the most recondite and sublime mysteries of the Faith without much personal study. But is it equally an advantage that these teachers of Christian truth should themselves be dispensed from a close and laborious study of the truths they teach? If it is made easy to convey exact formulas to the ears of the faithful learners, is it equally easy to impress these formulas on their minds; or to cause them to sink into the heart, which is only reached through the mind? Granted that doctrinal language is abridged, that the terms in which it is clothed are brought to the most perfect dogmatic precision, and above all that it is finally fixed in unalterable exactness. But is it really more accessible to ordinary intelligences? May we not, on the contrary, doubt whether a certain variety and copiousness of expression was not an advantage in bringing truth to bear upon the souls of the multitude; one word casting light upon another; the style or expression which did not suit one listener, being well adapted to another? In short, by thus calling into play all the resources of God's great gift of language, was there not more scope for trying every means by which words can penetrate the spirit of the hearers? Is it not true that a single unchangeable expression is lifeless as well as unchangeable, and leaves the mind and heart of the hearer lifeless also? Is it not true that a teacher who merely repeats what he himself does not understand, however scrupulously exact may be his words, gives us a sensation as though his lips were frozen, and scattered hoar-frost rather than the kindling rays of life over his listeners? The more perfect and full such words or sentences are, the more they require intelligence to make them reach their aim, the more they require thoughtful explanations. To the multitude they are like dry food given to a young child whose digestion cannot receive it until it is softened and prepared. Those formulas, imperfect if we will, by which the Christian doctrines were once taught, had this advantage from their very imperfection, that they did not put truth before men as a solid whole, but, so to say, broken up into fragments; while the comments made on them amended any possible defects of expression, and gathered together the seemingly separated parts, so that the absolute truth, formed and built itself up in the minds which received it, and was thus completed and perfected. It is certain that truth cannot influence hearts, if we are contented with a lifeless image of it, instead of the real living power; if we stop short in words, ever so precise in expression, which do not go beyond the ear, beginning and ending there. Certainly, in these days, when a child is to be admitted to the sacraments of the Church, we examine carefully if he knows the chief mysteries. He repeats the formularies, and that is the proof that he knows them. And yet there is often room for doubt whether a child who repeats the words of the catechism by heart, knows any more about these mysteries than another who has never learnt it. What then? Has the modern introduction of catechisms been more hindrance than help to the Holy Church? If so, it would be strange to see so perverted a result of that which promised so well in the abstract. But we must say of these admirable compendiums of Christian instruction, what the Apostle said of the law of Moses; "it is holy, and just, and good, if a man use it lawfully."[1] So that the defect lies not with the thing itself, but with men's use of it. Our modern catechisms are in themselves excellent, and a natural result of the law of progress to which all human things are subject, under the influence of Christianity. Let the clergy take heed: of them it will be required to give account of the good or evil produced by this, as by all other wonderful institutions with which the Holy Spirit continually enriches the Church of the Word; for these are, in themselves, dead, and must be

[1] Rom. vii. 12; 1 Tim. i. 8.

made to live, by the wise handling of the clergy.

XVIII. But it is not by rites alone that Christians are taught. In the institution of worship our Lord added to the language of actions, and that which taught the eye, the instruction of the ear, or vocal teaching; and His Church has followed in the same path. Necessarily this vocal teaching must vary with the diversity of nations. To remedy this hindrance to ready communication, Providence had raised up the Roman Empire, which, binding many nations into one, carried the Latin language wellnigh to the ends of the earth. Thus the peoples who were called to the Gospel found themselves possessed of a common speech, by means of which they understood those words which accompany sacraments and rites, explaining them, and setting them more fully forth. Seeing then that words are the form of sacraments, Christ willed by these certain and definite signs to speak as clearly as possible to the understanding, and while doing this, to work mystically. Therefore it was that the virtue of the sacrament was not to be attached only to the matter employed in it, which by itself is silent and cannot express any clear meaning, but rather to those words which set before the mind the use of the material substance, and the end which it is to further. Thus the understanding received light through the meaning of the things set before it, and strength by the grace given in the sacred rite. But wars and the intermixture of nations altered languages. In this way, the language of the Church long ago ceased to be the language of the people. By this great change the people found themselves in darkness. Their understanding was separated from the Church which went on speaking to them, of them, and with them, while they could make no better answer than the pilgrim exile in a foreign land, who hears all around him unwonted sounds that have no meaning whatever for him.

XIX. These two calamities, the decay of living instruction, and the disappearance of the Latin language from common use, fell at the same time upon the Christian people, owing to a common cause, namely, the general invasion of the south by the northern barbarians. Paganism and its spirit were deeply rooted in society; up to that time, the Christian faith had only taken hold of individuals. The conversion of the Cæsars themselves was but the winning of single persons, powerful as they were. And it was ordained in the unalterable destinies of Christianity that the Word of Christ should penetrate society, that it should control science and art as well as man; and that all culture, every flower of human life, every social tie should through it flourish afresh. Therefore Providence condemned the earlier social system to destruction, and tore it up from its very foundations. Carrying out this ban, the barbarian hordes, guided by the Angels of the Lord, poured down in masses one upon the other, not merely ruining the Roman Empire,.but sweeping even its ruins away. Thus was prepared a clear soil for the grand edifice of the new society of the faithful. In the history of mankind, the middle age forms an abyss separating the old world from the new; there is no more communion between them than between two continents divided by a pathless ocean. Weighed in the balance of Divine Wisdom the two misfortunes of ignorance and the loss of the Church's language, which thus visited the faithful, were shown to be more than counterbalanced by the radical destruction of the social institutions and customs of idolatry; and by means of this terrible visitation, the Eternal hastened the advent on earth of a society likewise baptized, so to say, in blood, and regenerated by the word of the Living God.

XX. But if it pleased God to allow His Church to receive so deep a wound by the separation of the Christian people from their clergy in the solemn acts of worship, is this wound incurable? Can it be that the people, who by primitive rule not only witnessed but took part in the services of the Lord's House, will now be satisfied with little more than bare attendance there? Scarcely so, I think; for it is too much to expect of an intelligent and civilized people that they will come mechanically to attend rites in which they have no longer any share, and which they do not understand.[1] And this their repugnance to frequenting Christian Churches is unjustly made by men's indiscretion an occasion for perverting most strangely the Redeemer's words, "Compel them to come in."

[1] The institution of the Oratories and of the Marian Congregations was the work of good men, who saw clearly that it was needful to feed the devotion of our Christian people with something more than the public offices of the Church. Some severe judges, holding fast to theories, and regardless of altered circumstances, raised a great outcry against these institutions, denouncing them as new to the Church, and unknown to venerable antiquity; and as calculated to disturb the ordinary action of the Church, since they imply that what sufficed to the first ages of the Church no longer suffices in these times. But these harsh critics do not bear in mind that in the intervening time the sacred services have become almost inaccessible to the people; while, on the other side, St. Philip Neri, St. Ignatius, and other eminently holy men who had no object but the good of souls, have borne strong testimony to the truth of our words.

Surely if nations are capable of being healed, much more are the ills of the Church curable. It seems an insult to her Divine Founder to imagine that He Who prayed the Eternal Father to make all His disciples "one, even as I and the Father are One,"[1] would suffer a perpetual wall of separation to exist between the people and the clergy, so that all that is said and done in the celebration of the Divine mysteries becomes unreal and meaningless; that He would permit the people for whom the Light of the Word was born, and who were themselves born again for the worship of the Word, to assist at the greatest acts of His worship in no other capacity, so to speak, than that of the statues and pillars of the temple, deaf to the voice of their mother the Church when in very solemn moments she addresses them or intercedes for them as her children : or that the priesthood, withdrawn from the people, on a height which is ambitious and harmful because inaccessible, should degenerate into an aristocracy, a peculiar society, severed from society in general, with its own interests, language, laws and customs! But these are the inevitable and deplorable consequences of a seemingly slight cause ; consequences to which a priesthood would be inevitably

[1] St. John xvii. 11.

exposed, when no longer united, except externally, to the people, and in reality absent from the great company of the faithful.

XXI. But if the wound can be healed, who is to apply the remedy?

The clergy. The Catholic clergy alone can first prepare, and then effect the cure. On their lips is the Word of Life, and Christ has given it to their charge for the salvation of mankind; they are the salt, the light, the universal salve of man. Why then do they not make ready, and administer the medicine? That arises from another Wound of the Church, which bleeds no less copiously than the first, namely, the insufficient education of the clergy themselves.

CHAPTER II.

Of the Wound in the Right Hand of the Holy Church, which is the Insufficient Education of the Clergy.

XXII. IN the happiest times of the Church, preaching and the liturgy were the two great schools of the Christian people. The former taught the faithful by words alone; the latter by words conjoined with certain rites; and, especially by those rites to which their Divine Author had given power to work particular effects upon human nature, namely, the Holy Sacrifice and the Sacraments. Both were full of teaching. They did not address themselves only to one side of human nature, but to the whole man; they penetrated, they subdued him. They were not merely voices to reach the intellect alone, or symbols which impressed the senses only; but both by means of the intellect and of the senses, they reached to the heart, and filled the Christian with an exalted sense of God's mysterious and superhuman works. This sense was as active and powerful as was the grace which gave it birth; for the words of evangelical preaching issued forth from saints who poured out upon their hearers the abundance of the Spirit with Whom they were overfilled; and rites, efficacious in themselves, became still more so through the good soil into which they fell. The hearts of the faithful were well prepared to receive them by the instructions of their pastors, and by their own clear apprehension of all that was done, or that they themselves did, in the Church. From among believers like these the clergy were chosen. They brought to the Church, which had chosen them to the high honour of her ministry, a groundwork of doctrine, as large as their faith, which they had imbibed in common with the rest of the faithful; praying the same prayers, visited by the same Divine Grace, by means of which they knew and felt intimately all the fulness of the sublime religion which they professed. Of a truth we may predict what the ministers of the Sanctuary will be, if we know the people whence they spring; and if we knew no more than the character of the faithful in primitive times, and of their holy assemblies, we should have materials for judging what their clergy must needs have been. This throws light on events which are so unaccountable in our eyes; as when we find a simple layman vehemently demanded by the multitude for their pastor, and, in spite of his resistance, transformed in a few brief days into a Bishop. This was by no means rare in early times. There are on record the instances of SS. Ambrose, Alexander, Martin, Peter Chrysologus, and others, who were raised at once from the humble condition of faithful laymen, living in obscurity or employed in secular offices, to the Episcopate. And no sooner were these lights set on a candlestick, than they shed a marvellous brightness over the whole Church.

XXIII. By the same rule, our modern clergy are such as are our laity. It cannot be otherwise; coming as they do from among Christians who have perhaps never understood anything of the Church services, and have assisted at them like strangers witnessing scenes in which they know not clearly what the clergy are doing. Perhaps they had never felt the dignity which belongs to members of the Church; and had never conceived or experienced that oneness of body and spirit in which clergy and people are prostrated before the Almighty, hold-

30   *Evils resulting from want of*

CHAP. II. ing communion with Him, and He with them. Probably many have looked upon the clergy as a privileged and enviable caste, living on the proceeds of the Altar; as an upper class, like any other highly placed laymen; as forming a separate whole, and not as the noblest part of the Church's Body, of which the laity, too, are members, while all obtain the same blessings, pray with the same voice, offer the same sacrifice, seek the same grace from Heaven. Hence has arisen the too-common saying that Church affairs are the priest's affairs. How shall we begin to teach and train, in a true and large clerical spirit, pupils who come to the Church's school so full of themselves! Lacking, as they do, the very first rudiments which we should suppose they would already possess, and of which Church education ought to be merely a development, such men do not even bring a definite idea of what is meant by a clerical temper; they do not know what they seek in seeking to become priests, or what they are going to learn in the school of the sanctuary.

XXIV. This want of fitting preparation in aspirants for a clerical training, is more to be regretted than appears at first sight. We cannot build where there is no solid foundation, especially where the instruction of the Catholic priesthood is in question. For this necessarily presupposes Christian instruction; Christian life being the first step towards the priesthood. Here is the reason why the pupils of the sanctuary enter there with such a lack of the true Church temper; or rather, with secular views, which they have contracted from want of the opposite teaching; and, with these views, a worldly mind which can hide itself under a black cloak and accompany outward decency of life. Thus it escapes the notice of those in authority. They fail to perceive that this will not suffice for the Church of Christ. He came to fill all things with Himself; especially the minds of His priests. They should know and impart to others the grandeur of a religion which should subdue and save man's entire nature. But the poverty and degradation of thought and feeling which characterize the training given in our modern Church institutions, only produces priests who do not even know what beseems the Christian laity, or the Christian priesthood, or the sacred bond that exists between them. Such ministers, men of a troubled spirit and sordid mind, in time become priests, and have charge of Churches, and educate other priests, who turn out weaker and more miserable than themselves. Then these again become fathers and teachers of others, who thus sink lower with each generation, since "the disciple is not above his master;"[1] until it shall please God Himself to lend us His aid, and take compassion on His beloved Church.

XXV. In truth, great men alone can form great men; and this was another gain in the ancient education of the clergy, which was conducted by the greatest men whom the Church contained. Now, however, the contrary practice is a second cause of the insufficient education of our modern clergymen.

In the early ages of the Church, the Bishop's house was the seminary of his priests and deacons. The presence and the holy conversation of their superior was for them a living, constant, and sublime lesson. His pious conversation taught the theory, his stedfast life of pastoral duty the practice, of religion. Thus Athanasius grew up beside Alexander, and Laurence beside Sixtus. Almost every great Bishop trained up in his own household a worthy successor, a fitting heir to his piety, his zeal, his learning. It is to this system that we owe the eminent Pastors for whom the first

[1] St. Matt. x. 24.

six centuries of the Church were so remarkable. By means of this full and perfect system the sacred deposit of Divine and Apostolic doctrine was faithfully transmitted from one to another through informal and oral communication. The system was itself Apostolic, inasmuch as Irenæus, Pantænus, Hermas, and so many others, had gained their knowledge from the disciples of the Apostles; just as these last—Evodius, Clement, Timothy, Titus, Ignatius, Polycarp,—had been brought up, in Scriptural phrase, at the feet of the Apostles.

In those days men believed in grace. They believed that the words of a Pastor, appointed by Christ to rule and teach His Church, derived a special and unique efficacy from the Divine Founder. This belief imparted supernatural life and energy to the doctrines taught, so that they made an indelible impression on men's minds. Everything combined to render them effectual— winning eloquence, holiness of life, grave and composed bearing, and the powerful influence of the presiding Episcopal mind. "I remember," says Irenæus, speaking of his first training under the great Polycarp,—" I remember what happened then, better than all that has happened since, for the things learnt in childhood, growing with our

CHAP. II. growth, are never forgotten; so that I could point out the very spot where the blessed Polycarp sat while he preached the Word of God. The gravity with which he ever came and went is yet vividly before my mind; the sanctity of his general life; the dignity of his countenance and his whole person; the exhortations with which he fed his people. I seem yet to hear him recount how he had conversed with St. John, and with many others who had seen the Lord Jesus Christ; the words he had gathered from their lips, and the details they had told him concerning the Divine Saviour, His miracles and His doctrine; and all this was in the fullest sense in conformity with the Holy Scriptures, as being described by men who had been living witnesses of the Word, and of His life-giving message. Of a truth by God's mercy I listened eagerly and diligently to all these things; graving them, not on tablets, but in the depths of my heart, and He has by His grace enabled me to remember them, and ponder continually upon them." [1]

XXVI. Such was the successful and wise mode of education whereby great Bishops trained their own clergy. As a result, there was a

[1] This passage, from a letter written by the holy Bishop to win Florinus from his errors, is quoted by Eusebius, Hist. Eccles., lib. v. c. xx.

constant supply of great men, deeply conscious of the weight of their office, and filled with the spirit of the priesthood. No need to say how strong was the consequent union between the chief Pastor and his disciples, his sons in the faith. The terms higher and lower clergy[1] were then unknown; a later age first uttered them. And it is difficult to describe what harmonious order in the Church's government arose from this communion in learning, this holy intercourse, this habit of life, this interchange of affection, whereby the Bishop of old diffused and reproduced himself in the young clergy, being to them teacher, pastor and father; adding dignity to the compact body of the priesthood, and securing a healthy influence over the people. Thus selected and educated, even a scanty supply of clergy amply satisfied the wants of the Church; while the order of presbyters was so venerated and esteemed, that even men of the most exalted rank deemed themselves honoured by entering it; the people and Churches gazed with attention on such as were destined to it by their Bishops;[2] while the

---

[1] ["Alto e basso clero." *Ital.*—ED.]

[2] In order to mark the importance attributed to the order of presbyters, it will suffice to recall the words of the Martyrs of Lyons, in their letter to Pope Eleutherius. St. Irenæus, then only a priest, was sent on an embassy to the Pope, and was thus

Chap. II. dignity of the priesthood served to exalt yet more that of the episcopate, which was raised on so noble a basis ; and thus the priest was entirely and heartily, and in the natural course of things, subject to his Bishop.[1]
XXVII. We cannot wonder if these Bishops commended by the Martyrs : " We beseech you to regard him as a man full of zeal for the testimony of Jesus Christ. It is by this title that we commend him to you. If we thought that rank and dignity could confer righteousness upon any one, we would certainly have recommended him as a priest of the Church, for such he is" (Euseb., Hist. Eccles., lib. v. c. iv.). It is evident that in our time a priest would not thus be commended to the pope! In proof of the interest taken by the people and the Churches in the ordination of a new priest, it is sufficient to recall the rumours excited when the celebrated Origen was ordained by the most renowned Bishops of Palestine, among others, Theoctistus of Cæsarea, and St. Alexander of Jerusalem—rumours which are attributed by St. Jerome to the jealousy of Bishop Demetrius of Alexandria. In our day the ordination of a priest could never be the subject of such jealousy or such commotion.

[1] In St. Ignatius' letters to various Churches we find strong commendation of this unity and submission to their Bishop, of both people and clergy. In the letter to the Trallians, after praising their perfect submission to their Bishop Polybius, he says that Polybius is "the mirror of the love which reigns among his disciples ; his mere exterior is a great lesson ; his exceeding gentleness is his strength, so that even wicked men cannot but respect him." Again, writing to the Church of Magnesia, he specially praises its priests for their submission "to their Bishop Damasus, although in years he is young." In a letter to the Ephesians, having highly lauded their saintly Bishop Onesimus, he praises them warmly because they "all were so closely united to him, especially the presbytery ($\pi\rho\epsilon\sigma\beta\upsilon\tau\epsilon\rho\iota\omicron\nu$), that is, the clergy, and because, by grace, they were joined in one accord with priests and Bishop in the Lord Jesus Christ, breaking together one bread, which saving remedy confers immortality and preserves from death."

kept jealously to themselves the instruction of CHAP. II. their clergy, when they rarely and with difficulty could be induced to entrust even that of the people to other hands;[1] believing, as they did, that Christ had committed to them the whole flock, both clergy and people; that to their lips He had entrusted the Word, and had conferred on their order, beyond others, the power of giving mission and grace.

XXVIII. Such being the habits and feelings of the clergy, the religion of the Crucified had triumphed over tyrants and heretics, and its invisible Head destined it to achieve no less noble a victory over the barbarian invaders. As I said before, in sending the barbarian hordes to destroy the very foundations of society, Divine Providence intended to set before the world the power of Christ's Word, which outlives the

[1] It was an extraordinary honour when St. Flavian, Bishop of Antioch, entrusted St. John Chrysostom with the instruction of the people. Such instances were not common in the Church: and those Bishops who first permitted presbyters to preach the Gospel, did so in consequence of the unusual holiness and learning of the men so trusted. The talents of St. Augustine induced Bishop Valerius of Carthage to commit to him the instruction of the people, as in the case of St. Chrysostom. This was the case in the famous school of St. Mark in Alexandria, where the teachers were always men eminent for learning and holiness. It was then well understood what men are worthy to teach the world, above all in the doctrine of Christ! By what misfortune is the influence of such a true and salutary principle forgotten among us?

CHAP. II. destruction of empires and of all the works of man, and has power to restore life to dust and skeletons, and to recreate a ruined society in a form worthy of itself. It is worthy of note, too, that when men, essentially social beings, find all the bonds snapped that bind them together; when they are scattered, degraded, resourceless, hopeless, shipwrecked amid a sea of disasters,—they will, by a spontaneous impulse or as a last resource, seek supernatural aid, and will throw themselves upon religion. Religion is ever welcome to all who are in trouble; it can bid a new hope shine before their eyes, a hope as vast as God Himself, because it can promise that out of their utter loss shall spring their eternal gain. Thus Religion, which must always precede the development of all social institutions, and which outlives their destruction, is ever found guiding the peoples, whether in their infancy or in their recovery from ruin. And this Providential order, which from the beginning caused all social links, all cultivation to spring from Religion, was preparing the way destined of God for the work of Christianity in the Middle Ages. The one true religion was not inferior in its results to false and imperfect religions; and inasmuch as the latter had promoted social union and national progress according to the little portion of truth that they contained, so was this done far more effectually by the Faith which owned the whole Truth, a pure and full revelation, the grace of Redemption.

The peoples then, oppressed and harassed with temporal calamities, had recourse to the sheltering arms of that Religion from which they had already learnt the awful beauty of things spiritual and Divine. They sought for the first time from it earthly succour. And the common Mother of the faithful, full of love and pity, was deeply moved by the wants of the harassed and disorganized peoples, so that she became their comfort, their shield, their ruler.

Thus the clergy beheld themselves at the head of the nations, almost without knowing how. Having yielded to the irresistible pressure of compassion in coming to the rescue of a ruined society, they found themselves suddenly installed as the fathers of orphaned cities, and as rulers where government had forsaken its duties. The Church was all at once overwhelmed with worldly honours and riches, which flowed in upon her as it were by their own weight, even as the waters pour in where landslips have made way for the advancing sea.

XXIX. It was in the sixth century that these

CHAP. II. new duties first devolved on the clergy. They were very unwelcome to saintly prelates, who saw the Church laden with worldly possessions, thereby losing that holy poverty so much praised by the early Fathers.[1] And they themselves were weighed down with secular cares, which drew

---

[1] See a famous passage in Origen. As an historical evidence of the opinions held in his time by the most eminent members of the Church as to the poverty and liberty of the clergy, it cannot be set aside. This great teacher of Bishops and martyrs, in one of his Homilies, publicly delivered at Alexandria, after speaking of the idolatrous priests to whom the King of Egypt had given possessions, proceeds, "The Lord does not give earthly portions to His priests, inasmuch as He Himself wills to be their portion ; and this is the difference between the two. Give good heed, all ye who exercise priestly functions ; beware, lest ye be rather Pharaoh's priests than the Lord's. Pharaoh wills that his priests should possess lands, and should be occupied with them more than with souls, or with the Law of God. But what does Jesus Christ appoint for His priests? He saith that whoso doth not leave all and follow Him, cannot be His disciple. I tremble as I utter the words, for I accuse myself first of all. I speak my own condemnation! What are we doing? How dare we read ai. preach such truths to the people?—we, who not only do not renounce that which we possess, but who even seek to acquire more than we had before we were the disciples of Jesus Christ? But if our conscience condemn us, can we therefore conceal what is written? I will not be guilty of a further crime! I confess before all the people this is what the Gospel prescribes ; but I cannot affirm that I have as yet fulfilled the precept. Since, however, we know our duty, let us from this moment seek to fulfil it ; let us seek no longer to resemble Pharaoh's priests, but let us become priests of the Lord, even as Paul, as Peter, as John, who had neither gold or silver, but who possessed such riches that not the whole world could give the like " (In Genes. Hom. xvi. § 5). This quotation needs no commentary ; every one knows how Origen himself fulfilled the profession of poverty.

them away from the study of Divine things, and robbed them of time and strength which were needed for dispensing the Word of Christ to the faithful, for the education of the clergy, and for perseverance in public and private prayer.

St. Gregory the Great, the great ecclesiastical ruler of that age, was deeply afflicted by the perils which, as he foresaw, must attend upon the new career thus opened to the Church. His letters are full of lamentations over the hard circumstances of the times, which forced him to be more a treasurer or adjutant of the Emperor than the Bishop of his flock. " Under the pretext of Church administration he was tossed on the waves of worldly affairs, and often even buried beneath them."[1]

This he repeats several times, especially in a letter to Theoctista, sister to the Emperor Maurice. In it he describes the peace which he had enjoyed as a humble monk, in order to mark the contrast of his present troubled life in the Pontificate. " Under the guise of the Episcopate," he writes, " I have returned to the world, since in the new state of things in the pastoral office [2] I am burdened

---

[1] Epist., lib. xi. ep. i. Nos enim sub colore ecclesiastici regiminis, mundi hujus fluctibus volvimur, qui frequenter nos obruunt.

[2] This expression, "ex hac modernâ pastoralis officii continentiâ," shows how new this burden of secular affairs was to the Episcopate, hitherto unaccustomed to it.

CHAP. II. with many more worldly cares than I can remember to have had while a layman. I have lost the lofty pleasures of my quiet life, and, while to those without I seem to have risen, I feel that I have really fallen. Therefore I bemoan myself, as cast forth from the Presence of my Creator. In those days I continually sought to forsake the world and the flesh ; to chase all earthly visions from my mental sight, and to see only the things of God ; crying not with my voice only, but from the depths of my spirit, ' My heart hath talked of Thee, Seek ye My Face ; Thy Face, Lord, will I seek ' (Ps. xxvii. 9). Thus, fearing nothing, and desiring nothing that this world can give, I seemed to be raised above all earthly cares, so that I almost believed that the promise given by the Lord through His prophet, was made good in my own case, ' I will cause thee to ride upon the high places of the earth.'[1] For he is truly raised upon the high places of the earth, who in his mind spurns all that the world esteems high and glorious." Having thus described the happiness of his earlier life of privacy and thought, he goes on to speak of the episcopal burden laid upon him, " But from this new elevation I fell into fear and anguish, not indeed for myself, but for those committed to me. Thus finding myself buffeted by

[1] Isa. lviii. 14.

the waves of business, and sunk by fortune, I say of a truth, 'I am come into deep waters, so that the floods run over me.'[1] I seek to retire within my heart when business is over, but the vain tumult of thought excludes me. He Who is within me is thus far from me, and I can no longer obey the voice which cries, 'Turn ye even to Me with all your heart.'"[2] Thus the holy Father continues to lament that "amid these earthly cares he cannot think over the miraculous works of the Lord, much less preach them publicly," and that "oppressed by the tumult of secular affairs, he is as one of those of whom it is written,[3] 'Thou dost set them in slippery places, and castest them down.'"[4]

XXX. Meanwhile it was thus that the Providence of God, which never fails in its purposes, brought about the introduction of Christ's Religion into society, or, more strictly speaking, created a new Christian society. In the Middle Ages the Religion of Christ penetrated every section of society: and was spread as healing oil over its festering wounds, infusing a new life and strength into the human race which was crushed by cen-

[1] Ps. lxix. 2. [2] Joel ii. 12. [3] Ps. lxxiii. 17.
[4] Epist., lib. i. ep. 5. The same lamentations are found throughout the letters of the first book, in letter 121 of the ninth book, and in letter 1 of book xi.

CHAP. II. turies of disaster. Religion took human nature under her maternal care; until, in its old age, it had passed through a strange course of long and cruel trials and had become once more a little child. Religion educated this pupil, this child of her tender love. And henceforward a new seed was sown in the earth; it blossomed into all modern civil institutions. It was public justice; a thing essentially Christian, and unknown to the ancient world. Although human passions ceaselessly try to shroud it, it will shine for ever. For the Providence of the Great King has pledged Itself to maintain His works; and, while disposing of all things by the Word of His power, It has but one aim, the greater glory of the Beloved Son, and the glorious destinies of His kingdom, so nobly won. Hence, as might be expected, the heads of these newly formed nations felt the strength of a religion which had given them political being and had blessed their crowns; and they displayed hitherto unknown examples of Christian virtues. This explains why the Middle Ages produced so many illustrious saints among the reigning sovereigns of Europe. Their proudest boast was that they were sons and subjects of the Church; they made it the study of their lives how they might temper a naturally fierce power by the gentleness of the Gospel, which they had received eagerly from the lips of their Bishops; and by the equity of their laws and the piety and splendour of their royal estate, they sought to promote the same object. But herein, too, we find the reason why, when kings had entered on the path of holiness, the clergy, on the contrary, strayed into the ways of corruption, which in the end cost them the saddest reverses.

XXXI. It was in the natural course of things, that the clergy, who had at first with bitter lamentations struggled to free themselves from the pressure of secular interests and worldly possessions which were thus forced upon them, should, after a time, begin to take pleasure in them and in the occupations which they involved. These occupations were new to them, and they were not sufficiently on the alert to guard against the perils which were close at hand. Thus little by little they forgot the gentleness and un-worldly habits befitting pastoral influence, and there appeared instead, only too plainly, the rough and earthly temper of civil governments. They sought to associate with the nobles, and to emulate their habits, and from that time they became unwilling to associate with the humble flock of Christ. From that time political and financial business became their chosen occupation, and, with the sophistry common to self-indulgence, they easily persuaded themselves that they were thus consulting the Church's best interests. The Bishops made over to the inferior clergy the instruction of the people, and the pastoral duties, which had now become a burden to themselves. Hence arose the formation of parishes, which in the tenth century were first introduced into cities, under the eyes of the Bishops. The Bishops' houses ceased to be so many flourishing schools of ecclesiastical learning and holiness for the young students who were the hope of the Church; they became instead princely courts, over-crowded with soldiers and courtiers. The glory of these houses was no longer to be found in the ardent Apostolic zeal, the deep meditation, or the eloquent instructions for which they were once renowned; the best praise that could be given them was that they kept in check the rude military temper, and imposed moderation upon the prevalent license. All pastoral care of the people was little by little abandoned to the subordinate clergy, so that before long they grew to look upon the parish priest as their Pastor, to the entire exclusion of the Bishop,[1] who by Christ's appointment is

---

[1] Thus, up to the time of St. Gregory, by " pastoral knowledge "

alone their true Pastor. Thus, as the duties and interests of the Bishops and the lower clergy became so divergent, and almost opposed, they constantly drew more and more apart. The familiar intercourse of a common life ceased. And the interviews which took its place were as rare and brief as possible, having no attraction for either party; as is the case between persons in different ranks of life. The old veneration and filial love of the priest became a timid subjection, and the kindly paternal authority of the Bishop took the airs of a superiority which was by turns contemptuous and patronizing. Meanwhile the lower clergy sank in popular esteem, and the higher clergy acquired a proportionate grandeur which was more apparent than real.[1] Can we

the knowledge of the Bishops was meant; but now in our seminaries "pastoral knowledge" means that of the parish priest, and the Bishop is never even mentioned in books treating of it. This application of the word Pastor to the parish priest, to the exclusion of Bishops, is principally to be attributed to the Protestants, who cast aside the Episcopate mainly because the Bishops had departed from those duties which were entrusted to them by Christ, and which in themselves bore testimony to His having instituted the office. Hence the people lost the idea of the Episcopal office, and this ignorance was the foundation of Protestant errors and separations from the Church.

[1] In all this, I have said already and would repeat once for all, I am speaking of the general state of the case. There were many exceptions. There have always been most saintly Bishops in the Church.

48   *Secularization of the clergy.*

CHAP. II. wonder that much evil should have crept in amongst a clergy thus degraded; and that, when they had become contemptible in the eyes of the people, their own estimate of the priestly character should be lowered? No doubt the holy occupations of the care of souls, and of preaching, now given up to the inferior clergy, might have served to keep up their tone; but from the moment that the highest rank of the ministry became an object of ambition for the sake of its power and wealth, the presbyter naturally gazed longingly at it. He envied his Bishop. And thus the Word of God, the sacrifice, and the sacraments became merely a lamentable trade, in which the sin of Judas, who sold his Divine Master, was daily renewed. In the same way sacred rites, devotions, prayers, even the very doctrines of the Faith, were recommended and ministered to the people according to the return which they yielded to the clergy. Thus, while the people were ignorant of much Christian teaching, they were intimately acquainted with what was taught about suffrages, benedictions, precepts of the Church, and indulgences, which afforded a revenue to the ministers of the altar. Of a truth they knew more concerning these matters than about many other parts of Christian knowledge. Thus the priests sank so low, that they were soon no longer held worthy of CHAP. II. the Bishop's attention; he need not trouble himself about an education which was thought unnecessary for them. Vice abounded; the attempt was made to stay it by means of laws and penalties. Such measures are better suited to secular than ecclesiastical governments. Although unable to uproot the moral evil, they did for a while restrain it within bounds. But, in time, the restraint gave way before the pressure, and the torrent overflowed the whole Church, threatening and visiting with ruin even her worldly pomp and her temporal greatness. The Mother of the Faithful was no longer recognized by her own children; whole nations fled from her face; for the time it was hidden from their weak sight. The Episcopate saw itself chastised by God after an unexpected and unforeseen fashion. It had persuaded itself that its interests were forwarded by every foot of ground that it could grasp, by every addition to worldly power that it could secure. But while thus absorbed in petty calculations, it was blind to the fact that the nations were withdrawing from it. While the Bishops were forsaking the care of their people for secular concerns, the people were in turn forsaking the Bishops, carrying away with them those interests which are never disjoined from

E

human lives. The Episcopate suddenly found itself rejected, set aside, almost effaced, scarcely discoverable, in hundreds of dioceses. Then, self-despised, the Bishops voluntarily stepped down from their thrones. In Germany, France, and England it was the Bishops themselves who threw aside the coronet of their regal priesthood;[1] they shook off their lethargy; they trembled at their own peril. For although the Episcopate may be chastened, it cannot wholly perish; Christ has promised that it shall last to the end of the world. And one of the first causes of the evil which presented itself to the Bishops was, the neglected education of the priesthood; and, in order to meet this difficulty, they resolved to provide the teaching of seminaries.

XXXII. Seminaries were invented to provide some kind of education for the clergy, as catechisms were invented to provide some kind of instruction for the people. The Bishops had not courage (it was hardly to be expected of them) to return to ancient customs, and themselves be the teachers of their people and clergy. They continued to depute these duties to the inferior clergy. But their vigilance was rekindled, and there was a great restoration of discipline, and reformation in

[1] [The author's meaning is somewhat indistinct here; but the fortunes and conduct of the episcopate in Germany, France, and England have been too various to be thus summarily described.—ED.]

manners. The lower clergy showed great zeal in the limited and largely unspiritual sphere of duties then open to them. But the art which had of old supplied the Church with great men, with priests alive to the vastness of their mission, had disappeared. The men were wanting who saw in the Church her sublime grandeur and universality, and who were, as it seemed, possessed and swayed by that felt presence of the Word which had formed the character of the primitive clergy. That living sense was no longer found which absorbs the powers of the soul, draws it away from a passing scene to that which lasts, and teaches it to snatch from the eternal mansions a torch wherewith to kindle the whole world. Only great men, I repeat, can train great men. It is enough to compare the teachers, if we would estimate the difference between the disciples. Alas! on one side are the ancient Bishops or some men of the highest distinction in the Church; on the other, the young principals of our seminaries. What a contrast!

XXXIII. Let it be considered with what hesitation and reluctance any school other than the Bishop's was set on foot even for the people in better times.[1] A separate school for the clergy

[1] Yet the popular school of those days did not resemble that of

52 Failure of modern seminaries

Chap. II. was only allowed in consideration of the great learning and saintliness of the men to whom it was entrusted. Thus, for instance, the school of Alexandria, already mentioned, probably the first of the kind, was established in the time of St. Mark.[1] On the other hand, consider how masters fit to teach the religion and doctrine of Christ to the clergy now abound, or at least are thought to abound! Not only has every diocese its seminary, and every seminary many teachers, but by reason of this abundance, and of the facility with which in these days Bishops can find priests to train their young clergy, the teachers are usually changed after a few years of work, in order that they may be promoted to a less unremunerative post. Others take their place who are as yet quite inexperienced, and who perhaps have not yet acquired the first principles of common sense. But then they have gone through the routine of the seminary, that *ne plus ultra* of modern ecclesiastical wisdom. When it is over, the

our time. The whole scheme of Christian doctrine was unfolded before the eyes of the Christian poor, so that both people and clergy were taught together; that is, those who aimed at the priesthood received the necessary preparation to enable them later on to profit by an ecclesiastical education. So far off from this are we, that many of our modern ecclesiastics could not understand what I am saying, and will assuredly be displeased at it.

[1] St. Jerome affirms it, De Vir. ill., c. 36. [But cf. Moehler, K. G. iii. 10, ch.—Ed.]

young ministers of the Altar are, without delay, sent to their work, and thus honourably dispensed from study. Meanwhile, the theological knowledge which very young teachers have acquired in a seminary is fragmentary, or probably limited to whatever may be necessary in order to enable them to acquit themselves perfunctorily of those ecclesiastical duties which are exacted of them by the authorities and by public opinion. And this weighty knowledge has neither root nor coherence in the young priest's mind; it has hardly reached his mind at all. Yet devoid, as he is, of the sympathies of knowledge, and of its true value, knowing what he knows as a mere matter of memory, he nevertheless considers himself better fitted for the office of teacher than a really learned man who might be promoted to it. Certainly, if mere memory is required, his pupils may have that! But the educational method of his master which St. Clement of Alexandria describes was far other than a mere training of memory. "He was as a Sicilian bee, which sucked the flowers of the apostolic and prophetic fields, in order that he might form within the souls of those who heard him the honey of a pure and uncorrupt knowledge."[1]

[1] Strom. lib. i. Eusebius thinks that the master of whom St. Clement speaks is Pantænus, who presided over the famous Alexandrian school (Hist., lib. v. c. 11).

CHAP. II. Finally, in these times, when the rate of salary attached to an office is a sure test of the class of men who fill it, may we not well doubt the efficiency of the masters in our seminaries, whose labours are so ill paid that they are over-joyed when the day comes for them to leave the seminary for some parochial benefice, which has all along been their aspiration, rather than continue their educational career?[1]

XXXIV. If the instruction of the clergy is entrusted to such feeble hands, it can cause no wonder that the writings of the saints and the learned should be set aside in favour of little books, "adapted for youth," as they say on the title-page, and put together by persons not much wiser. It is all after the same fashion, one evil leads to another; and the use of these meagre empty

[1] It is most essential that in these days the stipends of our Seminarist teachers should at least be equal to the best parochial charges, and that these teachers should not be removed from their collegiate chairs, except to be promoted to some canonry or capitular dignity, or to the Episcopate. In the celebrated school of Alexandria, St. Dionysius, St. Heraclas, and the great Saint Achillas, all three went from the teacher's chair to the Bishop's throne in that city, which was second only to Rome. But in those days men had present to their hearing and their minds the words of the Apostle to Timothy, bidding him find "men able to teach others also," the doctrines of the Gospel. The Apostle characterizes such men as "faithful," and bids Timothy "commit" the faith to them: "et quæ audisti a me per multos testes, hæc commenda fidelibus hominibus qui idonei erunt et alios docere" (2 Tim. ii. 2).

manuals in our schools is the third cause of the inadequacy of the education which is given there.

XXXV. There are two kinds of books. There are solid and classical books, containing the best wisdom of man, and written by its true representatives. These books are free from all that is arbitrary or barren, whether in method, style, or teaching. We find in them not merely exact facts and erudition, but those universal truths, that healthy fruitful information, which conveys all that is truly human, all common human feelings, and needs, and hopes. On the other hand, there are petty onesided books, the product of individual thought, thin and cold; in which great truths are minced up and adapted to little minds. The authors have been so exhausted by producing them that they convey no impression but that of effort, and have no power save to mislead. From such books all who have passed childhood turn away with contempt, finding in them nothing that answers to their natures, thoughts, or affections. Yet our youth is cruelly and obstinately condemned to the use of these books. Their natural sense would resist. But too often the want of something better leads them to the use of bad books; or else they acquire a downright dislike for study, as well as a concealed but deep aversion for all teachers and superiors; not to say a life-long hatred for books and for the truths contained in them. This hatred, hardly perceived by those who feel it, works for the most part under other forms than that of hatred. It is apt to conceal itself under any pretext, and when it becomes manifest is a source of astonishment to him who cherishes it. He was not aware of its existence and cannot account for it. It has the semblance of impiety, or of ingratitude towards teachers, who in all else have been good to their pupils, and have freely bestowed upon them their care, their advice, and their love.

XXXVI. In the Church's early days Holy Scripture was the only text-book on which instruction, both popular and ecclesiastical, was founded. This Scripture is really the book of mankind, *the* Book ($\beta\iota\beta\lambda\iota\alpha$), the Scripture proper. In this volume human nature is portrayed from the beginning to the end. It begins with the origin of the world, and ends with its future destruction. Here man recognizes himself in his changeful history. Here he finds a clear, sure, and final answer to the great questions which he is ever asking himself; and while his mind is satisfied by its wisdom and its mysteriousness, his heart is provided for by its rules of life and its revelation of grace.

It is that "great" book which the Prophet says is written, "With a man's pen."[1] In it the Eternal Truth speaks according to all those modes in which man's speech is fashioned: at one time it narrates, then it teaches; now it speaks in proverbs, now in song; the memory is fed with history, the imagination charmed with poetry, the intellect enlightened with wisdom; and the feelings kindled by all these at once. Its doctrine is so simple that the unlearned man may think it framed specially for himself; and so sublime that the wisest doctor cannot hope to fathom it. The words seem to be human, but it is God Himself Who speaks. Thus St. Clement of Alexandria says, "Holy Scripture kindles a fire in the soul, and at the same time guides the mind's eye to contemplation, now casting the seed into our hearts, as the husbandman sows it in the earth, now causing to germinate that which we already possess."[2] If such words are applicable to general literature, much more properly may they be applied to the Word of God.

XXXVII. Such was the Book of our Christian schools. And this great Book, in the hands of the great men who expounded it, was the nourishment of other great men. As long as the

[1] Isaiah viii. 1. [2] Strom., lib. i.

Bishops were themselves the teachers of the people and the clergy, they were also the authors who wrote for the Church and the public. Hence nearly all the chief [Christian] works of the first six centuries are the works of Bishops. It is an exception to the rule when we find any work of those times which had not an Episcopal origin. The exception occurs only in the case of some remarkable minds, as were Origen, Tertullian, and others, who attained to the post of Christian teachers by reason of their great merits. These Episcopal writings mark a second stage in the history of the books used for the instruction of youth in our Christian and ecclesiastical schools. These works were bequeathed as a legacy to the lower clergy, when the Bishops were forced, by the general collapse of government and society, and by the widespread demands upon their sympathy and assistance, to forsake labours hitherto considered inseparable from their pastoral office. The training of the people and the clergy gradually fell to the inferior clergy;[1] at first chiefly to those who

[1] I say gradually, for such changes are never made rapidly or generally. Fleury, speaking of the five centuries that followed the first six, says, " The method of instruction continued the same as in early times. The cathedrals or monasteries were the schools, where the Bishop himself taught, or else some of his clerks, or some learned monk appointed by him, so that the disciples at once obtained knowledge of Church truths, and were trained in the

Education conducted by canons and monks. 59

were most closely connected with the Bishops, and most venerated for their religious lives, that is, the canons, and the monks, who at this period were enabled by Providence to meet the pressing wants of the Church.[1] This section of the clergy, succeeding to the Bishops as trainers of Christian youth, lay and ecclesiastical, reverently received the precious inheritance from the venerable Fathers of the Church, and looked upon it as a safe

CHAP. II.

duties of the ministry and in devotional habits, under their Bishop's eye " (Eccles. Hist., from the year 600 to 1100).

[1] " Most of the schools were in monasteries; and the cathedrals in some countries, England and Germany, for instance, were served by monks. The canons, whose government dates from the middle of the eighth century, with the Rule of St. Chrodegang, led a monastic life, and their houses were called monasteries. I consider the monasteries to have been the chief means used by Providence to preserve religion in those miserable times. They were a refuge for learning and holiness, while ignorance, vice, and barbarism overflowed the outer world. Then the old traditions were followed in the sacred offices, and in the practice of Christian virtues, which were handed down from the elder to the younger. They also preserved the writings of earlier ages, and multiplied copies of them. This, indeed, was one of the chief occupations of religious houses, and without the monks' libraries we should have preserved but few books " (Fleury, ibid. § xxii.). The Bishop lived with his canons, thus preserving for a long time the primitive tradition of episcopal life. When secular distractions put an end to this pious community life, councils, led by zealous Bishops, endeavoured to reform the ecclesiastical life upon the old model, so that the same spirit has survived in the Church, and she strives ceaselessly to repair her losses. We all know that St. Charles wished to live in community life with his clergy: in short, the desire has never been forgotten by the Church, and her wishes and aims have always tended that way.

model for their guidance. Thus for a long time the ancient Bishops continued to teach through their writings. But there was a wide difference between the living presence and voice, and the mere written words, in themselves lifeless, and not often rekindled into life by the teachers of those hapless times. During the next five centuries, the clergy of the second order did not attempt anything original. They merely repeated the lessons and teaching which they had received from the early Fathers;[1] either because they knew themselves to be no masters in Israel, as the Bishops had been, or because their mental activity had suffered from the sad circumstances of the times, when the world was filled with wars, devastation, and misery. When the invasions had ceased, and the barbarians had established themselves in the countries which they had overrun, the new teachers began to write books which corresponded with the condition of the writers. The books fell as far short of those of the ancient Bishops in authority, dignity of language,

[1] Fleury, speaking of the monks, says, "They studied the doctrines of the faith in Holy Scripture and the Fathers, and the discipline in the Canons. They had little craving for knowledge, and little originality, but a profound veneration for the ancient authors, confining themselves to the study of these, copying, compiling, abridging from them. We see this in the writings of Bede, Rabanus, and other mediæval theologians; they are wholly taken from the Fathers of the first six centuries, and this was the surest way to preserve tradition" (Hist. Eccles. § xxi.).

Mediæval compendiums of theology. 61

and accurate thought, as the authors were inferior CHAP. II.
in weight and bearing to those old leaders of
the Church. Such works could not have the
stamp of originality. They were compendiums or
summaries in which the Christian doctrines were
scientifically registered. They were required to
furnish an easier method of learning the old
tradition of the Church ; with the lapse of time the
documents had greatly multiplied and the study
had become too vast. These compendiums mark
the epoch of scholastic theology, which may be
termed the characteristic work of the presbyters as
teachers. The first and most celebrated was compiled in the twelfth century by the Master of
Sentences, Peter Lombard. The idea of epitomising
the doctrines scattered through the vast literature
of ecclesiastical tradition was excellent. Those
documents were inevitably full of repetitions,
which add not a little to the student's labour.
But the compendiums did not confine themselves
to stating succinctly that which had often been
repeated ; they also stripped Christian doctrine of
all that referred to the heart and other faculties,
content if they satisfied the intellect.[1] Thus these
new books failed to impress mankind as had the

---

[1] St. Bernard, St. Bonaventura, and some others, are noble
exceptions ; they wrote with all the dignity of the early Fathers.

older writings. They touched a single side or faculty of man's nature, not man himself. Thus scholasticism acquired that narrow onesided character, which separated its disciples from the rest of the world; they gave up common sense for the subtleties of reason. It was a natural result. It was natural that the Bishop, who is not a mere teacher, but also a father[1] and pastor, whose mission is not only to demonstrate truth, but to make men love it, and save men through it, should in his instructions be explicit, persuasive and searching. The priest can do less; he feels himself to be less responsible; he is content with putting truth with cold exactness before disciples who almost argue with him as with an equal;[2] his method is scientific; it is not persuasive, adapting itself variously to various minds; it is moulded upon the objective sequence of doctrines which is absolute and unvarying; it avoids all amplification; and it introduces that element of rational-

[1] St. Clement of Alexandria says, "We call those who catechized us fathers. He who is taught is the son, who gathers up the substance of that in which he is instructed; and in this sense the Scripture says, 'My son, forget not my law' (Prov. iii. 1)." (Strom. i. 270 b.).

[2] This is the reason why the doctors of these later centuries followed the philosophy of Aristotle, while those of the first six centuries had greater sympathy with that of Plato.

by scholastic teaching.

ism which in the sixteenth century was fully developed into Protestantism,¹ under which sacred

¹ Protestantism, which in our time has forsaken revelation, and takes its stand on pure reason (that is, on a systematic reason which is *not* reason), is the full and perfect development of that rationalistic element which the schoolmen introduced into the Christian faith. This element of rationalism has not been without its influence among Catholics, that is, among that portion of the Christian world which did not venture to follow this development on to its extreme point, which involves forsaking the Church and revelation itself. It bore, even among these, some of the fruit we might look for from such a root. In dogmatic theology it generated the disputes between Catholic schools, which became irreconcilable, chiefly concerning the doctrines of Grace ; while in civil and canonical law, it produced such cavils as marred the usefulness of the best laws. In morals, the effect was not dissimilar, for it led to all that was said and done with respect to the subject of probabilism, which had much to do with the lowered tone of morals among Christian peoples, a falling away to be attributed as much to the influx of what was called laxity, as of what was called rigorism. The theological battles which so greatly marred union among the clergy are too well known to need dwelling on. Fleury writes thus concerning the cavils of the men of the law in the thirteenth century : "Examine the Canons of the great Lateran Council, and still more those of the first Council of Lyons, and you will see to what an extreme point the subtlety of litigants had attained in eluding the laws, and making them serve as clokes for injustice, the which I call the spirit of sophistry. The advocates and practitioners who were ruled by this spirit were clerks, who then alone studied civil or canonical jurisprudence, medicine, and the other sciences. If mere vanity and ambition could suggest to philosophers and theologians such evil sophistries, over which they contended ceaselessly, how much more would the greed of gain excite lawyers? And what could be hoped for from such a clergy? The spirit of the Gospel is sincerity, candour, love, disinterestedness. These clerks, who were devoid of such virtues themselves, were little qualified to teach them to others" (Discours v. Hist. Eccles., § xvii.). As to the effect on morals of the predominance given to human reason in the schools, Fleury

64 *Subsequent imitation of the schoolmen.*

Chap. II. knowledge and the religion of Christ were taken from the hands of the clergy, and were completely secularized.

XXXVIII. Scholastic summaries and compendiums reached their climax of perfection in the work of St. Thomas Aquinas, in the thirteenth century. Later teachers in the schools of Christianity, down to our times, while they have doubtless made great advances in history, criticism, languages, and elegance of style, have done nothing for doctrine but follow the schoolmen, repeating, glossing, abbreviating, much as the teachers in the ages following the first six centuries had done with respect to the Fathers. Nor is this an invidious comparison; every one who

expresses an opinion in which some do not agree: "The worst result of the logical method (that is, the method which teaches us to seek everywhere the *pro* and *contra*, as the schoolmen did) is a despair of finding the truth, which led to the introduction and authorization in morals of the probabilist opinions." The evil was not their introduction, but their abuse. "In fact, this side of philosophy was not better treated in our schools than elsewhere. Our doctors, having the habit of contesting everything, and of finding out all probabilities, did the same as to morals, and they were often tempted to stray from the right path by flattery of their own or other men's passions. This was the origin of the laxity so evident in the more recent casuists, which did not begin till the end of the thirteenth century. Those doctors were satisfied with a certain calculation of proportions, the result of which did not always agree with the Gospel or with good sense; but they forced all to harmonize by the subtlety of their distinctions" (Hist. Eccles., dis. v. § ix.).

looks below the surface will find it to be true. The restoration of letters, in the fifteenth and sixteenth centuries, drew the attention of men, who, forsaking speculation for the charms of imagination and feeling, let go the nervous fibre of Christian philosophy. It died out, as before, the dignity and fulness of doctrinal statement had died out. The importance of the leading intrinsic reasons for Christian doctrine was overlooked, though these were still retained by the best of the schoolmen; just as they themselves had lost sight of the importance of the grand and full exposition of truth in use among the Fathers. The schoolmen had impoverished Christian philosophy by despoiling it of all that belonged to feeling and that gave it moral power. Their disciples (how should they be superior to their teachers?) curtailed it still further, casting aside everything in it that was deepest, most central, most real, avoiding its noblest principles under pretext of facilitating study, but really because they themselves did not understand them. Thus they reduced the science of religion to materialized formulas, isolated deductions, practical remarks such as the clergy could not dispense with, if they wished to present religious matters to the people, under the outward guise which had always been customary in past times. And this is the

CHAP. II. fourth and last epoch in the history of books used in the schools of Christianity: the epoch of *theologians* succeeding to *schoolmen*. By these steps—Holy Scripture, the Fathers, schoolmen, and theologians—we have come at last to those marvellous text-books now used in our seminaries, which instil so much would-be wisdom, so poor an opinion of our predecessors. These books, I believe, will, in the more hopeful future days of the imperishable Church, be considered to be the most meagre and the feeblest that have been written during the eighteen centuries of her history. They are books without life, without principles, without eloquence, and without system;[1] although by a set and regular arrangement of materials, which takes the place of system, they show that the authors have exhausted their intellectual resources. They are the product neither of feeling, nor talent, nor imagination; they are not episcopal nor priestly, but in every sense lay; they

[1] To cite some most learned writers, Tournely, or Gazzaniga. Certainly they wrote a large, very erudite work on Grace. But it is only quite at the end that they just glance at the question, "In what the essence of grace consists;" leaving it unsolved, as rather a matter of curiosity than one of importance. But is it not of foremost importance to know the essence and nature of the thing treated of? Is it not necessary to know the nature of a thing, in order to give a good definition of it? And is not definition the fertile source from whence should issue all further discussions on a subject?

require only masters able to read mechanically, and pupils who can listen as mechanically.

XXXIX. If the little books and little teachers go together, can a great school be formed out of such elements? or can they aim at a dignified system of instruction? No. And this defect of system is the fourth and last cause of the Wound in the Church now under review, the insufficient education of the clergy in our times. We said that the habits of the clergy became demoralized when the schoolmen separated the education of the heart from that of the intellect.[1] Later the attempt was made to correct the excessive demoralization which had naturally ensued; and then in our well-regulated seminaries we find a good, or at least decent manner of life. But the root of the evil was left untouched; no one tried

---

[1] Fleury, speaking of the young students of the twelfth and thirteenth centuries, says, "Dare I call attention to the customs of our students, such as I have described them in my history, following the testimony of contemporaneous authors? You will see that they were constantly fighting, either among themselves, or with the citizens; that their privilege was to deny the right of the secular judges to try them for their misdeeds; that the Pope was obliged to concede to the Abbot of St. Victor power to absolve them from the excommunication pronounced by the Canon law against all such as struck a clerk; that their disputes began, for the most part, with drinking and debauchery at the common inns, often leading on to violence and murder. In short, you will find the hateful portrait drawn from life by Jacopo di Vitri. Yet all these students were clerks, destined to serve or govern the Church" (Discours v. § x.).

CHAP. II. to counteract the fatal separation of theory and practice, or once more to make fathers of the teachers. St. Chrysostom says, "To be a father, it is not enough to have governed, but you must also carefully educate a young man."[1] Nothing was done beyond propping up and strengthening the failing morality. But assuredly this is not enough for the Church. The morality of the clergy ought to spring from and be sustained by the fulness and solidity of their knowledge of the doctrine of Christ, inasmuch as we want not merely respectable men, but Christians and priests enlightened and sanctified by union with Christ. This was the leading principle and foundation of the system followed in the first centuries; knowledge and holiness were closely combined, the one springing from the other. It may be truly said that knowledge sprang from holiness, since the former was sought solely out of love to the latter; knowledge was sought after so far as it was essential to holiness, and no other knowledge was desired. Thus all was combined. In this combination we find the true spirit of that doctrine which is destined to save the world: it is no ideal doctrine, but practical and real truth. Once

[1] Οὐ τὸ σπεῖραι ποιεῖ πατέρα μόνον, ἀλλὰ καὶ τὸ παιδεῦσαι καλῶς (De Anna, serm. i. § 3). [Ros. transl. σπεῖραι by "aver governato."— not accurately.—ED.]

take away from it its holiness, and can we believe that the wisdom taught by Christ remains? It would be a delusion to think it; esteeming ourselves wise, we should be but fools; we should mistake a vain and lifeless shadow for the living doctrine of Christ.

XL. Let us see with what a holy longing after practical truth Papias, a celebrated disciple of the Apostles, pursued his studies. Eusebius, in his history, quotes Papias as saying, that he sought not the society of those who talked much, but of those who could teach him the truth. He did not seek those who published abroad new doctrines invented by men, but those who adhered to the rules our Lord had left for the support of our Faith, and observed by the Truth Himself. Whenever he came upon any who were disciples of the first Fathers, he eagerly gathered up all their words. He would ask them, what St. Andrew, St. Peter, St. John, St. Philip, St. Thomas, St. James, St. Matthew had said, or any other disciple of Jesus Christ, such as Aristion or the aged John. For he held the teaching gathered from books to be less profitable than that which he received from the lips of those with whom he spoke. And he noted in his writings that he was the disciple of Aristion and John the aged, often quoting

CHAP. II. them, and repeating things he had learnt from them.[1]

· In this description given by Eusebius, we see how strongly that characteristic of Christ's doctrine—the love of truth which improves us, apart from idle curiosity—induced holy men in primitive times not so much to seek knowledge, as to gaze with the soul's eye into truth; to feed on it inwardly, as on living bread. Hence they greatly preferred oral instruction to that of books, especially as to the sacred mysteries.[2] And their disciples felt the practical benefit of the system. One of the most valuable points in this system employed by those great minds in forming other great minds was that the instruction did not end with the brief daily lesson. It was continued in the constant intercourse of the disciple with his master, of the young ecclesiastic with his venerable Bishop. This advantage was lost when education was given up to the

[1] Euseb., bk. iii. c. xxxix.
[2] The *disciplina arcani* was expressly intended to prevent the most sublime truths being set before those who were unworthy to hear them. Those great doctrines were only taught orally, and then to none save to long-tried disciples, who had proved themselves worthy by their consistent perseverance in aiming at a holy life. The early writers allude to this caution and reverence for revealed truth; it is enough to cite Clement of Alexandria, who speaks of it in the first book of the "Stromata," as well as in other works.

inferior clergy; to mere instructors who were not pastors.[1]

XLI. Knowledge may be had by all, good and bad. But the truth and practice of the Gospel are found only among the good. Hence where knowledge only is taught, there is no need for anxiety as to the morals of the teachers. But of old this point was carefully investigated. The truth which was to be taught was holy truth, and it was held to be indispensable that he who taught it should himself be holy.[2] Nor will the selection of dis-

[1] Even in seeking to remedy the deficient education of the clergy, the root of the evil was not reached. One remedy was the foundation of universities; but these only divided clergymen still more from their Bishops, as they do still. Fleury says, "Another defect in universities is, that masters and pupils are all clerks, some beneficed. But they were all occupied with their studies, to the exclusion of duties belonging to Holy Orders, except those in church. Thus the pupils never learnt those things which are taught by practice—the art of instruction, the administration of the Sacraments, the guidance of souls. They might have learnt these in their own country, by watching the priests and Bishops, and serving under them. The doctors of the university were doctors and nothing more, absorbed in speculation, and having full leisure to write endlessly upon all manner of useless questions, which were so many subjects of strife and dispute, every one seeking to subtilize more than the rest. In the primitive times the doctors were Bishops, who were engrossed with weightier occupations" (Discours v. § x.).

[2] Another instance which shows how all things work together, and the bad system involves bad teachers. How unlike the noble views entertained of old of the Christian teacher! How much was required of him! In a celebrated sermon of St. Gregory Nazianzen, "Of Theology," he describes at length what he who teaches theology should be: "Not every one," he says, "is fit to philosophize concerning Divine truths; those alone should do so who are pure in body and

ciples be good, where the main object is only scientific, instead of being truly moral as well. Wherever, on the contrary, the wisdom of holiness is chiefly considered, great pains would be taken to remove from a school all those who are not actuated by a holy desire for this wisdom. This was done in early times, when a wise selection of men for the service of the sanctuary was easier. This was the received test which showed who had a vocation or not, and the young men who sought admittance into the schools, knew what was expected of them, and what they came to learn. Moreover holy and practical truth has this superiority over merely ideal truth, that it inspires respect and veneration in those who learn and in those who teach, by reason of its own sacred and Divine nature. And therefore such as hold the sublime mission of communicating it to others, ought wholly to shrink from wasting it on those who are unworthy, as in so doing they join in profaning its holiness. They must feel the force of our Lord's words, when He forbade His disciples to "cast pearls before swine."[1]
soul, or who at least seek to be such, and are advanced in contemplation of holy things "(Orat. xxxiii. and Orat. xxxix.). St. Clement of Alexandria (Strom., lib. i., Pedag. in f.) treats at length of the disinterestedness, the spiritual light, and the holiness necessary for those who would teach sacred things.

[1] St. Matt. vii. 6.

Alexandrian reserve in teaching. 73

For this reason the primitive teachers, as described by Clement of Alexandria, " made long trial, choosing from among their pupils the one who was most apt to listen to their words ; watching his conversation, his way of life, his movements, his dress, his manner, and investigating whether he were sand or rock, or trodden footpath, or fertile ground, or thicket, or good field, fruitful and well tilled, wherein the seed might multiply." " They imitated Christ," says the same St. Clement, " in that He did not reveal to the many those things which were not meant for the many, but to the few, for whom He knew they would be suitable ; because these could not only receive but model themselves upon them ; that is to say, they could correspond to the truth which they received in their minds, by the rectitude of their lives."[1] According to this plan, there would be but few priests. Well ; Clement makes no other answer to this objection save, " Pray ye the Lord of the harvest, that He would send forth labourers into His harvest."[2]

XLII. Another result followed from the principle, that " ecclesiastical instruction should convey the living Word of Christ, and not human and lifeless words." All the sciences were voluntarily

[1] Strom., lib. i., 273 c. sqq.   [2] Strom., lib. i.

CHAP. II. subject to religious truth. In it they found a point of unity; and thus they paid their debt of service and homage to Christ, and the minds of men were better disposed to appreciate the beauty and value of Gospel wisdom. There were not in those days two educations; one pagan and the other Christian; one teaching profane science in a profane spirit, and the other teaching ecclesiastical science; one opposed and hostile to the other. Young men were not corrupted by an infusion of the spirit of heathen authors, and by crooked and worldly aims in work which were later on to be counteracted and corrected by the maxims of the Christian Church. One sole aim was set before them, and one only doctrine was to guide them, that of Christ; and thus even profane studies did but serve to strengthen their faith. It was owing to such a system that we find Origen coming forth from the school of Pantænus, and Gregory Thaumaturgus from the school of Origen.[1]

[1] St. Jerome says that Origen made use of profane knowledge to lead into the faith the philosophers and learned men who came to hear him (D. V. M. c. 54). In the oration delivered by Gregory Thaumaturgus (the most illustrious of Origen's disciples), at the close of his studies, he describes the method by which Origen had trained him; by which it appears that the first step had been the correction of his manners, passing on to various sciences all so ordered as to strengthen and mould the pupil's faith. Origen used no compendiums, but read all the chief philosophic writings with

XLIII. At the same time that all education gained unity by the unity of its principle, and the single aim of really Christian studies, all other studies were completed and perfected by its means. All was gathered together, especially Religion; her secret mysteries, her profound principles, her noble precepts; in a word, her whole system. There were no arbitrary exclusions, no unjust preferences of one point of doctrine to another. The Word of Christ was loved; it alone was sought; and hence the desire to discover in it all that could be explored. And inasmuch as men sought in that Word the hidden life, it was

his pupil, pointing out to him wherein they were in error and wherein true. After these preliminary studies, by which he formed the young man's mind, he inspired him with a longing for the highest and most perfect doctrines; and ended by setting the Holy Scriptures before him, by which he was to attain to the doctrines of God. I know that in our day we cannot give up compendiums, but I know, too, that we shall never do anything with them alone; we shall not even succeed in starting the student on the highroad of true learning. Their true use is to sum up briefly what has been studied fully in great authors; these must be read and explained. Certainly all cannot be read, but some part may be; and that part will suffice to inspire the student, to give him an idea of the grandeur of Christian knowledge, even as from the foot of Hercules it could be seen what the whole man was.—But in this way we should not get even the outlines of science in general ?—If mere outlines are required, no doubt these may be found in compendiums: this, and no other, is their proper use. The knowledge which such a system will give the student will be as though a painter's disciple saw his master design a picture and partly colour it, leaving the pupil to finish it after his master's style of colouring.

CHAP. II. communicated amidst prayers and tears, and sacred services : whence was derived the grace that supernaturally fed with the light of truth souls that were craving for righteousness.[1]

[1] St. Clement of Alexandria, when discussing the acquisition of knowledge, always joins thereto the Sacraments of Christ. He would have the Master not a mere teacher, but a husbandman giving all his thought and care to the delicate plants he tends. He adds, "There is a double tillage—one without books, another with them. In both systems that husbandman of the Lord who has sown good seed, watched the ears grow, and gathered in the harvest, will be indeed a labourer for God. The Lord says, ' Labour not for the meat that perisheth, but for that which endureth unto life eternal.' We may understand by that meat food, and also the Word. Of a truth blessed are the peacemakers who draw those hitherto lost in error from their miserable condition, teaching them what is true, and leading them into peace, which is found in the Word, and in the life of God ; blessed too are they who feed with good food those who hunger after righteousness " (Strom., i. 272 c). Here we see how this disciple of the Apostles united together the giving of bread with the teaching of the Word ; he had before compared instruction with the Eucharist. He always describes the teacher of holy things in a similar way—saying that he should be a heavenly labourer, a pastor, a minister of God, and as he says soon after, "even one with God Himself ! " Origen, Clement's disciple, holds the same language. " None," he says, "should listen to the Word of God who is not sanctified in body and soul, since he is shortly to enter in to the wedding feast ; he is to eat the Flesh of the Lamb, and to drink the cup of salvation " (In Exod., Hom. xi.). Is not this a noble union of the Divine Sacrament with the Word? One more passage from the same author ; it is in a Homily taken down from his lips : " O ye who are wont to be present at the Mysteries, well do ye know with what care and respect ye receive the Body of the Lord, fearful lest the least particle should fall, since ye would esteem yourselves most guilty, were the smallest crumb to be lost ; and if ye use so many precautions to preserve His Body, think ye it is less guilty to despise His Word ? " (In Exod., Hom. xxiii.).

XLIV. Ah, who will restore such a system to the Church, the only system worthy of her? Who will restore to the schools of the priesthood their great books, and their great teachers? Who, in a word, will heal the deep Wound of an insufficient education of the clergy, which daily weakens and grieves the Bride of Christ? None can do it save the Bishops. Theirs is the commission to rule her; theirs the miraculous gift of healing her when she is sick: but it is theirs when they are united, not when divided and scattered asunder. We need for this great work the whole episcopal body joined together in one, both in will and deed. But it is precisely this union which is lacking in these evil times among the Pastors of the Holy Church. And herein lies the third Wound of the Church, which is by no means less cruel than those of which we have already spoken.

CHAPTER III.

Of the Wound in the Side of the Holy Church, which is the Disunion of the Bishops.

XLV. BEFORE the Divine Founder of the Church left the world, He prayed His Heavenly Father that His Apostles might be joined together in a perfect union, even as He and the Father were perfectly One, having one and the same Nature. This sublime union, of which the God-man spake in His wonderful prayer after the Last Supper and just before His Passion, was chiefly an inward unity, a unity of faith, of hope, of love. But to this inward unity, which can never be wholly wanting in the Church, there should correspond an external union; as the effect follows on its cause, as the expression on the thing expressed, as the fabric embodies the type or design to which it is due. "One body and one spirit," the Apostle says.[1]

[1] Eph. iv. 4.

Unity of the Apostolic Church. 79

This includes everything; inasmuch as the body signifies union in the sphere of external and visible things, and the spirit union in respect of things which are invisible to our bodily sight. He adds, "One Lord, one Faith, one Baptism, one God and Father of all, Who is above all, and through all, and in you all."[1] Here, once more, is the Unity of the Divine Nature set forth as the momentous foundation of that union which should exist among men; those scattered believers whom Christ has gathered under His wings, "as a hen gathereth her chickens," and has formed them into His one Church. Here too is the ground of that unity in the Episcopate of Christ's Church, of which the first Bishops thought so highly, and of which St. Cyprian treats so eloquently in his book "on the unity of the Church."

XLVI. Very remarkably did the Apostles maintain this twofold unity. As to the inward unity, they shared in common one and the same doctrine, and one and the same grace. As to outward unity, one among them was first,[2] and the origin of the one Episcopate, as the great Bishop and Martyr of Carthage says, which all possessed

[1] Eph. iv. 5, 6.
[2] "Deus unus est" (so writes St. Cyprian in a letter), "et Christus unus, et una Ecclesia, et Cathedra una super Petrum, Domini voce fundata" (Ep. xl.). [Ed. Fell. xliii. ad plebem].

CHAP. III. in its entirety.[1] To one alone was given in particular that which was given to all in general, and upon one, as upon a single and individual rock, was built that Church of which all, together with him, were equally the foundation.[2]

XLVII. The consciousness of this perfect Unity in the hierarchy, in itself the beautiful expression and faint reflection of their inward spiritual union, strengthened the first successors of the Apostles. Scattered as they were throughout the world, they yet felt themselves to be a single commissioned authority. Thus they realized the Divine Ideal of a beneficent Power, which, like God Himself, was found everywhere. This wonderful unity they knew to be the last heritage of Christ to His chosen ones, before His death ; that is, before He shed the blood which sealed this His new and eternal testament. Of a truth, the unity of His chosen ones, typified in the Eucharistic Bread and in · the seamless garment which covered His Sacred Flesh, was the ultimate aim of the prayers of Christ, the desired fruit of His infinite sufferings. For He had asked of the Father, " Keep through Thine own

[1] "Episcopatus unus est, cujus a singulis pars in solidum tenetur" (Lib. de Unit. Eccles. § 4).
[2] [But cf. Langen, Vat. Dogm. p. 13, sqq.; Hussey, Rise of Papal Power, Lect. I. ; Macaire, Theol. Dogm. Orth. ii. p. 246 sqq.—ED.]

Name those whom Thou hast given Me, that they may be one."[1]

CHAP. III.

XLVIII. This great idea of Unity having entire possession of the minds of the early Bishops, and still more of their hearts, they neglected nothing which might bind them together. They were not content that all should maintain an absolute oneness of Faith, and an equal love for the body of Pastors. They went further,—and this was of the highest importance to the wise government of the Church— they desired nothing more ardently, they had, we may say, nothing more at heart, than a perfect unanimity of action. Any one who considers the vast extent of the Church's rule—scattered as she is among all nations—cannot but marvel to behold everywhere such unity of doctrine, of discipline, even of usages; while the points of difference are few and unimportant.

XLIX. But whence arose this Unity? How was it rendered permanent?

1. By the personal intercourse of the Bishops. It began for the most part before they became Bishops, as a natural consequence of the lofty type of education of those great men from among whom the Church selected her prelates. They had

[1] " Pater sancte, serva eos in Nomine Tuo quos dedisti Mihi : ut sint unum, sicut et Nos " (St. John xvii. 11).

G

generally been fellow-disciples under other great Bishops,[1] or they had sought to become known to each other by journeys arranged for that especial purpose. In those days men did not spare long and wearisome journeys, in order to obtain the sight of any one celebrated for his holiness and his teaching, to enjoy the privilege of hearing him, and of sharing his intercourse. This was because in those times it was held that books alone did not suffice for wisdom, in the sense then attributed to the word, which was, not a barren knowledge, but a living intelligence, a deep feeling, a practical conviction. On the contrary, it was believed that the presence, the voice, the

---

[1] For instance, St. John Chrysostom was trained under St. Meletius of Antioch, and Socrates records that the holy Bishop, perceiving the good dispositions of the youth, kept him ever at his side, baptizing him after three years' instruction, appointing him reader, and later ordaining him subdeacon and deacon. With St. John Chrysostom, were Theodorus and Maximus, who later became Bishops of Mopsuestia in Cilicia, and Seleucia in Isauria. Diodorus who trained them in the ascetic life, was Bishop of Tarsus. Basil, St. John Chrysostom's friend, was early raised to the Episcopate. Here we find a whole nest of Bishops, who had been friends before they attained that dignity. To take an instance from the West. Look at the School of St. Valerian of Aquileia :—at the time he visited St. Jerome, besides Heliodorus who was later a Bishop, that school contained many learned and pious priests, deacons, and lower ministers, such as the celebrated Rufinus, Jovinus, Eusebius, Nepotian, Bonosus, etc. It is well known that the house, or rather the monastery of St. Augustine in Africa was a nursery of future Bishops.

gestures, even the commonest actions of great men [1] Chap. III. had a virtue which communicated itself to others; a virtue able to kindle sparks of fire in young minds which, without such contact, would remain passive. St. Jerome went from Dalmatia to Rome to seek his early education; thence he travelled in Gaul, visiting all the well-known men who dwelt there; thence on to Aquileia in order to hear the Bishop St. Valerian, around whom were gathered so many celebrities. After that he went to the East to see Apollinaris at Antioch, enrolling himself among the disciples of Gregory Nazianzen at Constantinople. Later on he did not esteem it unworthy his grey hairs to learn that truth, which in those days was sought after to the last hour of life, from the lips of the blind Didymus of Alexandria. At that time, men travelled over half the world, only that they might thoroughly understand a single point of the Church's doctrine. Take, as an instance, the priest Orosius, who went from Spain to Africa in order to learn from St. Augustine how best to confute the heresies then infesting the Church. He was referred by Augustine to

[1] This is still more the case in the order of supernatural things. The saints communicate and pour forth the spirit of holiness on all those around them; as Christ Himself has declared in those words, " He that believeth on Me, as the Scripture hath said, out of his belly shall flow rivers of living water" (St. John vii. 38).

St. Jerome, whom he then sought in Palestine. It was thus that the priests of those ages studied theology, and thus that the leaders among the clergy diligently kept up their mutual intercourse.

L. 2. The second means by which episcopal unity was preserved was the constant intercourse maintained by correspondence even between Bishops who lived widely apart from each other. The means of communication were very different from those in our times. It surprises us to find Vigilius, Bishop of Trent, sending as a gift, accompanied by a friendly letter, part of the relics of the Martyrs of Anaunia to St. Chrysostom at Constantinople, and the other part to St. Simplician at Milan. Besides the letters of private friendship that passed between the Bishops, the Churches wrote one to another, especially the chief Churches to those which were subject to them. In this pious correspondence both the presbytery and the people took part; the treasured letters were reverently read in public on festivals. In thus acting they were following the example of the Apostles. Witness the Epistles of St. Peter, St. Paul, St. John, St. James, and St. Jude, yet preserved to us in the Canon of Holy Scripture. Witness, too, the letters of the Pontiffs,[1]

[1] [This epithet is an anachronism.—ED.]

St. Clement and St. Soterius to the Church of Corinth, as also the epistles of St. Ignatius, and of St. Dionysius, Bishop of Corinth, to various Churches, specially that of Rome;[1] together with many more.

LI. 3. Another means of preserving unity was the frequent visits of the Bishops to one another, either from zeal in the affairs of the Church, or in order to a mutual interchange of affection. A Bishop's zeal was not confined to his own special charge among the Churches; it was yet greater for the Church Universal. He knew that he was a Bishop of the Church Catholic,[2] and that a diocese can no more be severed from the whole Body of the faithful than can a limb from the living human body. Every member of

---

[1] Among other things in this letter of Dionysius to the Roman Church, the saint says, "This day we kept the holy feast of the Lord's Day, and we read your letter, which we shall read continually for our instruction, as well as those previously written to us by Clement" (Euseb., Eccles. Hist., lib. iv. c. 23). We know of seven epistles written by that eminent Bishop of Corinth to the faithful of different Churches, i.e. besides that to the Romans, one to the Lacedæmonians, the Athenians, the Nicomedians, the Church of Amastris in Pontus, the Church of Gortyna in Crete, and to the Gnossians also in Crete. Still better known are the six beautiful epistles of St. Ignatius which we yet possess—to the Ephesians, the Magnesians, the Trallians, the Romans, the Philadelphians, and the Smyrnians. So far did the relations between these holy Bishops, their priests and people extend!

[2] They always signed themselves with this denomination.

the human body must needs be supplied by the blood which flows through the whole body, penetrating to each extremity by means of arteries, veins, and capillaries. This blood perpetually passes from one vessel to another, so that it is impossible to say that any portion belongs to one arm or leg; since it belongs to the whole body. So it is with other vital juices which circulate through the frame; the simultaneous action of the various parts produces a single result, namely, life. In this life each particle of the body shares, not as having a life of its own, but because the life of the body is the life of each of its members. Thus, too, in the Catholic Church, each individual diocese must live by means of the life of the Universal Church, keeping up a continual living intercourse with it, and receiving from it healthy influences. Any member that separates itself, becomes as one that is lifeless. If free communication with the whole Church is hindered, a languid feeble life only remains as a natural consequence. So it would be, were an arm tightly bound round with cords, which must needs impede its movement and sensation; or if it were paralysed or stiffened with cold, so that circulation was hindered, and all living functions arrested or suspended. But such notions as these are strange to the greater part of our clergy. CHAP. III. And the result is that we have Bishops, who are rarely to be seen at the further boundaries of their dioceses, and who suppose themselves to be satisfactorily fulfilling their episcopal duty if they have not failed to appear on the usual formal occasions in their cathedral churches, or in their seminaries; if the external management of the diocese is somehow provided for, so that there are no complaints from the laity; and finally, if they have outwardly gone through all the functions of the "Pontifical" or of the "Ceremonial"[1] prescribed for Bishops.

LII. 4. Unity is secured by frequent gatherings, especially in provincial Councils. Unity of will and unity of intention are essential to the unity of the Church; and these are not promoted by the exercise of individual authority. This too often provokes an element of invidious or hostile feeling, which causes less of enlightenment than of irritation. Wherefore the Apostle himself said,

[1] St. Cyprian writes thus of the Bishop's office in caring for the Universal Church: "Copiosum corpus est sacerdotum concordiæ mutuæ glutinæ atque unitatis vinculo copulatum, ut si quis ex collegio nostro hæresim facere, et gregem Christi lacerare et vastare tentaverit, subveniant cæteri. Nam etsi pastores multi sumus, unum tamen gregem pascimus, et oves universas, quas Christus sanguine suo et passione quæsivit, colligere et fovere debemus" (Ep. 68, ad Steph.).

CHAP. III. "All things are lawful unto me, but all things are not expedient."[1]
Hence also it arose that the wishes of the people were constantly ascertained. In those days the people may be said to have been a faithful counsellor to the Church's rulers.[2] An account was rendered by the Bishop to the people of all that he did in the government of the diocese.[3] This consideration for the popular wishes whenever it was practicable—a course in itself so charitable—was well suited to the spirit of Episcopal government. This lofty and powerful

[1] 1 Cor. vi. 12.
[2] Fleury says, "Everything in the Church was done with counsel, so that reason, rule, and the will of God, might alone bear sway." "Assemblies have this advantage, that there is always some one present able to point out the right course, and to lead others to see it too. Thus mutual respect is produced;—men are ashamed to be publicly unjust; and those whose virtue is weakest are upheld by others. It is not an easy thing to corrupt a whole assembly; but it is an easy thing to gain one man, or whoever rules him; and an individual decision is apt to be biassed by personal feelings, which have no counterbalancing influence. No Bishop took any important measures without the council of presbyters and deacons, and the chief among his clergy. Often, too, the whole people were taken into council, when they had an interest in the transaction, as in the case of ordinations" (Discours i. § 5).
[3] St. Cyprian used to give account to his people of all that he did; and when, in the times of persecution, he could not do so personally, he still did the same by letters, some of which are still extant (see Ep. 38, Pam. 33). Two centuries later, St. Augustine did the same. In his sermons he tells them all the wants of the Church, and gives a minute report of his doings. These sermons, 355, 356, are specially worthy of attention.

rule is so unlike that of earthly kings, inasmuch CHAP. III. as it is only thus powerful for good, and not for evil. Its very essence is the adornment of humility, modesty, and vast charity. It must be above all things just, and strong by means of its gentleness.[1] Hence also arose the intimate union of Bishops with their presbyters, whose advice they sought in every matter concerning the government of the Church. The presbyters had a share in plans and measures, which were carried out according to the general wish, and the object and reasons of which were thus understood by those who were to give them practical effect.[2] Hence also those Councils in which all

[1] Fleury says, "Such heed was paid to the assent of the people, in the first six ages of the Church, that if they refused to accept a Bishop, even after his consecration, they were not constrained, and another more acceptable was provided" (Disc. i. § 4). St. Augustine gives the reason in these words, addressed to his people : "We are Christians for our own sakes, and Bishops for yours" (Serm. 359).

[2] St. Cyprian, writing to his clergy from his place of concealment in time of persecution, accounts for not having answered a certain letter written by some of his priests, by saying that he was alone : "And I determined from the beginning of my Episcopate to do nothing by myself, without your counsel and the assent of the people" (Ep. 14). This determination was founded on Apostolic example. Remember the Apostolic proceedings as to the election of deacons. Assuredly the Apostles had power to elect whom they would. Yet with what gentleness and consideration they set the matter before the faithful, that they might nominate those fittest for the office! "Wherefore, brethren, look ye out among you seven men of honest report, full of the Holy Ghost and wisdom, whom

CHAP. III. the Bishops of a province met twice a year,[1] as so many brothers, to discuss their common interests, to take counsel respecting difficulties occasioned by particular cases, and to unite in framing such measures as were best calculated to put an end to disorders. They decided causes; they appointed successors to deceased Bishops. These successors were not only known but acceptable to them, and they thus contributed to preserve the perfect harmony of the Episcopal body. Hence also the greater Councils of several provinces, and national and Œcumenical Councils.

LIII. 5. Unity was preserved by the authority of the Metropolitan who presided over the Bishops of a province, and by that of the Chief Sees to which several provinces and Metropolitans were subject. By this well-ordered system of ecclesiastical government the Body of the Church was admirably united and bound together. There was no risk of its high offices becoming merely honorary and useless.

LIV. Lastly, unity was, above all, due to the

we may appoint over this business" (Acts vi. 3). "And the saying pleased the whole multitude," Holy Scripture says further, and they chose the seven first deacons of the Church.

[1] The Fifth of the twenty disciplinary Canons of the Council of Nicea ordains that in every province the Council should be held twice a year.

authority of the Supreme Pontiff, the chief stone CHAP. III. of the Episcopal edifice — ever and alone immovable; and therefore the true foundation-stone, securing to the whole Church militant identity and endurance. All Bishops and Churches had recourse to him in every need, as to their father, judge, teacher; as to a centre, a common source [of authority]. From him persecuted pastors received consolation, and those who were pillaged and despoiled received alms; and the faithful of every nation, nay, the Catholic world, found at his hands light, direction, protection, safety and peace.[1]

LV. Such were the six golden links forming that powerful chain, which, in the better days of the Church, bound together the Episcopal body. Golden they were, in truth, forged out of no other material than that of holiness and love; of faithfulness to the pattern of Christ's Word and to the Apostolic examples; of zeal for the Church which was founded by the Blood of Christ, and by Him entrusted to the Bishops' hands; of fearfulness and trembling, because ever conscious of the in-

---

[1] [This is inaccurate. In the earliest times no such authority as the Papacy existed in the Church; and when it was developed, after the fall of the Western Empire, the assertion of its claims occasioned the division of East and West.—ED.]

exorable account to be one day required by that same Lord, the Invisible Head and Pastor, Jesus Christ.

We have seen that the invasion of the barbarians, who overthrew the Roman Empire, gave rise within the Church to one of those new periods which may be described as periods of movement. At such times the Church rose and made a fresh advance. There was developed in her a new activity, which had hitherto lain dormant from lack of any exciting cause. When aroused it exercises a new influence on mankind, and produces a new series of beneficial results.

The character which marked the period of which we are treating was that of "the introduction of Bishops into political government." The end which Providence had in view in so great a change, may surely be said to have been that the Religion of Christ should penetrate the innermost recesses of society, and should by ruling sanctify it. This end was attained, inasmuch as the order of Providence is unfailing and sure. But it was attained at the cost of serious evils. The human means, with which Providence deigns to work, are all necessarily limited and imperfect. And in addition to those already enumerated, one noteworthy evil was the disunion of the Episcopate. This sharp spear went far to tear the breast and pierce the very heart of the loving Bride of Jesus Christ.

LVI. Let us trace the steps by which so bitter a trial came about. But first let me say a word concerning the laws according to which God tempers the vicissitudes of His holy Church. There is both a Divine and a human element in the Church. The eternal plan is Divine. And the chief means whereby that plan was carried out—the Redeemer's aid—is also Divine. Divine, too, is the promise that this aid shall never fail; that the holy Church shall never be left without light to know the true Faith, or without grace to practise holiness, or without a Supreme Providence disposing of all earthly things as they affect her. But besides this the principal element, there are other and human elements which take part in carrying out the designs of God. This is inevitable, since the Church is a society composed of men, and of men who ever, while they live, must be subject to the imperfections and ills of humanity. Thus the human element of this society obeys the ordinary laws which regulate the course of all other human societies, in its development and in its progress. And yet those laws to which human societies are subject cannot be altogether applied to the Church, precisely because it is not a purely human society, but also, in part, Divine. Thus, for instance, the law that "Every society begins, advances to its perfection, and then fails and perishes," is not wholly applicable to the Church, which is sustained by a Power far out of the reach of human vicissitudes. That Infinite Power repairs her losses, and pours new life into her when she is faint. And thus this singular and unique society does not move in the sphere of the ordinary life of human societies, simply because it contains an element which is extraneous and superior to all societies that are merely human. In a word, the Church is as lasting as the society of the whole human race, which, created contemporaneously with man, will not perish until the last individual of the species perishes.

Since, then, other particular societies are formed, destroyed, and formed again, they have a period of destruction succeeding a period of formation, to be succeeded in its turn by another period of new formation. But these periods of *organization*, and of *crisis*, cannot be applied to general human society, nor to the Church of Jesus Christ, both of which endure perpetually. They are only applicable to the *accidental conditions* of either: these alone are organized, destroyed, CHAP. III. and re-organized. The moment in which the presiding force of organization begins to act, may be called the *epoch of movement*; that in which the work of organization is completed, the *stationary epoch*. The Church finds herself by turns in these two epochs; at one time moving towards some new and mighty development, at another resting as though she had come to the end of her journey.[1]

LVII. We may make a further remark with respect to the laws which govern the progress of society, as applied to the Church. In ordinary societies reconstruction succeeds to destruction; the tendency is to build up after a better fashion that which has been destroyed. But in the Church destruction and formation are contemporaneous. Not that, as elsewhere, the same object is destroyed and reconstructed, but that while one order of things is destroyed, another is formed. Let us take as

[1] Let us distinguish two *epochs*, and two *periods*. The point at which a new order of things begins, is the *epoch of movement;* the point at which that order of things is formed, and sufficiently established, is the *stationary epoch*. Between these two epochs there is a period in which society works at its own organization, with a view to perfecting the new order of things, and this we may call the *period of organization*. This organization completed, and thus the stationary epoch having arrived, human affairs cannot remain motionless, and consequently there speedily arises a movement in the opposite direction, that is to say, towards destruction, and this we may call the *period of crisis*.

an example that memorable period when the invasion of the barbarians[1] forced the clergy to take part in temporal government. This *epoch of movement* in the Church of God is the principal object which claims our attention.

At that time the movement in the Church, the new order of things which was being organized, was the sanctification of civil society. This society, hitherto pagan, was to be converted to Christianity; that is, it was to conform all its laws, its constitution, and even its habits, to that new code of grace and love, the Gospel. But simultaneously with this progress there was the destruction of a former order of things, and a retrograde movement within the Church. The new movement which the Church carried into civil society, brought with it the evil alluded to, namely, that

[1] There were many causes which forced the clergy against their will into temporal affairs. Fleury writes, "The Romans had a profound hatred and contempt for their new masters (the barbarians), who were not only rough and fierce, but were also heathens or heretics. On the other hand, the people increased in trust and respect for the Bishops, who were all Romans, and for the most part members of noble and wealthy houses." He adds, "In course of time, however, the barbarians became Christians, and helped to fill the ranks of the clergy, among whom they introduced their own customs ; so that not only clergymen, but even Bishops became hunters and warriors. They also became territorial lords, and as such were obliged to attend the assemblies which regulated State affairs, and which were at once Parliaments and National Councils " (Fleury, Discours vii. § v.).

the Episcopate was withdrawn from its natural CHAP. III. duties, Instruction and Worship,[1] and was plunged into a sea of secular business. Such occupation was, for the clergy, an untried, unforeseen temptation. Its danger was easily foretold,[2] but in resisting it they as yet possessed no experience. Hence, in course of time, human nature failed under the severe trial : the standard of holiness among the clergy was lowered, and the best customs, and traditions of the Church perished. This was the work of destruction which worked on side by side with that of organization. Such, I repeat, is ever the measure of human capacity. We find it even in the Church, which in its progress and development is subject to havoc and change.

LVIII. And what follows? When the intended organization has been effected, when the

[1] In Apostolic times, when the question of "serving tables" arose, the Apostles appointed seven Deacons, to fulfil that office, saying of themselves that "it was not reason" that they should undertake temporal affairs. They singled out the two truly Episcopal functions with the words, "Nos vero orationi, et ministerio verbi instantes erimus" (Acts vi. 4). Prayer corresponds to *Worship* and Preaching to *Instruction*.

[2] This is proved by the fears expressed in the writings of St. Gregory, and the other Bishops, who were the first to be dragged into secular affairs. Little by little these fears and lamentations died away among the clergy, a symptom that they were gradually becoming attracted by worldly business.

period of destruction has been traversed, and has devoured all that seemed to be given up to it by Providence, then for a short time it appears as if this completed destruction would imperil the very existence of the Church, and that the yawning abyss would also swallow up all which had been won and organized. In such a predicament the Church is troubled, her faith hardly sustains her. In her extreme perturbation she turns with piteous supplications to her Divine Master, Who is asleep in the storm-tossed vessel; until the moment when He shall awake, and control both the wind and the sea. By this time experience has been gained. The fatal effects of the principle of destruction have been exhibited, and at last the remedy is sought. Then begins the new period in which an attempt is made to repair the breaches wrought in the noble vessel during her long and difficult voyage. It is a *stationary* epoch; for these repairs do not advance the Church, they do not secure to her any new development. They merely restore her so far as she may have suffered in her fatiguing journey. But meanwhile she has traversed a long reach of her course, and when the imperishable vessel is repaired, she must once more confront new seas, and gales, and storms.

LIX. Providence has so ordered and ruled the

Church, that the force of organization is ever stronger within her than the destructive force. The two forces always act simultaneously, so that events may come to pass speedily, and no time may be lost.¹ When their work is once finished, there may succeed within the Church a season of repose. In this she neither makes much progress, nor attempts great enterprises, but she may diligently seek to repair her breaches, until the time comes for her to weigh anchor, and once more start on a sea of perils. For many centuries after the memorable year 1076, and with renewed vigour since the Council of Trent, she has laboured earnestly at the work of careful restoration in Church discipline and practice. Who knows if we are not now approaching a time, when the great vessel will once more leave her shores, and unfurl her sails for the discovery of some new, possibly larger continent!²

¹ We may perhaps find an exception to this law only in the first six centuries. Then the force of organization was alone in operation, but antagonism was not lacking, and opposing forces worked from without the Church, through heathen society.

² Thus to the period of destruction, a period of *reparation* succeeds. This reparation concerns, not the motion, but the condition of the Church. Contemporaneously with destruction we find a period of organization; this belongs to movement, it is a time of enterprise. Then there follows a weariness—the time of rest. Thus in the time of movement there are two very active forces at work, one building up, the other pulling down.

CHAP. III. LX. To resume, in the preceding chapters we have considered the indefatigable activity of the destructive force which worked upon the Church with respect to the education of the people and of the clergy[1] during the centuries immediately following the first six. Let us now see how this unfriendly force operated so as to dissolve the union of the Episcopate.

The first successors of the Apostles, poor and unknown, communicated with one another in the simple manner which the Gospel inspires, and which is the expression of the heart alone. It is thus that man imparts himself to his fellow-man, and it is thus that the conversation of God's servants is so easy, attractive, useful, and holy. Such was the conversation of the first Bishops. But when they became surrounded and hedged in by temporal power, it became difficult to approach them. Worldly ambition invented fixed titles and a code of outward usage, exacting from men as the price of communication with their Prelates, at least a considerable sacrifice of self-love, if not some degradation, because some insincerity and falsehood. At last things

In the time of rest, also, two forces are in operation, but neither with much energy. The one seeks to repair losses, the other injures afresh, but rather from carelessness than from design; much as one who, having built a house, neglects to keep it in good repair.
[1] Chaps. i. and ii.

reached a point when the intercourse of ordinary Chap. III. Christians with the heads of the Church was thoroughly complicated by empty questions of form, which, in fact, often admitted of no reasonable or possible solution. The Pastor's mind, instead of being devoted to meditating on sublime truths and to devising wise counsels, was distracted with the study of all these new rights and claims within the Church, which arose from the new code of usages. Hence the character became suspicious, anxious, and disingenuous, from precautions and from recriminations. The complication increased, and henceforth an assembly of Bishops, naturally so kindly and unassuming a meeting, necessitated long and serious consideration, inasmuch as before taking part in it, a man required a long study of the accompanying ceremonies, a long purse to meet the expenses, an abundance of spare time, and great strength to endure the fatigue and weariness of the etiquette, which alone was sufficient to kill feeble old men.[1]

LXI. Such hindrances separating the Bishops,

---

[1] Fleury says, "The Bishops' intercourse was carried on as between brothers, with much love and little ceremony; and the titles of Holiness, Venerable, etc., with which they addressed one another, are to be attributed to the custom which had been introduced at the fall of the Roman Empire, of giving to every one the title suited to his condition" (Discours i. § v.).

CHAP. III. and surrounding them with an atmosphere of estrangement, were a sure sign that ambition had made its stealthy way into their hearts. And what could be a more powerful source of division, and even of schism, than ambition, which is never found without its satellites, the lust of wealth and of power? It is an unfailing fact in Church history, that, "wherever an Episcopal see has been joined for any length of time to a considerable temporal power, causes of discord are also sure to follow." An example occurs at once to the mind in Constantinople. Not a century after its foundation, the Bishops of the New Rome, grown powerful through being neighbours to the Emperor, sought to overreach the most ancient and most illustrious sees of the Church, and after many struggles they succeeded in obtaining the second post of honour.[1] But not content with this, they entered into a rivalry with Rome, which resulted in the fatal Greek schism.[2] Thus the loss of the East to the

[1] In the [Œcumenical.—ED.] Council of Constantinople, A.D. 381, that see obtained the post of honour next to Rome, to which her self-appropriated name of *New Rome* contributed not a little.

[2] It was the protection of the State which encouraged these Archbishops to rebel against Rome. They succeeded in obtaining from the Emperor an ordinance called the Type by which they were withdrawn from the authority of the Roman Church. [Muratori, Scrip. Rer. Ital. ii. 149; iii. 145. Ducange, *s.v.*—ED.] This document was afterwards given up to Pope Leo II. when they submitted.

Church may be plainly traced as one of the terrible consequences of the annexation of temporal power to the See of Constantinople.[1] In the West we find an instance in the Exarchate of Ravenna, established in the sixth century. Its Archbishops speedily grew indocile and insubordinate to Rome, and were at last only reduced by extreme measures.[2] But above all other sources of discord and disunion in the Western Church, were the numerous Antipopes who arose; and, finally, the great Western schism, in the fourteenth century, which even after its extinction left deep roots of division and hatred among Christian nations. These germs of evil won new life through all that took place on occasion of the schism from the ever-memorable Councils of Pisa, Constance, and Bâle. It was this schism which paved the way for the defection of the North from the Church, a century later. Although now extinct outwardly, it still exists, its ill-omened spirit works continually under the disguise of Gallicanism

[1] [It would be more accurate to read 'Rome' for 'Constantinople,' in this sentence. But the excellent author is only repeating the traditional Roman account of this passage of history.—ED.]

[2] Ravenna returned to obedience under Pope Donnus, A.D. 677. These Archbishops rebelled again, A.D. 708, and it was by a dispensation of Providence that this Exarchate came to an end, having existed only 180 years, through the means of Astolfus, King of Lombardy, who destroyed it A.D. 752. Thus Divine Providence made use of these barbarian invaders of the Church's territories, to consolidate the Roman dominion by destroying that of Ravenna.

and Aulicism: and its fruits are the ill-advised ecclesiastical enterprises of an Emperor and a Grandduke; the blind ambition of four German Archbishops, who, contending with the Apostolic See, the only and faithful protector of their temporal dominions, lost those dominions; and all that was wished, said and attempted more recently, in a Catholic Capital, in order to establish there a Patriarch and to produce a fresh schism in the Church.

LXII. We cannot wonder at the miserable divisions which tear the breast of the Spouse of Christ, if we reflect that, whereas the first Bishops who were constrained to plunge into temporal concerns were so holy-minded, so imbued with the true episcopal spirit, that they did this with pain and tears, such was by no means the case with all their successors. Those who were animated by the secular temper, the love of money and of power, were thereby widely removed from the Episcopate of earlier days. It was poor, and it spent itself in preaching the Gospel and in tending souls. For the office involved little save labour and care; oftentimes persecution, exhaustion, and martyrdom. So great was the courage and the spirit of self-sacrifice which it demanded, that men might well say, in the words of St. Paul, "If a man desire the office of a Bishop, he desireth a good work."[1] But holy men of old shunned the office for a very different reason. They saw in it a dignity altogether Divine, such as it wears to the eye of faith, to which God alone could call and raise them; while, possessed by a humble estimate of themselves, they did not deem themselves endowed with the high qualities required by so great and sacred a ministry. Thus it came to pass that, as no candidates for the Episcopal sees offered themselves, the Church was free in her choice. She herself sought, without prejudice, the holiest men, unfettered as she then was by the inclination of electors, or the manœuvres of candidates. The result was that such men as were pre-eminent for holiness and learning were elected. But this desirable state of things was changed as soon as the Episcopate ceased to be a purely spiritual power, and undertook the administration of great wealth and the cares of temporal government. The office then became an object of dread and avoidance to holy men. They shrank earnestly from it, even binding themselves with vows in order to elude the charge; as did those Apostolic men under Loyola,[2] who, some

[1] 1 Tim. iii. 1.
[2] Many have found fault because religious orders have done so much in the Church, without being Pastors, and even with privileges which to a great extent set them free from Episcopal authority. But is it not evident that this was a means whereby it pleased God to strengthen His Church, at the very time when her Bishops were

106   *Degradation of the Episcopate.*

Chap. III. three hundred years since, founded a company of indefatigable labourers in the Lord's Vineyard. At the same time, there arose only too many candidates for the Episcopate with which it might well have dispensed; namely, all who were seeking a worldly fortune, and against whom all easier and better opportunities for making one were closed.

Then arose the formal and materialized devotion of the upper class of the clergy; and among the lower, the virtue of dexterous management of business and knowledge of the Canon Law, instead of zeal and earnestness in wielding the sword of the Divine Word, and in guiding souls heavenward. Henceforth the lords and princes of this world looked on the larger and wealthier sees merely as rewards for their ministers and flatterers, or as provision for their younger or illegitimate children. That which had at first been done from an instinct of inconsiderate covetousness, became before long a political system, well-nigh a recognized State procedure. I might cite almost any Christian nation in Europe as an illustration.

distracted by secular dignities? Evidently the mission of the Mendicant Friars in the thirteenth century, and that of the Regular Clerks in the sixteenth, was to fill up and supply that which was left undone by those who are but too fitly called the secular clergy. [The later history of the Jesuit order shows that the secular spirit was not a monopoly of the secular clergy.—Ed.]

Attentive study will show in each case that the CHAP. III. final confusion in the Church's government had its beginning in the spirit and maxims which during its later years prevailed in the republic of Venice. There all the Bishops were younger sons of patrician families. They must apparently have received their vocation to the Episcopate before they were born. For they were condemned to be Bishops before their birth by rapacious, cruel, presumptuous men ; who, by way of compensation for this treatment, would dispense the Pastor of Christ's Church from his most sacred duties, willingly consenting to see him lead a life of ignoble indolence, or of still worse dissipation. Could we expect among such Bishops as these, to find large endowments of love and moral strength, and that truly pastoral union which springs from a mutual zeal for the welfare of Christ's dear Spouse, the Church, and from a wisdom which grows deeper and stronger by the force of concurrence in common rules and by uniformity of action ?

LXIII. It was easy to bind together in close intercourse and hearty friendship, men who had but one object and aim, that of the progress of mankind in truth and goodness. Truth is universal and immutable. A union among men which aims at that heavenly blessing cannot but be itself universal. There need be no limit to the number of its members. When it is bound together by truth, it cannot fail to be firm and enduring; it is not to be overthrown by trials, or by the changes and chances of life. Such was the brotherhood of the early Bishops. Its aim and bond was evangelical truth; God Himself was its foundation. But when a man's mind turns towards worldly wealth, and his aim is the enjoyment, and consequently the preservation and increase of such wealth, he ceases to be free. He can no longer be wholly devoted to that Chief Good Who can be freely shared by all without taking away aught from any, Whose value is wholly contained in Himself and not derived from anything external or changeable. Then men become unreal; they have no longer the power to be heartily loyal in their social relations, or to contract a lasting, indissoluble friendship with each other. Their intercourse cannot but be conditioned by circumstances. Whatever may be the outward formalities and the conventional signs of a restricted affection, there is always an understood limit to union. It is shackled with fears, cautions, and reserves, which greatly weaken it, and altogether change its nature. "*If at all, with whom? how? how far? is not union contrary to other interests? what is the object or the conditions of such union?*" these questions are always understood to be asked. If, then, these rich and powerful Bishops are not paragons of extraordinary virtue, but rather men whose hope and longing through life has been to gain a wealthy see, what must be the inevitable result? What can we expect from such successors of the Apostles? Who can doubt that their anxious efforts will be devoted to their temporal power and possessions? Content with the sufficiency of their worldly position, they cannot feel any burning desire to maintain spiritual intercourse with other Bishops. Absorbed in secular business, they have neither time nor inclination for earnest correspondence on Church questions, which moreover requires a different frame of mind, and other studies than theirs. If perchance they do attempt some sort of union and intercourse, it is certain to be embarrassed with all the hindrances alluded to above, of fashion, persons, rank, and season; and it will not be allowed to interfere with the Prelates' convenience, to disturb their comfortable ease, or to run the least risk of lowering their secular grandeur.

LXIV. Church history shows that the Bishops, having become possessed of temporal baronies, soon quarrelled among themselves. They were involved in factions, in wars, and in all the horrible discords which for whole centuries distracted the world. These discords were cruelly hurtful to mankind, fatal to the Church whose very foundation is love, and painfully scandalous where men are concerned to whom Christ has said, "Behold, I send you forth as sheep in the midst of wolves."[1] Yet it was but natural that such Bishops, having become a constituent part of the political body, possibly its most influential part, and clinging eagerly to their temporal fortunes, should be involved in the struggles and contentions which perpetually embroiled the great personages of the world. For riches and power are of themselves occasions of conflict, whether for those who seek to keep what they have, or those who take offensive measures to add to it. Thus the holy, continuous, universal union of the early Bishops came to an end, and was succeeded by partial and temporary unions, such as arise out of secular interests, mere confederations, leagues and factions. What a difference! Could the unity of the Episcopal body be preserved thus? Was it not inevitable that little by little that general isolation of Bishops should take place, which, unhappily,

[1] St. Matt. x. 16.

is one of the deepest and most cruel wounds CHAP. III. which ceaselessly afflict the Church of God ?

LXV. It is evident that Bishops who are immersed in secular affairs must continually mingle with princes and great personages. It is also evident that this intercourse cannot long continue, without leaving on the Bishops an impress of the manners and customs of the world. This impress is seen in their personal tastes, their households, their dwellings. Moreover it is clear that a worldly habit of life is widely different from the life of the Church. Any man who adapts himself to the pomp, the turmoil, and license of the one is likely to shrink from the lowliness, the regularity, and the strictness of the other. Thus it was inevitable that a Prelate who was taken up with worldly greatness, should be disinclined to return to the poor of his flock, and to his inferior clergy, and to devote himself to the lowly offices of the Church and the special care of souls. He would prefer the society of great persons in the world to that of his Episcopal brethren, as being more lively, less critical, and, according to his views, more profitable.

LXVI. Hence such Pastors forsook their dioceses, not merely in order to attend parliaments or national Councils, but because they preferred residing near royal Courts, whence the voice of many Councils vainly sought to recall them.[1] And what had they to do at such Courts? Some, perhaps, sought to share in their pleasures; some to seek aggrandizement of that earthly prosperity which always kindles insatiable longings in the heart of man; others to satisfy their vanity, by receiving homage and appearing great in the eyes of men. They mingled, perhaps, in the tricky and rough work of politics; or they even made war on the Church herself, on her doctrine, or on her discipline; or they filled the infamous post of spies, satisfying personal animosities against their brethren in the Episcopate, or kindling a perfidious and sacrilegious war against their common father and master, the Roman Pontiff; or they basked with their degraded natures in the prince's smile, perhaps flattering him, winking at his infamous pleasures, or his ruthless enterprises, with

[1] In the year 341 the Council of Antioch, not content with condemning Episcopal residence at Court, treats it as an almost unknown irregularity, and ordains that no Bishop, priest, or other clerk, should even pay an ordinary visit to the Emperor without letters of permission from the Bishops of the province, signed by the Metropolitan; and whosoever infringed this ordinance of the holy Council, should be excommunicate, and deprived of his office. Such was the holy jealousy of those times for the freedom of the Church! such the fear of contagion from earthly greatness! In A.D. 347 the Council of Sardica ordained that Bishops should not go to Court even for charitable objects, but that they should send one of their deacons as a commissioner.

good-natured indulgence ; or, worse, they blessed CHAP. III. such enterprises, and sanctioned such pleasures with a Bishop's solemn words—thus prostituting the Gospel and all the ordinances of religion.[1] Would that I were speaking of mere possibilities! Of all my statements there are too many terrible illustrations to be found in history. There they are, written in clear, indelible characters, which neither the bitter tears of the Church nor long-continued efforts to obliterate them can ever efface.

LXVII. Doubtless one end for which Providence permitted the ecclesiastical power to gain so much influence in civil governments was to provide mediators between the governors and the governed, between the strong and the weak. The Church, after preaching for six centuries submission and unexampled meekness to the weak, was to teach the strong how to moderate the use of power. She was to subject rulers to the Cross, and, through the Cross, to justice, thus making them ministers of justice and beneficence to the people of God, and not merely judges of earthly things. This

---

[1] The history of the tyrant Christian of Sweden, and his adulatory Bishops, is a sufficient illustration. The Church owes her loss of that nation to such Prelates ; and the same may be said of Germany and England. [Whatever the character of some of Henry VIII.'s Bishops, the English Reformation is due to causes independent of any individuals concerned in it.—ED.]

office of the ecclesiastical power, this noble mission of Christ's Church, was exercised by many Bishops, who maintained the truth, or, as Holy Scripture has it, the testimony of God, before kings. Amidst the perversion of many among their brethren, such Bishops were never wanting. The first outbreaks of fierce resentment were often braved by them. Crowned monarchs were taught the existence of a moral power, utterly unlike their own merely material resources. That peaceful, gentle power could, nevertheless, direct and rule brute force. Although hitherto unheard-of, it issued in the Christian legislation which occasioned so many struggles, which was the object of so many reproaches and calumnies, which led the Pontiffs of the Middle Ages to fight the battle of the people against kings, and the result of which was a wholly new sovereignty, a monarchy of an entirely new character, the Christian monarchy. Thus the Eternal God willed that the savage government of earthly lords should be modelled upon the peaceful rule of the Church's Bishops, and that slavery should cease in the Christian world, since the Church of Christ owns only sons; that arbitrary power should cease, since the Church's power is holy and reasonable; and, finally, that the few should no longer treat the many as mere machines, because the Church's power is but a ministry and a service by which the few sacrifice themselves for the good of their fellow-men. All this God secured for man through Christ; He secured it by the course of events, and, where events failed, it was won by the public condemnation of those who acted in a contrary sense, and who were not screened from condemnation by a great position. Hence the precepts of the Gospel, taking possession of the public mind, laid the foundation of a new general feeling which dealt justice freely to monarchs, and that with a severity not to be found save among Christian nations. But this noble mission of the clergy is over; the period of the *conversion* of society ended in the sixteenth century. At the present time everything proves that a new epoch is before the Church, which during the last centuries has been labouring to amend her minutest defects. A clergy which has become the slave and flatterer of princes can no longer mediate between those princes and the people who reject its mediation; and thus arise such times as our own, when irreligion and impiety prevail. The Church's power is out of joint; it is no longer an intermediary between the legal power of kings and the moral power of the people. Absorbed by the former, it

CHAP. III. becomes identified with it; and the royal power itself loses its natural character. It is double-faced, cruel on one side, fraudulent on the other; presenting here a military aspect, there a clerical one. And so the world is overdone with military forces and with an excessive number of useless ecclesiastics. Kings are face to face with the people; they have either to receive a capital sentence, or, worse still, to pronounce it. There is no longer any one to give counsel, to join the two parties together, to bless their contracts, and receive their oaths, now faithless and unsanctioned; both sides fear and threaten, they make ready for battle, and in a battle everything is at stake. Who can be surprised if, when in Russia, Germany, England, Sweden, Denmark, and other countries, princes[1] once Catholic, under the tyranny of some caprice or passion, chose to declare themselves the religious heads of the nation, and to separate their realms from the Church, they found no resistance from the Episcopate? or, if on the contrary, they found among the Bishops their most active servants in carrying out their designs of racking the Body of the Holy Church? These schisms existed practically before they were actually made: there was only

[1] [This is rhetorical. Russia was never in communion with Rome. And the incidents of the Reformation do not admit of this general description.—ED.]

the addition of some external forms, a change of name; the ecclesiastical power which alone could have prevented them, had already ceased to exist; it was lost in the temporal power. Bishops had ceased to be Bishops, in order to become courtiers; they were not only disunited among themselves, torn with jealousies and rivalries, but they had also separated themselves from their head, the Roman Pontiff, and from the universal Church, preferring to be united as individuals to their sovereign. Thus they had renounced the law of their existence, in preferring to be the slaves of men clothed in soft raiment, rather than the free Apostles of the Christ, despoiled of His garments. Alas, what a spectacle the Catholic nations present at this day! Where would be the union and the disinterestedness of our Episcopate, if a sovereign were to think of separating himself from the unity of the Church?

LXVIII. Observe, too, that even if the degradation of the chief Pastors stops short of such extremities (yet there is no standing still, and every social good and every social ill is developed with time, and reaches its extreme point gradually), still the obsequious adherence of Bishops to princes, and their continual immersion in secular business, tended throughout to diminish union among the Episcopal body. It was inevitable that the Bishop who was minister to his prince, or who at all events had a powerful influence in political affairs, should use great circumspection in his dealings with men around him, not excepting his Episcopal brethren. He would naturally become cautious, reserved, silent, difficult of access. Thus every political party in the nation, every successive system of administration, helped to divide the Episcopal body and break it up into sections. These sections might indeed hold together externally in times of public tranquillity, since the ancient ecclesiastical forms of brotherhood and love are still retained. But nevertheless they are inwardly split asunder all the more disastrously because they are superficially covered with the cloak of pastoral harmony. What, again, can we say of the union of Bishops of different nations? Having practically ceased to be Bishops of the Church Catholic, they are no longer more than national Pontiffs; and, as the Episcopal order has changed to a mere magistracy, an office like any other political office, the Bishops treat each other as strangers, making peace and war, truce or strife with one another, and even with the Church of God. As early as the fifteenth century this strange scandal was seen in the Church, when a Council was assembled, CHAP. III. divided into nations.[1] The authority committed by Christ Himself to His Bishops to be judges in the faith and masters in Israel was practically denied. The dogmatic controversies of Christianity were decided, not by the Bishops' votes, but by the votes of "nations." At each meeting of "nations," the laity voted with the Bishops and priests. Disastrous forerunner of the diets and congresses of secular princes which took place in Germany in the sixteenth century on the question of Reformation, and of the decisions through which so many civil magistrates, undertaking to judge in religious matters, ended by renouncing the faith of their fathers! The Bishops had lost their voice in the decision, it was swallowed up by the lay power. After that, who can wonder at the constitutional priests of France, or at the monstrous system of its national Church!

LXIX. Yes, indeed! the natural end is a national Church, when the Episcopate ceases to be regarded as a body of pastors and only as a first estate; when it has become a political magistracy, a council of State, an assembly of courtiers. And this nationalism of Churches, which existed

[1] [Lenfant, Concile de Constance, ii. 46. Hallam, Midd. Ages, ii. 42.—ED.]

in fact before it was formally acknowledged, is opposed to, and destructive of all Catholicity.[1] How can the head of the Church Catholic, jealous for the well-being of the Bride of Christ, make common cause with such national or royal Bishops? Is not this at once an ample reason for the limit placed by the Roman Pontiff to the Episcopal power, and for those Pontifical reserves which have occasioned so many quarrels, and so much calumny?[2] What other means were there of saving the Church amid the divisions of her Bishops, and the general dissolution of her constituent elements, but that of concentrating strength and energy at her centre? Was it not an urgent necessity that in such circumstances the head of the Bishops should gather up in his own hand the reins which they had let fall in so cowardly

[1] [But cf. Freeman, Norman Conq., i. 31.—ED.]

[2] Thus the French kings took it into their heads that, when a Bishop of the State died, they succeeded to his rights as patron of benefices, etc. Is it desirable for the Church that the rights of Bishops, reduced to such a condition, should be extended? Is it not better that they should be diminished, so that the Church may preserve at least some remains of her liberty, and may say to a king as Gregory IX. wrote to the Emperor Frederick II., " Esto quod in collatione beneficiorum morientibus succedas, ut dicis, Episcopis: majorem in hoc ipsis non adipisceris potestatem " (cf. Oderic Raynald, *ad ann.* 1236). These words were addressed by the Pontiff to a sovereign who claimed a greater right over a vacant see than had its living Bishop! The French lawyers, called " pragmatists," assert that, even if the king neglects to appoint to the vacant benefices, and so ruins the souls of his subjects, his rights still remain good, and the vacancy cannot be otherwise filled.

a fashion, lest the chariot of heaven should be hurried into the whirlpool? In truth, if the Church yet retains any particle of liberty (and without it, she can no more exist than a man without air to breathe), it is not to be found among Bishops who are subject to Catholic princes; it is concentrated in the Roman See. We may perhaps except such liberty as the Church enjoys in the United States of America, or in other Catholic countries, where it yet has some modified existence. I say advisedly "some;" for everything possible has been and is being done, in order to drag the Roman Pontiff into the chains of the general slavery. If he is free, he is only free from day to day. He is wearied with perpetual struggles; he is free, but like Samson in the midst of the Philistines, on condition that he is perpetually and with a mighty effort bursting through the bonds which are continually woven around him. He is yet free in spite of all the transactions on which he is constrained sorrowfully to enter with " the kings of the earth who stand up, and the rulers who take counsel together, against the Lord, and against His Anointed."[1] Because he is free, and indomitable, and upheld by a more than human strength, therefore the "nations furiously

[1] Psalm ii. 2.

CHAP. III. rage together, and the people imagine a vain thing." Therefore the whole world rises against him; hell launches all its weapons against that impregnable fortress, and all dissensions among men are speedily quieted, so soon as they unite together against the visible Head of the Church. And therefore it is, that the Roman Bishop, the common father, is an object of such hatred, not only to the heretic and the impious, not only to monarchs and rulers, but, in their secret hearts, to Bishops, and to a clergy who are "national" and courtier-like; for he is the only obstacle they encounter in the destructive course on which they have entered, whether from ignorance, weakness, prejudice, corruption, or diabolic malice,—a course which leads to apostasy, to the betrayal of Christ, and to the despair of Judas. Yet they will not perceive it! Amid the sorrows which surround the Spouse of the Redeemer, the faithful disciples of a Betrayed Master would indeed be comfortless, had He not said before His Agony, "Thou art Peter, and upon this rock I will build My Church, and the gates of hell shall not prevail against it."[1]

[1] S. Matt. xvi. 18. [In passages like the foregoing the excellent writer's Ultramontanism blinds him to the fact that the secular spirit, which, as he says, has so degraded sections of the Episcopate, has been equally fatal to many Popes. What is gained by concentrating power in the hands of a Julius II. or a Leo X.? Quis custodiet?—ED.]

LXX. Another deplorable result of this false position of the Bishops, which divided them more and more, from each other, was the jealousy of their sovereigns. As they became temporal lords, they incurred jealousies, and shared in vicissitudes like the nobility. When the Government feared or strove with the lay lords, the Bishops suffered even more. Thus they were more and more watched and circumscribed in their work, fettered at every step, shut in and guarded as prisoners, not only within the State, but within their dioceses. Divisions among them were fostered for State reasons; they were hindered from attending Councils, and from meeting together; they were subjected to endless humiliations. Their political power soon fell with that of the nobles. But, weaker than the nobles, they were more easily plundered of their baronies, which the nobles grudged to them. The measure of their degradation was filled up when they were made stipendiaries. Of the centre of Christian unity nothing was said; it was a thousand miles away. Every dissension between the Bishops and their chief was encouraged; the tares were sown; rebellion was upheld, promoted, and rewarded. Thus the Pope, the father of fathers, the supreme judge of the Faith, the universal

CHAP. III. teacher of Christians, could no longer communicate freely with his brethren and sons, with men commissioned by Christ to govern the Church with him and under him. He could not correct them, or summon them before his tribunal. Nor could his oppressed children appeal to him for redress.[1] His decisions in matters of faith, in questions of morals, were submitted, before their promulgation, to a lay tribunal, which assumed superiority over all ecclesiastical tribunals. Nay

[1] When the clergy had acquired great temporal wealth, the sovereign assumed to dispense it, and to convey it to the Prelate, who received it from the king as *a gift*, according to the wording of the forms of Investiture of the Middle Ages. On such occasions the king exacted an oath from the Prelate, by which he was made to promise whatever the sovereign pleased. Eadmer (Hist. Novorum. lib. ii.) relates among other things, how William II. of England made new Prelates swear that they would neither appeal to the Pope, nor go themselves to Rome without his sanction. All Christians have the right of appeal to the Head of the Hierarchy, as part of the intrinsic constitution of the Church, and opposition to it is an attempt to destroy the Church. If abuses creep in, these should be remedied, but the appeal itself should be intact. In like manner, every Christian should have free access to the common father, the Roman Pontiff—these are the *rights* of Christianity. Rulers should defend, not destroy such rights; and to hinder them, under the pretext of evil consequences, is destruction. It is true also that, under the pretext of putting a stop to these evil consequences, princes introduced temporal despotism into the Church,— a mere brute force, where moral force alone should rule,—thus securing impunity for their wickedness. [This language, like that in the text, is only accurate if the Papal supremacy be a part of the revealed will of God. English Churchmen must necessarily regret it, as weakening the argument of the chapter.—ED.]

worse, they were submitted to a prince, who was no Jew or Turk, but a baptized Christian, and consequently a son and a subject of the Church.[1] She had taught him his faith, and he had vowed at his Baptism to support her. As her son and subject, he was as liable to be warned, rebuked, punished as any other of the faithful. The Church does not respect persons. All men are really equal before the laws of Jesus Christ. At length, as time advanced, a new department of police was specially organized for ecclesiastics. It proved to be a most minute and irritating system, under which the Catholic clergy suffered a martyrdom like that of the early Christians, who were covered with honey, and then exposed to the sun, to die a lingering death from the countless stings of flies, wasps, and gadflies. Such a system as this could not be perfected all at once. The vast edifice was the slow, tedious, and learned work of the lawyers, those subtle flatterers of all rulers. But the first general idea of this achievement of earthly power was naturally suggested to the policy of governments by the false position of a degraded clergy.

[1] S. Gregory Nazianzen (Orat. xvii. ad Civ. Naz. § 8): Τί δὲ ὑμεῖς, οἱ δυνάσται καὶ ἄρχοντες; . . . τί οὖν φατε; . . . καὶ ὁ τοῦ Χριστοῦ νόμος ὑποτίθησιν ὑμᾶς τῇ ἐμῇ δυναστείᾳ καὶ τῷ ἐμῷ βήματι. Ἄρχομεν γὰρ καὶ αὐτοί· προσθήσω δὲ ὅτι καὶ τὴν μείζονα καὶ τελεωτέραν ἀρχήν. This is the doctrine of the Catholic Church.

CHAP. III. Here was one of those thoughts which act upon and influence the minds and the conduct of rulers long before they are developed into shape, or reduced to a theory. Some clever statesman at length makes the idea his own, and thus.it is digested into a system and takes its name from the minister who noticed and elaborated it. Then the system is worked with untiring industry, and developed to its extreme consequences. Who would have believed that we should owe a system, ruinous to the liberties, nay, to the very existence of the Church, to a Prelate ? This Prelate was animated by all that looked like piety, but he was a king's minister. When Richelieu depressed the nobles in order to set free the supreme power which he held in his own hands, he knew not that he was moulding that monarchy of modern Thrones which has become intolerable to the people, who, being strong, rebel against it.; intolerable, too, to the clergy, who, being weak, submit to it. Nor is there any hope of deliverance save in the secret prayer which implores God to send a new Moses, who may deliver His people from their Egyptian bondage. May He Who dwells in the bush that is not consumed, send such an one speedily to His oppressed Church !

LXXI. It is obvious that ecclesiastical wealth,

if not spent in works of charity, will be an object of envy to the lower orders; of hatred to the nobles, who look upon such wealth as so many patrimonies alienated from their houses; and of covetousness to governments. Thus we find here another copious source of disunion among the people of God. We must also bear in mind that, from the natural order of things, the unarmed clergy have no power to protect their possessions. And all unprotected wealth will, sooner or later, be the prey of the strong, whose covetousness is powerfully excited by the spectacle of treasures easy to seize. It is evident that the repeated spoliations of the Church in all ages are due to the weakness of those who possessed her wealth. This explains why the nobles were so much less frequently pillaged than were the ecclesiastics. The nobles were much stronger: but whenever they were weak in comparison with a hostile power, it did not fail to pounce upon them, as was finally seen in the French Revolution—not so novel a catastrophe as people in general are apt to think. But the most deplorable circumstance in the spoliation of the clergy is, that ignorant men have conceived the false impression that the wealth of the Church is one and the same thing as the Church herself, and as the

128　　*Mistaken use of excommunication.*

CHAP. III. Christian Religion. The clergy themselves helped to foster this mistaken belief. Having no means of defending their temporal goods from the spoilers, save by depriving such persons of spiritual privileges, they made the guilt of a sacrilegious robbery the same thing as the renunciation of religion. Hence those princes who had resolved at all hazards to despoil the clergy, took counsel together how to separate themselves entirely from the Church. Assuredly if the clergy are prudent, they will take a more cautious line at the present day. The excommunications which followed on the seizure of ecclesiastical property, served to increase its guilt, inasmuch as the guilt of theft is increased when those who commit it openly and wittingly incur separation from the Church. The crime is greater, the impiety deeper, and a religious people, among whom the Faith yet lives, would be chary of committing such a double sin; and thus at certain times and in certain places, excommunications might protect the Church's possessions.[1] But in

[1] In the better times of the Church these Canonical punishments, which cut the offender off from her, were used with great reserve, lest he should be reduced to despair. In the Council held at Carthage by St. Cyprian, after the Decian persecution, A.D. 251, the cases of those who had apostatized during it were investigated, and, after long debate, it was decided "not to take away from them all hope of communion, lest, being desperate, they

unbelieving times, as indeed wherever passion and wickedness are in excess and ready to brave anything, excommunication does not restrain the sinner, but rather provokes and incites him to pass all bounds. Perhaps in some countries Catholicism might have been saved from shipwreck, had it laid aside the ill-used wealth which imperilled it; just as in a hurricane, men cast into the sea the most precious cargoes, if by so lightening the ship they may save her and the lives of the sailors. Had the Church yielded in time to Gustavus Vasa, or to Frederic I., or to Henry VIII., the great wealth, or even a part of it, which she held in Sweden, in Denmark, and in England, the impoverished clergy of those nations might possibly have saved both her and themselves. They might have rekindled the Faith by the very means whereby the Apostles at first had planted it. But where shall we find a very wealthy clergy courageous enough to become voluntarily poor? When is their mental vision clear enough to see that an hour has come in which to impoverish the Church is to save her? Possibly a long and sad experience—

should become worse; and, seeing the Church shut against them, they might go back to the world and paganism." Such was the tenderness for human weakness of those days!

CHAP. III. possibly the generous cry of liberty raised lately by one who, whatever may be thought of him in other respects, is governed by a noble aim which raises him above everything petty, and by a Catholic temper which is really uncommon and which pervades all that he says, may not have been uttered in vain. Not in vain it may have reached the ears of the sentinels who are placed by God to watch over Israel![1] The disquietude

[1] I allude to the proposition made by a priest to the clergy of France that they should renounce all government stipends, and thus regain freedom ; a generous proposal, worthy of the first ages of the Church. It recalls that liberty of which St. Paul was so jealous, that for fear of damaging it he would not be maintained at the expense of the faithful. He had the right, like any other Apostle, to such maintenance. But he preferred to add the fatigue of daily manual labour, whereby to supply his own necessities, to the enormous labour of his Apostolate. "Omnia mihi licent," he said, "sed ego *sub nullius redigar potestate*" (1 Cor. vi. 12). Such noble thoughts are strange to our times, yet surely some hearts will receive them ; the seed sown will not perish without bringing forth fruit, and the Word of God shall not return unto Him void.

But he who uttered this Divine saying, he who prized thus highly the liberty of the Church, why did he lavish it on the wicked ? why did he not see that liberty belongs to truth alone ? why did he make over the rights of unchangeable truth to falsehood? why did he raise a godless humanity to that rank which belongs solely to humanity rendered God-like by Christ? Why did he not bring himself reverently to recognize in the Church, that is, in the company of the sons of God, "the pillar and ground of the truth," instead of hoping to find that pillar and ground among the sons of Adam ? Undoubtedly the system is coherent. If truth belongs to sinful humanity, so may liberty. But I do not believe that truth and righteousness can be separated. I believe that truth appertains to good men only, and that the right of

of the people may express itself in materalized forms. A feeling which is struggling for expression does assume the first form which it meets with, however inadequate and even contradictory to its own idea. But perchance this very disquietude and these murmurs may have a secret source, undiscovered as yet by the peoples themselves. Even where irreligion seems most triumphant, a latent craving for the faith may lie concealed. Men may feel the need for a religion that can be freely imparted to the heart of the people without

freedom does not accompany error. Therefore man is not born free, but is made free by Christ, through Whom he receives the light of truth and righteousness. To those who know that they do not possess the truth, but are ever seeking it, while they cannot even deceive themselves into thinking that they have more than a vain hope never to be fulfilled, to such as these belongs that doctrine of despair which asserts that "all thoughts issuing from the heart of man have an equal right to propagate themselves, and to attack the weak and yielding convictions of the people." A Catholic cannot hold such a doctrine. He knows that he possesses the truth; he appreciates its dignity, its priceless value; he feels that he has no power to alienate its rights. And for this reason the Chief of the Church made his voice heard when a doctrine was set forth as Catholic, which he denied to be such . . . . May God give light to that man's soul! We cannot speak of him without unbounded esteem and affection. May He give him such victory over himself, such strength of mind, that, conquering his own self-love, and the flatteries of his friends and enemies, he may return loyally to the way of truth. He has done it such good service, and has testified towards it so much love and devotion, that, if he would be consistent with himself, he has involved himself in a positive necessity of recanting his errors and submitting himself fully to the imperishable Chair, to which the teaching of truth is entrusted.

CHAP. III. any intervention of princes and rulers. It may be that the irreligious cry lies even to itself, and, in its hatred of the enslaved ministers of religion, confuses true religion with the object of its hatred. Divine Providence may be preparing a re-ordering of nations with a purpose far other than that of diminishing taxation; since heavier taxes are endured with patience by the people in times of revolution. It may be intended by such means—little as we can understand what heaven designs,—to give freedom to the Church of Him, in Whose hands are all things.

CHAPTER IV.

Of the Wound in the Right Foot of the Holy Church, which is that the Nomination of Bishops is given up to the Lay Power.

LXXII. EVERY free society has an inherent right to elect its own officers. This right is as essential and inalienable as that of existence. A society which has given up to others the election of its own officers, has in so doing parted with itself, and has no independent existence; those with whom the election of its officers rests, can from moment to moment maintain or put an end to its existence. It only exists for the pleasure of another, and by his permission. Thus it has only an apparent and precarious, not a real and lasting, existence.

LXXIII. Now, if there is on earth one society that has a right to exist, and this is the same thing as having a right to be free, all Catholics will certainly agree that it is the Church of Jesus Christ. For she derives that right from the

CHAP. IV. undying promise of her Divine Founder. And that promise, which will outlive heaven and earth, is guaranteed by the words, "Lo, I am with you alway, even unto the end of the world."[1] The Church of God cannot give up her government into the hands of others. She cannot in any way barter away or alienate the election of her rulers. For she cannot destroy herself; and every concession of the kind referred to is in itself null and void; it is a contract invalid from the first, a mere bond of iniquity.

LXXIV. Our Lord first chose the Apostles; they chose their successors.[2] And the right of electing[3] those who should receive the deposit which they are bound to transmit through the world to the end of time, has always appertained[4] and always must appertain to the successors of the Apostles. They alone must give account for it to the Master Who has deigned to place that deposit

[1] St. Matt. xxviii. 20.
[2] We read in the Acts of the Apostles, that Paul and Barnabas "ordained elders in every Church" (xiv. 23); that is, Bishops and priests.
[3] [The author seems here to be confusing the right of election with that of ratification.—ED.]
[4] St. Paul had consecrated Titus Bishop of Crete, and writes to him, bidding him do the like for other cities: "For this cause left I thee in Crete, that thou shouldest set in order the things that are wanting, and ordain elders in every city" (that is Bishops), "as I had appointed thee" (Titus i. 5).

in their hands. Thus the guilt of the evil selection of the Church's Bishops falls on the head of those earlier Prelates, who first let the election of their successors pass out of their keeping; or who did not use every means in their power to discover others with clean hands and fitted to receive the sacred deposit of the Word and the institutions of our Lord Jesus Christ.

LXXV. It is true that the government instituted by our Lord in His Church is not an earthly rule, but a service of good will to men, a ministry of salvation to their souls.[1] Accordingly it is not governed at the will of a stern authority. It does not stand on harsh right. It is flexible, and based on humility and reason. It may be said to take its laws from the subjects for whose benefit it was established. Such is its constitution as to have large capacities for good, and none for evil; the only right of which it boasts, is the right to aid mankind. Hence arose that gentle principle of ecclesiastical government, which was universally

[1] Origen says, "He who is called to the Episcopate, is so called not that he may command, but that he may serve the Church; and he must serve her with such modesty and humility as may benefit him who renders and those who receive the service." He adds this reason: "that such is the character of all Christian rule, and specially of the Church, inasmuch as the government of Christians should be altogether different from that of the heathen, which is hard, insolent, and vain" (Hom. in Matt. xx. 25). All the Fathers held this evangelical doctrine.

acted on in the first ages of the Church, and especially in the election of her chief Pastors. It was, that "The clergy judges, the people counsels." Of course, as a matter of strict and rigid right, the Christian people could have no share in the election of Bishops. But wisdom and charity guided the rulers of the Church in their exercise of the power which they had received from Christ, softening and tempering it. Therefore these wise Prelates avoided all secret or arbitrary decisions. They desired the counsel and testimony of others, and they held the advice of the whole body of the faithful to be the most trustworthy and the best. Thus the Church of believers acted as one man; and, although in this "man" the head was distinguishable from the members, it did not reject the services of those members, or cut itself off from its trunk out of a desire of being alone or independent. Thus it arose that the wishes of the people designated both Bishops and priests.[1] Nor was it unreasonable that those who were to entrust their own souls (and what greater trust could a believing people give?) into the hands of a man, should know what manner of man

[1] The Roman Pontifical still retains the ceremony in which the Bishop asks of those about to be ordained whether they have witnesses to their fitness among the faithful. But, alas! what an admission I make, when I say that the *ceremony* is retained!

he was, and should have confidence in him, in his holiness and his prudence.[1] But when the Bishop and the priest cease to be pastors save in name; when they cease to be the confidants, the friends, the fathers of the faithful, who with hearty trust give into their hands not only all they hold dearest, but themselves also; when the clergy confine themselves to the forms and outward ceremonies of religion, bringing themselves almost to the level of the ancient pagan priests;[2] when it has come

---

[1] Origen says (Hom. xxii. on Num. and vi. on Levit.) that "in the appointment of Bishops, besides the election of God, the presence of the people is desired, in order that all may be assured that the newly elected Pontiff is the best and most learned to be found; the holiest, and the most remarkable for all virtue. The people should be present, so that none may have any cause to complain, and that every scruple may be done away."

[2] Such a view of the priesthood is but too prevalent: men believe, or affect to believe, that the functions of the Christian priest are confined to the material walls of the Church! Listen to what M. Dupin said not long since in the Chamber of Deputies of France (séance Feb. 23, 1833): "J'ai le plus profond respect pour la liberté du prêtre, tant qu'il se renferme dans ses fonctions : si cette liberté était attaquée, je serais le premier à la défendre ; mais que le prêtre se contente du maniement des choses saintes, *et qu'il ne sorte pas du seuil de son Église;* hors de là, il rentre pour le moins dans la foule des citoyens, il n'a plus de droits que ceux du droit commune." Is it the Catholic priest, the priesthood founded by Jesus Christ, that is thus spoken of? When did He limit the priesthood to the Church's walls? Did He not rather say, "Go, teach all nations"? Did He not say, "Ye are the salt of the earth"? When did the Divine Founder, Who taught that the true believer must "worship the Father in spirit and in truth," speak of material temples? Did He not give His priests power to

CHAP. IV. to this pass in a religion which teaches men to worship God in spirit and in truth; then it is easy for the people to receive with indifference any Pastor who may be imposed on them. And the right of electing such Pastors passes as easily from hand to hand, from one authority to another, as might be the case with the ownership of houses or lands. Yet we hear invectives against the public indifference in religious matters. And all the while the people are trained, and required to receive as their Bishop any unknown individual whatsoever, with whom they have no common interests, no ties created by past benefits, whose good works they have never witnessed, never even heard of! Well indeed is it if his works are only good works. But when the people are required and taught to be indifferent about their own Pastors, is it not equivalent to teaching them indifference to the doctrine which may be set before them, and to the course of conduct in which they may be led? Is it not teaching them that it is no longer necessary for men to

bind and to loose? and was that power valid only inside the Churches? When He bade them teach His truth from the housetops; when He commissioned them, saying, "As the Father hath sent Me, so send I you;" when He bade them confront the lords and tyrants of the world with His Gospel, did He confine the Christian priesthood within such restrictions as M. Dupin would now impose? But his ignorance or prejudice is in a measure excusable, as the result of the sad state of public affairs, and of the difficulties raised in the way of religion by politics.

have confidence in the ministers of religion; that CHAP. IV. they may set aside the needs of their souls and repentance; in short, that they can do without religion, or that at all events they may rest satisfied with its purely outward and material aspects? And what else is this than to lay upon the people a blind, irrational obedience, which is but the synonym for religious indifference?[1] It is true that when once a Christian people has been brought to this pass, it must be really perverted. Christianity must be well-nigh extinct in souls, and only the habits of religion left. Of such an unfortunate people, which, by dint of a secret, slow, steady corruption, has unconsciously lost

[1] The great St. Leo knew well that to force the people to accept an unwelcome Bishop was to demoralize them, and this was one reason why he persisted in upholding the ancient discipline of the Church concerning the election of Bishops, as carried out by the clergy, the people, and the provincial Bishops. For instance, he writes thus to Anastasius, Bishop of Thessalonica, A.D. 445 (Ep. xiv. § 5): "When it is a question of electing the chief priest, let him be preferred above all others who is required by the consent of both clergy and people; and if the votes should be equal, let the Metropolitan prefer him who has obtained most affection, and is a man of greater merit; only give heed that none shall be elected who are not wished or asked for; lest the people, being thwarted should despise or hate their Bishop, and *lest they should become less religious than is fitting, not having obtained him they desired.* 'Ne plebs invita Episcopum aut contemnat aut oderit; et fiat minus religiosa quam convenit, cui non licuerit habere quem voluerit.'" So thought St. Leo. See further what the same Bishop writes in his letter to the Bishops of the province of Vienne, cap. 3, and in that to Rusticus of Narbonne, c. 7.

its religious principles, become dead to its religious interests, practically independent of its Bishops,[1] indifferent to the ecclesiastic who may preside in the choir and perform the sacred rites which it does not understand, we may well quote what was said by a Father of the Church in the third century, "that God provides pastors for the Churches according to the deserts of the people."[2]

LXXVI. But if we wish to discover the origin of this sore trouble, we must go back to the fatal epoch when the period which I have termed that of the conversion of society began in the Church. It is an epoch which explains all ecclesiastical history after the first six centuries, since it contains the seeds of all its prosperity and of all its woes. It is an epoch when the clergy counted for much in the balance of temporal power, because they were both strong and correspondingly wealthy.[3]

[1] One fact suffices to show how close was the union and dependence, in primitive times, of the people on their Bishop; namely, that not merely priests, but the faithful laity also who moved from one province to another, were expected to take with them letters from their own Bishops, in proof that they were in the communion of the Church. A Council of Arles accordingly ordains "that even the governors of provinces, being of the faithful, shall like others carry letters of communion from their Bishops, and the Bishop of the place where they are in authority shall bear them in mind, and excommunicate them if they are guilty of any breach of discipline." It was the same with respect to all holding public offices.
[2] Origen on the Book of Judges, Hom. iv. § 3.
[3] At a still earlier period, when the emperors had but just

Of course, so soon as the clergy was powerful CHAP. IV. and rich after the manner of worldly greatness, it became the interest and policy of monarchs to keep the upper hand over them, and with this object to take part in the election of Bishops. Thus the first sees in which the lay power seized upon the right of election were Antioch and Constantinople, where the emperors resided, and where the Patriarch's power was more widely extended.[1]

become Christians, they made some attempt to interfere with the election of Bishops, but in reality this was not so much their own fault as that of unworthy ecclesiastics, who induced them thus to aim at subverting the Church's constitution. It is so easy for a secular prince to be deceived by the hypocrisy and effrontery and ignorance of bad clergymen, above all in ecclesiastical matters! The great Athanasius himself had but too good cause to complain of some such attempts on the part of Constantine the Great. That mighty champion of the Divinity of the Word writes thus of Constantine, "He, seeking to alter the laws, to dissolve *the constitutions of our Lord transmitted to us by the Apostles*, and to change the customs of the Church, invented a new way of appointing Bishops! He sent them to an unwilling people from strange regions, even fifty days journey off. They were escorted by soldiers. These Bishops, instead of being received and judged of by the people, themselves bore to their judges letters of menace " (Epist. ad solitariam vitam agentes). Here we see how important a place the right election of Bishops by clergy and people held in the Church's constitution, and how the institution was considered as Divine, and maintained by Apostolic tradition. St. Cyprian, too (Ep. lxviii.), affirms that this manner of electing Bishops is of Divine right, "de traditione *divina* et apostolica observatione descendit." Observe well likewise the blame expressed by St. Athanasius to Constantine because he sent Bishops " ex aliis locis et quinquaginta mansionum intervallo disjunctis!"

[1] Nevertheless the Canonical election by clergy and people was

CHAP. IV. LXXVII. The struggle with the secular arm, striving to appropriate the election of Bishops, lasted for many centuries. The Church promulgated her Canons in self-defence. But the value of such instruments depends upon the religious feeling that may exist among princes and people. Thus the proportion in which freedom in the election of the clergy was lessened, may be taken as a sure gauge of the decline of faith, of morality, and of piety, both in the rulers and in the nations. The history is briefly this :—

required, as well as the emperor's command. For instance, Epiphanius, Patriarch of Constantinople in the beginning of the sixth century, giving an account of his election to the Roman Pope Hormisdas, after recounting that he was elected by the Emperor Justinian and all the nobles, adds, "nor was the consent of the priests, the monks, and the people, wanting." (*"Simul et sacerdotum et monacorum et fidelissimæ plebis consensus accessit."*) Again, in the same century, the epistle of the Pope Agapetus, which was read in the Synod of Constantinople, held under the Patriarch Mennas, speaking of that Patriarch's election, says expressly that the imperial assent was given, but only as an accessory, dwelling on that which was according to the Canonical law, namely, the election by clergy and people. The Pope's words are as follows :—" Cui, licet, præter cæteros, serenissimorum imperatorum electio arriserit, similiter tamen et totius cleri ac populi consensus accessit, ut et a singulis eligi crederetur ; " breathing the true spirit of ecclesiastical liberty.

What was the reason that at certain times the Patriarchate of Constantinople became avowedly open to purchase ; and, again, that the Papacy itself at other times was sold? What, indeed, but the temporal goods which were no longer devoted to charity, but to the pomp of these sees? Men of the world are not inclined to spend without receiving an equivalent.

the freedom of Episcopal elections.

Already in the sixth century the sovereign's favour had begun to weigh more with the Electors than the merits of the candidate, and the Councils were eager to meet the danger by means of Canons, designed to protect the freedom of such elections.

In the year 500, in a Council held at Rome, where 218 Bishops were assembled, Pope Symmachus published a decree confirming the Canonical elections of Bishops, in opposition to the lay power, which was continually striving to interfere. The decree began thus: "We will not that they should have any power to set up in the Church those whom it behoves them to obey, not to command;" and after this preface, he confirms the ancient manner of electing Bishops by the votes of clergy and people.[1]

---

[1] From the first ages to the present time the Church has ever attached the greatest importance to keeping the old form of Episcopal election inviolable; that is to say, the assent of all, and the decision of the clergy. While on a subject of such deep interest to the Divine constitution of the Church, I will cite several documents prior to the sixth century, which confirm the ever-watchful care of the Church to maintain her elections uninfluenced by any secular power whatsoever.

As early as the date of the Council of Nice it was found needful to fix the Apostolic and Divine form of election by a Canon (the sixth), and this proves that the emperors had hardly become Christian before they threatened the liberties of the Church. For similar reasons the ensuing Councils did not fail to publish decrees in order to preserve intact the ancient and lawful method of electing

CHAP. IV. In the year 535, the Council of Clermont[1] enacted that Bishops should be appointed by the election of the clergy and citizens, and with the consent of the Metropolitan, without the intervention of the favour of great men, without intrigues, and without the employment of violence or bribery to obtain the writ of election. If it were done otherwise, the consenting candidate was to be deprived of communion with the Church he sought to rule.[2]

We find a similar care to keep the elections free from secular influence in the second Council of Orléans, A.D. 533;[3] in the third, A.D. 538;[4]

Bishops by the clergy and people; among others, see the decrees of the Council at Antioch (Can. 19, 23).

Among the Apostolic Canons we find the twenty-ninth speaking thus: "If any Bishop has obtained his See by the influence or favour of secular princes, he shall be deposed, and cut off, as shall be all those who communicate with him."

Early in the fifth century, Pope Celestine I. put forth a decretal with the same object: "Nullus invitis detur Episcopus; cleri, plebis et ordinis consensus et desiderium requiratur."

St. Leo the Great, who filled the Chair of St. Peter from A.D. 440 to 461, was constantly bent on guaranteeing the free and Canonical election of Bishops. It will suffice to quote the injunction to Anastasius, Bishop of Thessalonica, where he says, "Nulla ratio sinit, ut inter Episcopos habeantur, qui nec a clericis sunt electi, nec a plebe expetiti, nec a Provincialibus cum Metropolitani judicio consecrati."

[1] Can. 2. [2] Can. 4. [3] Can. 7.
[4] Canon 3. Fleury, giving an account of this Council, says that "in it was recommended the ancient form of election of the provincial Bishops, with the consent of clergy and citizens, probably by

Royal assent made necessary.

as well as that in Clermont, A.D. 535, and others; all of which plainly show how much need the Church already had to protect herself against the worldly power, which pressed more and more heavily on her, and seized upon her rights.

Soon after this there was a successful effort in France to obtain the sanction of the law of the Church for the necessity of the Royal Assent. It had already become a practical necessity in Episcopal elections. This was done by means of the celebrated Canon of the fifth Council of Orléans, A.D. 549, in which, however, the rights of the people and clergy are guarded.[1]

Nor is it other than reasonable to require the Royal Assent; on the contrary, it is obviously agreeable to the temper of the Church. Eager for peace and unity she would have the Ministers of the sanctuary acceptable to every one, above all to the rulers of the people. But the danger involved in the Assent is lest it should become a command,[2] or a *sovereign grace*; in which case the

reason of the unfit men who began to be thrust in by the temporal power" (lib. xxxii. § 59).

[1] Can. 10. "Nulli episcopatum præmiis aut comparatione liceat adipisci, sed cum voluntate regis *juxta electionem cleri ac plebis.*"

[2] As it only too soon fell out. Among the forms in use in France under the Merovingian kings, which are preserved by Marculfus (lib. i., formula 5. See also Sirmondus, "Concilia Antiqua Galliæ," vol. ii. App.), we find not that of the *consent* of the king

L

CHAP. IV. Church which is free as a matter of *grace*, is a slave as matter of *justice*.[1] The *grace* of kings is of its nature arbitrary. And whether the Church was to have more or less worthy Pastors would depend on the will or caprice of laymen merely because

to the Bishops' election, but that of his *precept*. It is thus worded : "With the counsel and will of the Bishops, and of our nobles, according to the will and consent of the clergy and people of the same city, in the aforesaid city N——, we commit to you in the Name of ,God the pontifical dignity. Therefore with this same *precept*, we decide and command that the aforesaid city and the properties of her Church, and her clergy, be subject to your rule and authority." Nothing is more common among the writers of that period than the phrase "*by command of the king*," such and such a one was made Bishop. We find also the forms of supplication presented by the people to the king, asking him to exercise this power; supplications, forsooth, for such an exercise of power!

[1] Vanity and flattery invented these terms, which at first are unimportant, but they quickly acquire only too real an importance. Such language is not merely the expression of the steady faithful respect due to kings ; it becomes, from time to time, bitterly satirical. Surely that is a bitter irony of a learned author of the last century, who, being censured for having said of the times we treat of, that it was " a benefaction of the king which allowed the clergy to enjoy freedom of election, and that the king was the judge and arbiter of the elections" (as if the two assertions were compatible !), defends himself by replying that the royal "benefaction " meant that the kings had left off their usurpations! Is not this something like the benefaction of highway robbers, who spare their victims' lives ? I give the words of the author, who is heartily devoted to the secular power. "Jus eligendi penes clerum erat. Sed quia sæpe reges electionum usum interturbaverant, assensum in merum imperium vertere soliti, Ecclesia Gallicana his qui veterem electionum usum restituerant, ut Ludovico Pio, plurimum se debere profitebatur. Eorum certe beneficiorum erat asserta et vindicata sacrarum electionum libertas," etc. (Natalis Alex. ad calcem Dissert VI. in sæc. xv. et xvi.).

they were powerful, and of such and such men or women who might have acquired influence with them.

This is exactly what came to pass. Not the royal assent only was reckoned a *grace*, but even the royal command. And at last it became a *grace* which was sold very dearly, the price being nothing less than the property of the Church,[1] her degradation, and the loss of souls.[2]

In consequence of this danger, the third Council of Paris, which was held four years after that of Orléans, A.D. 553, reinstated by a Canon the ancient freedom of elections, without making any mention of the royal consent. The eighth Canon of that Synod says, "No Bishop shall be appointed contrary to the will of the citizens, but he only whose election has been *heartily and voluntarily* demanded by the people and the clergy. No one shall be thrust in by royal command, or

[1] St. Gregory of Tours wrote, A.D. 527 : "Jam tunc germen illud iniquum cœperat fructificare, ut sacerdotium aut venderetur a regibus aut compararetur a clericis." He writes thus after citing various instances of ecclesiastics who had obtained sees from monarchs, not by reason of their virtues, but by purchase.

[2] The Gothic kings even usurped the nomination of the Pope, interrupting the Canonical election. After they were driven out of Italy, Justinian assumed the right of confirming the papal election, and his successors exacted from each new Pope a heavy mulct as the price of this confirmation, which was paid up to the time of Constantine Pogonatus, A.D. 668.

CHAP. IV. by any other means, contrary to the will of the Metropolitan, and of the con-provincial Bishops. And if any one by an excess of audacity shall dare to invade this dignity under pretext of the king's appointment, he shall be counted unworthy to be received by the con-provincials of that country, who shall hold him to be unduly appointed."

Towards the end of this same sixth century, the great Pope St. Gregory felt how much was involved in the Church's freedom; and at the same time he saw plainly that such Bishops as owed their exaltation to the secular power would be the slaves of that power. On the occasion of the death of Natalis, Bishop of Salona, the metropolis of Dalmatia, he wrote thus to the Subdeacon Antoninus, in charge of the patrimony of that province, A.D. 593 : "Give notice at once to the clergy and people of the city, that they unite to elect a Bishop, and send hither the decree of election, in order that the Bishop may be consecrated with our consent, as of old. Above all, give good heed that neither royal nor any other power take part in this matter, since whosoever is appointed by their means, is constrained to obey his patrons, at the expense of the Church's property and discipline."[1]

[1] Ind. 11, bk. iii. ep. 22. St. Gregory was most vigilant with

In the year 615 the fifth Council of Paris also proclaimed the freedom of elections. But Clothaire II. modified its decision by an edict in which he protested his desire that the Canons concerning Episcopal elections should be carefully observed except in the case of such Bishops as he chose to have appointed, or whom he should send as chosen from among the worthiest priests of his Court: an edict which was maintained by his successor Dagobert.[1]

The Council of Châlons-sur-Saône, however, under Clovis II., A.D. 650, once more declared null and void, without exception, all such elections as did not proceed according to the forms prescribed by the Fathers.[2]

At this period we find a continual struggle, although a secret and guarded one, going on in France between the King and the clergy; the King striving to usurp the Episcopal elections,

respect to the freedom of Episcopal elections, and we find this argument often reiterated in his letters. Among others see iii. ep. 7.

[1] The language of the edict, which is a contradiction in terms, is as follows, "Ideoque definitionis nostræ est, ut canonum statuta *in omnibus* conserventur. . . . Ita ut, Episcopo decedente, in loco ipsius, qui a Metropolitano ordinari debet cum Provincialibus a clero et populo eligatur." After these fair words, there follows immediately, "Et si persona condigna fuerit, *per ordinationem principis* ordinetur: vel certe, si *de palatio* eligitur, per meritum personæ et doctrinæ ordinetur." This was how the civil power meant the 'Canonum statuta' to be maintained *in omnibus!*
[2] Canon 10.

150 *Opposition of Church and State in France.*

CHAP. IV. the clergy to maintain their freedom.[1] This struggle was attended with various vicissitudes, in which, however, the Church, if not altogether conquered, was at least always hardly pressed and weighed down by the heavy force opposed to her.

Assuredly the Popes were not blind to the

---

[1] To instance facts. Gregory of Tours (Lib. iv. c. 5, 6) relates how the Bishops entreated Cato, who had been canonically elected to the Bishopric of Clermont, to allow himself to be consecrated without waiting for King Theobald's nomination, A.D. 554. He also relates (Lib. vi. c. 7) how Albinus succeeded to Ferreolus in the see of Uzès *extra regis consilium;* going on to tell how, after Albinus' death, the Royal Precept conferred this see on a certain Jovinus, but the con-provincial Bishops being summoned to make a Canonical election, they set Jovinus aside, and appointed the Deacon Marcellus (Lib. vii. c. 31). The citizens of Tours asked the King to appoint as their Bishop Euphonius, whom they had elected according to the Canons. The King answered, "*Præceperam ut Cato presbyter illic ordinaretur, et cur est spreta jussio nostra?*" (Gregor. Touron., lib. iv. c. 15). King Clothaire having appointed Emerius Bishop of Saintes, he was tolerated; but on the death of the King the Metropolitan Leontius called together the Bishops of the province, and deposed Emerius as being uncanonically appointed, A.D. 562 (Greg. Tours., lib. iv. c. 26). In a similar way the Bishops of Aquitaine made haste to consecrate the priest Faustinianus to the see of Aqui, although King Chilperic had destined it for Count Nicetius (Greg. Tur. vii. 31). Hence Constantine Roncaglia wisely observes that, "the fact that the Bishops held it to be a duty to oppose the King when he sought to meddle with Episcopal appointments, proves that princes were never in tranquil possession of the power they assumed of directing such appointments according to their will;" and that "the Church never gave her willing consent to such assumption, although she was often constrained to put up with many such trials, rather than expose her children to worse treatment."

Gregory II.; the second Council of Nice.

peril which was daily increasing, through royal invasion of the right of Episcopal elections. Its success would place the Church wholly in the power of the Crown. Early in the eighth century we find Gregory II. writing to the Eastern Emperor to admonish him not to infringe the sacred rights of the Church, with respect to the selection of her own Prelates.[1] But meanwhile the governing power was perpetually renewing its attacks, and the Church could do nothing in self-defence save by means of new laws and Canons.

The seventh Œcumenical[2] Council, which was held at Nice, A.D. 787, did not fail in one of its Canons to shield the Church from the secular power which considers itself free to do whatever it can. The Holy Council says,[3] "All elections of Bishops, priests, or deacons made by princes shall be null, according to the law which decides that whosoever obtains for himself a Church through the secular power shall be deposed and cut off, with all such as communicate with him. Thus it is necessary that all who are to be pro-

---

[1] Among other things he addresses the following remarkable words to Leo the Isaurian: "Quemadmodum pontifex introspiciendi in palatium potestatem non habet ac dignitates regias deferendi: sic neque imperator in Ecclesiam introspiciendi et electiones in clero peragendi" (Epist. ii. ad Leon. Isaur.).

[2] [So-called.—ED.] [3] Canon 3.

CHAP. IV. moted to the Episcopate should be elected by the Bishops, as was ruled by the Holy Fathers assembled at Nice."

The Synod held near the town of Thionville,[1] A.D. 844, sent a solemn monition to the royal brothers, Lothaire, Louis, and Charles, in order that the Churches should not remain any longer widowed of their Pastors. This was the case when the Episcopal elections depended on princes, who, distracted by their own quarrels, had neither time nor inclination to consider the interests of the Church. As a consequence, the Church shared all the vicissitudes of the civil government. The fathers of the Synod speak with dignity and freedom. " As the ambassadors of God, we admonish you that those sees which by reason of your discords now remain without Pastors should forthwith, and without any taint of heretical simony, receive their Bishops, who should be given them by God, conformably to the authority of the Canons, being duly designated by you, and consecrated by the grace of the Holy Spirit."

About the same time Pope Nicholas I., always a strenuous supporter of the Canons, did not fail loudly to protest against the abuse whereby the lay power had taken to interfere with Episcopal elec-

[1] Canon 2.

tions. This may be seen, among other documents, CHAP. IV. in a letter he addressed to the Bishops of Lothaire's kingdom, commanding them under pain of excommunication to warn the King to remove Ilduin from the See of Cambrai, which he had conferred on that person, albeit unworthy and irregular, and to allow "the Clergy and people of that Church to elect a Bishop in the manner ordered by the Canons."[1]

The eighth Œcumenical[2] Council of Constantinople was convened in A.D. 869, under the successor of the great Nicholas, Adrian II. At this time the liberty of the Church had already been seriously impaired.[3] The same protests were made in its defence; the same ancient rules respecting the Episcopal elections were repeated; there were prohibitions against the appointment of Bishops by the authority and command of princes, under pain of deposition;[4] and, finally,

[1] Ep. xli.   [2] [So-called.—ED.]
[3] The French Bishops could not at that time leave the kingdom without express permission from the King; neither could a Metropolitan send a Bishop as his legate beyond the kingdom, as we find from the letter of Hincmar of Rheims to Pope Adrian, A.D. 869.
[4] Can. 12. "Apostolicis et synodicis canonibus promotiones et consecrationes Episcoporum, et potentia et præceptione principum factas penitus interdicentibus, concordantes, definimus, et sententiam nos quoque proferimus, ut si quis Episcopus, per versutiam vel tyrannidem principum, hujus modi dignitatis consecrationem susceperit, deponatur omnimodis, utpote qui non ex

CHAP. IV. laymen in high positions were forbidden to interfere with Episcopal elections, unless invited to do so by the Church.[1]

voluntate Dei, et ritu ac decreto ecclesiastico, sed ex voluntate carnalis sensus, ex hominibus, et per homines, Dei donum possidere voluit vel consensit."

Can. 22. "Promotiones atque consecrationes Episcoporum, concordans prioribus conciliis, electione ac decreto Episcoporum Collegii fieri, sancta hæc et universalis Synodus definit et statuit atque jure promulgat, neminem laicorum principum vel potentum semel inserere electioni Patriarchæ, vel Metropolitæ, aut cujuslibet Episcopi; ne videlicet inordinata hinc et incongrua fiat confusio vel contentio : præsertim cum nullam in talibus potestatem quemquam potestativorum vel cæterorum laicorum habere conveniat, sed potius silere ac attendere sibi, usquequo regulariter a Collegio ecclesiastico suscipiat finem electio futuri Pontificis. Si vero quis laicorum ad concertandum et co-operandum ab Ecclesia invitatur licet hujus modi cum reverentia, si forte voluerit, obtemperare se asciscentibus; taliter enim sibi dignum Pastorem regulariter ad Ecclesiæ suæ salutem promoveat. Quisquis autem sæcularium principum et potentum, vel alterius dignitatis laicus, adversus communem ac consonantem, atque canonicam electionem ecclesiastici ordinis agere tentaverit, anathema sit, donec obediat ac consentiat quod Ecclesia de electione ac ordinatione proprii præsulis se velle monstraverit."

[1] Fleury says, "These Canons are the more remarkable, that they were published in the presence of the Emperor and of the Senate" (Lib. li. § 45). Other Canons in defence of liberty were framed by this Council. The principal among these are as follows : Can. 21. "Those who are powerful in the world shall respect the five Patriarchs and not seek to wrench from them the possession of their sees ; or do anything against their honour;" from which we see that the Patriarchates were more exposed than other sees, owing to their greater emoluments and temporal power. Can. 14. "Bishops should not go far from their Churches to meet generals or governors,—alighting from their horses, or prostrating themselves. They should preserve the authority necessary for reproving great personages, if needful." Can. 17. "Patriarchs have full right to convoke the Metropolitans to their Council, when they shall see fit,

But, alas! reason and justice exercise but a CHAP. IV. feeble influence upon mankind compared to that of the passions, above all when these are strengthened by external forces. The Christian princes, instead of giving heed to the exhortations, the commands, the threats of their mother the Church, only attempted fresh usurpations of her liberties, backed up with legal subtleties as well as with violence. I speak generally, for at all times there were some docile and respectful monarchs who obeyed her. Moreover, almost all royal personages were more or less influenced by the decisions and enactments which were perseveringly set forth by Popes and Synods concerning the Church's discipline. Among these the prominent point was always the right of election. This somewhat restrained their eager efforts to interfere with Episcopal appointments. They endeavoured to evade the Canonical laws by underhand means, while their usurpations were often accompanied with respectful words and assurances which contradicted and condemned their actions.[1]

---

without these latter excusing themselves on the plea that they are detained by the prince." These words are added, "We reject with horror that which some ignorant persons have said, *i.e.* that Councils cannot be held without the presence of the prince." Such was the language of Œcumenical [?] Councils!

[1] For instance, observe with what a strange medley of command

All this did not diminish the need for great vigilance on the Church's part, or for courage on that of her leaders. They were called to fight the battles of the Lord, and they were inevitably objects of the world's calumny. Their noble efforts to defend the deposit entrusted to them, and to escape the sentence of our Lord upon His unfaithful servants, was attributed to personal pride and ambition.

LXXVIII. One of these noble Prelates who, towards the end of the ninth century, defended the freedom of Episcopal elections with dignified firmness, was the celebrated Archbishop of Rheims,

and entreaty, of submission and authority, of piety and self-assertion, Louis II. writes to Adon, Bishop of Vienne, ordering or beseeching him to appoint a certain Bernarius to the see of Grenoble, merely because he was one of the Emperor Lothaire's clerks, and that Emperor wished him to be made a Bishop. "Our beloved brother Lothaire entreats our benignity (*mansuetudinem nostram*) to appoint a certain clerk called Bernarius to the see of Grenoble; which we of our benignity have done (*quod nos benignissime fecimus*)." Remark the authoritative action of his "benignity,"—first doing the thing, and then humbly asking leave of the Church! "Therefore we admonish (*monemus*) your Holiness to appoint him, and to obey (*obedias*) speedily (*mox*), being assured of our consent that he be consecrated in the Church of Grenoble." The recommendations of Charles the Bald and Louis III. are in the same style, with as many contradictions as there are words. Sometimes when recommending a person, they added the clause, "if he be found worthy,"—leaving it to the Metropolitan to examine into his fitness; but we may judge how much such a clause was worth by the occurrences at the Council of Fismes in the time of Louis III., of which we shall shortly have more to say.

Hincmar. Let us briefly review his dealings with Chap. IV.
Louis III.
The Council of Fismes was held A.D. 881, Archbishop Hincmar presiding. The see of Beauvais was vacant in consequence of the death of Bishop Odo, and a clerk named Odoacer presented himself before the Council with a decree of election by the clergy and people of Beauvais, which had been obtained by Court influence. The Council exercised its right of examining the candidate before confirming his appointment, and pronounced him unfit for it. The fathers then wrote a letter to the King, in which they set forth the reasons why they could not, in obedience to the Canons, proceed to consecrate Odoacer. It was taken to the King by a deputation of Bishops. This caused a great stir at Court, and people said that " when the King permitted an election, the object of his choice should be elected.[1] Ecclesiastical endowments were in his power, and he could give them

---

[1] Remark the progress of usurpation. First, the secular power hindered the Church's elections until she obtained permission from it. Secondly, this permission became wholly a *favour* on the sovereign's part, which he could arbitrarily concede or refuse. Thirdly, this *favour* was no longer gratuitously granted, but had to be bought. Fourthly, at last this *royal favour* having been bought, and permission to elect freely thus obtained, it was shackled with the condition that the election should still only fall on the candidate whom the monarch selected !

to whomsoever he would."[1] The King wrote to Hincmar in indistinct and self-contradictory language. He expressed his "desire to be guided by the Archbishop's counsels in the affairs both of Church and State, and intreated him to feel the same concern on his account, as for the kings his predecessors," adding, as a proof of his royal intention of following such counsels, "I beg that I may be enabled to give the Bishopric of Beauvais to Odoacer, your dear son and my faithful servant, with your assent and by your ministry. If you oblige me in this, I will in all things have respect to your wishes."[2] Is it fitting that Christ's Flock be committed to a Pastor in order to oblige a man? Should souls redeemed by the Blood of Christ be entrusted to a Bishop, not because he is wise and holy, but because he is a royal favourite, and therefore to be enriched with Episcopal endowments? What a reversal of all that is right!

Hincmar was not unequal to his duty. He replied "that the letter of the Council contained nothing that interfered with the respect due to the King or the welfare of the State. Its only object was to maintain the rights of the Metro-

[1] Observe the confusion of ideas among these courtiers. The possessions of the Episcopate were regarded by them, not as mere accessories, but as its very substance and reality.

[2] Hincm., ep. 12, tom ii. p. 188.

politan and the provincial Bishops in respect of the examination and confirmation of Prelates according to the Canons." He added, "The assertion that you are master of these elections, and of the Church's possessions, comes forth from hell and the mouth of the serpent. Remember the promise made by you at your consecration, signed by your hand, and presented to God on His altar before the Bishops. Read it over in the presence of your Council, and seek not to introduce into the Church that which was never attempted in the times of the great emperors who preceded you. I hope ever to maintain the fidelity and devotion which I owe you. I took no small thought for your election. Do not therefore render me evil for good, by seeking to induce me in my old age to forsake the holy maxims which, by the grace of God, I have followed up to the present time, through an Episcopate of thirty-six years. As to the promises you make me, I do not venture to ask anything of you, save what concerns your own soul and in behalf of the poor. But I entreat you to remember that ordinations contrary to the Canons are simoniacal, and that all who have any hand in them are partakers in the guilt. Nor do I speak out of my own head or set forth my own thoughts. I cite to you the words of Jesus Christ, of His Apostles and His Saints who reign with Him in Heaven. Beware how you heed them not! The Bishops are gathering together in council, in order to proceed to a regular election with the clergy and people of Beauvais, and with your consent."

Bishops who spoke the truth to kings, after this fashion and without disrespect, considered that they were giving the best proof of their faithful and inviolable attachment. How little do men know each other! Yet from whom should monarchs hope to hear the truth and the word of God, if the Bishops withhold it? Would that Bishops could learn the tone of that Apostolic freedom, which is anything but a want of respect or loyalty! Would that Catholic princes could appreciate it! and understand that it is a precious gift of God to have men who will speak conscientiously to them; men who are ready to face their displeasure, and the more active indignation of flatterers and servile ministers, rather than betray the truth or utter agreeable falsehoods. These insincerities may seem to honour royalty; but in reality they stealthily undermine its foundations, and prepare its ruin. The Church, which is the "pillar and ground of the truth," has always held it unlawful to deceive even those princes who seek to be deceived, and who punish men who will not deceive them. This friendly loyalty of the Church tends to strengthen the throne, by the support of piety and justice. How has her faithful voice been misinterpreted, misunderstood, calumniated by those who are seemingly the zealous friends, but really the deadly enemies of royalty! They know well enough that if a prince gives heed to the severe admonitions of the Church, both Church and State will prosper together; yet they persistently seek to persuade monarchs that the Church would fain trench upon their rights, and that the Apostolic liberty of Popes and Bishops is only ambition and an audacious infringement upon their royal dignity.

It was thus that the ministers of Louis III. misrepresented the faithful and dignified answer made to him by Hincmar. Instead of increasing the young prince's reverence for and gratitude to the aged Prelate, it only irritated him. He replied as follows: "If you will not consent to the election of Odoacer, I shall esteem it a proof that you refuse the respect due to me,[1] that you will not uphold my rights, and that

---

[1] In what was this respect to consist? In a vile act, in the betrayal of Christ's Church, and of the souls bought by Him with His precious Blood!

you purpose in all things to resist my will. With an equal, I should put forth all my power to maintain my dignity.[1] On a subject who insults me, I shall only bestow my contempt. I shall go no further in this matter until I have laid it before my royal brother and cousins, to the end that a Council of all the Bishops of our kingdoms,[2] may be summoned. It will decide what is conformable to our dignity. And if it be needful, we shall do that which is according to reason." If Hincmar had been actuated by motives of ambition or self-interest, such an answer, threatening him with the loss of royal favour, would doubtless have induced him to yield. But he who acts for conscience' sake cannot yield. No prince can lead him to betray his trust, inasmuch as his fidelity to his prince is built upon his fidelity to God. It is not a self-interested fidelity; it is based solely on duty. As to the reproach of failing in respect and obedi-

---

[1] A dignity which consists in arrogant injustice!
[2] The caprice of one man was to inconvenience all the Bishops of a kingdom by assembling them in Council. And for what? to oblige them to make a law not according to justice, but according to his own pleasure, which he styles his "dignity." It seems a strange thing to seek to avenge one's self on the uprightness of a provincial Council by corrupting a national Council! But have we not seen similar aims and similar results in our own times? Who has forgotten the National Council of Paris?

ence to the King, Hincmar contented himself with giving a solemn denial to the royal secretary. For the rest, he answered thus : " With regard to what you say you will do if necessary, I see plainly that your object is to intimidate me. But you have no power save that which is from on high. May it please God by your means, or by any other means, to release me from this prison—I mean from this aged and infirm body—and to call me to Him after Whom I long with my whole heart. It will not be my desert—for truly I merit nothing of good ; it will be His abundant mercy. If I sinned by consenting to your election, against the will and the threats of many, I pray God to let me be chastised through you in this life, rather than in the next. And since you are so anxious concerning the election of Odoacer, let me know when the Bishops of the Province of Rheims, with those who were sent to you by the Council of Fismes, can assemble. If I am still living, I will cause myself to be carried thither. Send Odoacer thither also, with those who elected him, whether they be of the palace or of the Church of Beauvais. Come also yourself, if you will, or send your commissioners ; and let us see whether Odoacer has entered the sheepfold by the door. But let him know, that if he does not come, we

CHAP. IV. will seek for him wheresoever he may be in the province of Rheims. And he shall be judged by us as the usurper of a Church, so that he shall nevermore exercise any ecclesiastical function in any part of this province; and all such as may have shared in his crime will be excommunicate, until such time as they make satisfaction to the Church."

But these noble words, well worthy of the primitive Bishops, did not influence the government. Louis III. was persuaded by his time-serving courtiers to use violence. Odoacer was thrust upon the see by the force of arms. The ill-starred Church of Beauvais had to endure the hireling. But she never inscribed him on the roll of her Pastors. And a year later, when Louis III. had departed this life to render account of his deeds to the Judge of all men,[1] Odoacer was excommunicated for this and other crimes, and deposed.

[1] All who believe that Divine Providence rules over human affairs, and that nothing happens save by His ordering, will observe the coincidence of this young sovereign's death with the warnings of the Archbishop of Rheims on this occasion. Commenting on the King's obstinacy in thrusting Odoacer into the see of Beauvais against the Canonical laws, he said, "If you persist in doing wrong, God will set it right in His own good time. The Emperor Louis did not live as long as his father Charles; your grandfather Charles did not live so long as his father, nor your father so long as his father. And when you are at Compiègne in their stead, look where they lie, and do not lift up yourself against Him Who died for you, Who rose again, and lives evermore. You will soon depart hence; but the Church and her Pastors, under Jesus Christ their

LXXIX. This persevering attempt on the part of the secular power to seize the right of controlling episcopal elections, was in no small degree aided by the division between the people and the clergy, already alluded to. As the people became more estranged from their Pastors, and more corrupted, they grew more indifferent to the character of those who were set over them. On the other hand, the episcopal sees had degenerated into posts of great worldly comfort by reason of their abundant wealth and honours. Hence they became the aim of the most covetous, and the prey of the most intriguing. It was thus natural that the injured people should be sold and bought, divided into parties, roused to tumults, as being tools of the unworthy flatterers, to whom they looked for the toleration of their own vices, rather than for the virtues which become a Bishop. These disorders led to the exclusion of the people from the elections. It first occurred in the East, where the lay authorities had seized upon the elections. The West followed. Thus the Canons were deprived of their sanction, which came chiefly

Head, will endure, according to His promise." Fleury, who is certainly not a credulous historian, after citing these words of Hincmar, adds, "This threat of the Archbishop might be regarded as prophetical, when we observe that the young King Louis died in the following year" (Lib. liii. § 32).

166 *Restriction of elections to the Cathedral clergy.*

CHAP. IV. through the people. And the clergy unconsciously seconded the views of the secular power, if not by deliberate counsel, by some unfailing instinct. They were not content to retain for themselves the right of election without taking account of the multitude of the faithful. There soon arose among them a supremacy of the few over the majority.[1] These few appropriated to themselves the right of electing their Bishops; and being the canons of Cathedrals, they succeeded in confirming this assumed right, by the sanction of Church law. Thus the elective body was weakened by the exclusion from the Episcopal elections of the mass of the people and of the clergy. It became power-

[1] This occurred in the twelfth and thirteenth centuries. We see from a letter of the famous Hincmar, Archbishop of Rheims, that in his time (the ninth century) the country clergy, as well as that of the towns, took part in the Episcopal elections. Writing to Edenulf, Bishop of Laudun, to desire him to preside at the election of the Bishop of Cambray, he expresses himself as follows : "Quæ electio non tantum a civitatis clericis erit agenda, verum et de omnibus monasteriis ipsius Parochiæ, et de rusticanarum parochiarum presbyteris occurrant vicarii commorantium secum concordia vota ferentes. Sed et laici nobiles ac cives adesse debebunt : *quoniam ab omnibus debet eligi, cui debet ab omnibus obediri.*" The fact of Hincmar's warning to Edenulf, is a proof that already there was a tendency to change the ancient custom. At the end of the twelfth century, Innocent III., in one of his decretals (de caus. possess. et propriet., c. 3) ascribes the right of election, "*ad Cathedralium Ecclesiarum clericos.*" Finally, in 1215, the fourth Lateran Council (can. 24-26) restricted that right wholly to the canons of Cathedrals.

Policy of the Avignonese Popes. 167

less to maintain its rights against those who sought to appropriate them.

LXXX. This state of things, when the French Popes were resident at Avignon,[1] led to the Pontifical reserves, reversions of rents, and annates as a natural consequence. These were at first winked at by the princes, and eventually required by them, because they tended to weaken still further the *sanction* of the Church's right to elect her pastors.[2] For the sanction which protects a right must be strong in proportion to the extent of that right; and no one person,

---

[1] Clement V., A.D. 1306, extended the Pontifical reserves to Bishoprics. Benedict XII., who became Pope A.D. 1334, soon made them universal. Towards the end of the fourteenth century Boniface IX. extended *annates* to the Bishoprics, making them perpetual. [Cf. Hallam, Middle Ages, ii. 14.—ED.]

[2] This explains a fact, otherwise inexplicable. The Council of Basle, supported by the lay power, annulled Pontifical reserves. What was the hidden motive which induced these princes to side with the Council of Basle? Did they seek to abolish reserves? No, but by gaining the mastery over the Church, they sought to weaken her. We find a proof of this in the line taken by the King of France. Charles VII. received the decrees of the Council of Basle with seeming exultation, and declared them to be laws of the State at the assembly of Bourges, where he published the *Pragmatic Sanction*. Why? Shortly after, this same king, and his successors, Louis XI. and Charles VIII. requested the Pope to reserve certain Bishoprics in order to bestow them according to their own desires. They wished to maintain the reserves, but in an attenuated form, and as bestowed by the Pope in accordance with their own wishes. Thus the real aim of politicians was to "abrogate" reserves only in the sense of weakening and then employing them to evade the laws of the Church.

CHAP. IV. albeit invested with ever so high a dignity, can possess power commensurate with the extension of such a right as the election of all Bishops throughout the world. Together with these world-wide reserves, the Popes assumed a responsibility beyond their strength. They undertook the exercise of a right so enormously vast, that it was impossible for them to guard it with any proportionate resources; and a right thus unguarded is held precariously, if it is not lost. Hence the lamentations of whole nations; hence the humiliation of concordats, wherein the Mother of the faithful was constrained by her discontented children to condescend to make terms with them;[1]

[1] During fifteen centuries, amid all her many trials, the Church was never brought so low as to be forced to make compacts with the faithful! The sins of the clergy incurred this humiliation. "If the salt have lost his savour, wherewith shall it be salted? it is thenceforth good for nothing, but to be cast out, and to be trodden under foot of men" (St. Matt. v. 13). It is useless to deny that concordats *are* compacts — a Pope himself gives them this name; Julius III. says, "Nos attendentes concordata dicta vim PACTI inter partes habere," etc. (Constit., 14 Sept., 1554, apud Raynald). No compact holds good when it begins to be sinful, nor should compacts with the Church be so stringent as to hinder her power of benefiting the Christian world—a power which, essentially free, cannot be bound. In saying this, I do not so much condemn concordats, as lament their necessity. Neither they nor any other human convention whatsoever can take away the Divine and immutable rights of the Church, or fetter the legislative power given her by Jesus Christ, or in any way diminish the fulness of her power for good—by means of which she can lay her injunctions on the faithful without limit where she sees it needful for their

hence, finally, a terrible Wound in the body of the Church. When her ancient elective rights were gone, when the clergy took no part in the elections, and the chapters were despoiled of their privileges, and the Popes of their reserves, the nomination of Bishops fell everywhere throughout Catholic Christendom into lay hands, although their confirmation, a matter of little consequence, was retained by the ruler of the Church. Thus was accomplished the work of the wolf in sheep's clothing, "the Church was enslaved under the outward garb of liberty."¹ But before I proceed to set forth the bitterness of this piteous Wound, of this fiction of liberty which is a real slavery, I have yet somewhat to say

Chap. IV.

eternal salvation, and for the enlargement of Christ's kingdom upon earth. [It is difficult to follow our author here. If a compact is sinful, it ought not to be made ; if any compact is made, and can be kept without positive immorality, it ought to be kept. Surely he does " condemn" some concordats.—ED.]

¹ When Pope Adrian I. wrote to Charlemagne (A.D. 784), to make him understand that the secular power had no right to take part in Episcopal elections, and that they must be left free, he was able to make use of an effectual and telling argument, namely, that he himself (the Pope) did not meddle with the elections, because they were better free. His words are, " Nunquam nos in qualibet electione invenimus nec invenire habemus. Sed neque Vestram Excellentiam optamus in talem rem incumbere. Sed qualis a clero et plebe . . . electus canonicè fuerit, et nihil sit quod sacro obsit ordini, solita traditione illum ordinamus " (Tom. ii. Conc. Gall., p. 95, 120). This telling argument could no longer be used by the Popes, when the day of reserves had arrived.

about other reasons which brought Episcopal elections to so pitiable a state. Something must be said of the weary struggles of Popes and Bishops, who did and bore much in the attempt to keep the Church as truly free as she was by the constitution of her Divine Founder.

LXXXI. When the northern chieftains fell with their barbarian hordes upon the South and conquered it, they styled themselves Kings of France, of Italy, and of England,[1] that is, of the possessions of Frenchmen, Italians and Englishmen, and thereby of their persons. But it was impossible for any one possessor, however great his strength, to keep a hold over such wide districts, while the received law enacted that "the power to protect a right must correspond with the extent of the right itself." Hence these chieftains, who were a new kind of kings, invented the feudal system, as a means of retaining a principal claim upon their new possessions, while ceding the present use of them to others. Their tenants became the faithful guardians of lands, which they would otherwise have endeavoured to wrest from the chiefs; whose companions in arms would never have submitted to be excluded from a share in the new conquests.

[1] [This is, of course, too rhetorical to be history.—ED.]

These men, who shared in the bounty of the king, and had to a great measure the same interests, were his *faithful* men (fedeli); whence was derived the name of fiefs (feudi), because they vowed fidelity to the king, and a vassalage of fixed services, chiefly of raising men-at-arms, and of serving themselves in the king's army. It was a clever arrangement. By this means conquerors were able to maintain a right in the conquered lands, and also to keep in subjection those to whom they were ceded; as, whenever a feudatory died, his fief lapsed to the king, who conferred it upon any one else, according to his pleasure.[1]

It was not long before these new masters of Europe perceived that it was more to their advantage to make over their lands in trust to Bishops and Churches, than to military dependants. And thus, as early as in the time of Clovis, began the system of ecclesiastical fiefs and baronies. Charlemagne especially appreciated the value of this plan. William of Malmesbury says, "Charlemagne, seeking to subdue the ferocity of the Germanic nations, gave nearly all the lands to the

[1] It was not till near the end of the second dynasty that lay fiefs became hereditary in France, as is shown by Marc. Anton. Dominicy (De Prærogativis Allodiorum, c. 15, Strasbourg, 1697); but out of respect to ecclesiastical feudatories, who had no succession, they were always more or less personal.

Church, reflecting, with consummate wisdom, that men in Holy Orders would less easily cast aside their fidelity to the Emperor than would the laity; and that, moreover, if the laity rebelled, they would be able to control such rebellion by the terrors of the spiritual power, and the authority of excommunication."[1]

Such liberality, shown by princes towards Bishops, closely resembled bribes offered to judges by parties to a suit. Moreover, the very nature of these royal bounties involved the Church's servitude. The Bishops became so many vassals, constrained to take the oaths of fidelity and to do feudal homage to the king.[2] As his

[1] De gestis regum Anglorum, lib. v. "Carolus Magnus pro contundendâ gentium illarum (Germanicarum) ferociâ, omnes pene terras Ecclesiis contulerat, consiliosissime perpendens, nolle Sacri Ordinis homines tam facile quam laicos fidelitatem domino rejicere. Præterea, si laici rebellarent, illos posse excommunicationis auctoritate et potentiæ severitate compescere."

[2] Nor did it stop here. The oath that at first was exacted from the Bishops as feudatories, was soon exacted from them as Bishops, *per extensionem*, as the lawyers said, and by this clause they thought to justify the usurpation. The Church was not inactive; she forbade such Bishops as held no temporal possessions at the king's hands to take this oath. At the fourth Lateran Council, the solemn decretal of Innocent III. on this point was published (Can. 43): "Nimis de *jure divino* quidam laici usurpare conantur, cum viros ecclesiasticos, nihil temporale detinentes ab eis, ad præstandum sibi fidelitatis juramenta compellunt. Quia vero, secundum Apostolum, servus suo domino stat aut cadit, sacri auctoritate Concilii prohibemus, ne tales clerici personis sæcularibus præstare cogantur hujus modi juramenta."

associates, sharing his earthly interests, and joining in his enterprises and wars, it was impossible for them any longer to appreciate the Apostle's rule, "No man that warreth, entangleth himself with the affairs of this life."[1] They inevitably learnt to look upon the king solely as their temporal lord, and themselves as his servants, sharing his wealth and his power as a matter of favour. They forgot that their king was but a layman, a son of the Church, a sheep of their fold; and that they were Bishops chosen by the Holy Spirit to govern the Church of God. In a word, it was impossible that, having become *King's men*,[2] they could have ever before them that they were *men of God*; forasmuch as "no man can serve two masters."[3]

LXXXII. The use of earthly advantages for earthly ends rarely fails to blind men. All the Church's power, all her liberties, belong to the spiritual and invisible world. Who can wonder, if, when power of an outward and imposing

[1] 2 Tim. ii. 4.
[2] He who held an investiture from the king was called "homo regis." There could be no expression which more fully describes the king's absolute lordship over such a man, who became, so to say, a royal possession. Who could imagine St. Peter, St. Paul, St. Chrysostom, or St. Augustine converted from "homo Dei," into "homo regis"! And in those days the word "homo" had become a synonym for soldier; cf. Du-cange; Glos. med. et infim. latinit. Voc. *Miles*.
[3] St. Matt. vi. 24.

Chap. IV. character and worldly and civil duties were added to the spiritual office of the Episcopate, the Bishops—who, after all, were but men—should, like their princes, be dazzled and absorbed by such accessories, and speedily learn to seek in them the essence of their Episcopal dignity? Who can wonder that this secular rank which royalty had bestowed, was mingled and confused in men's minds with the spiritual power conferred by Christ, until the invisible gift, through its confusion with the earthly, vanished by degrees quite out of sight? Hence the benefice annexed to the office was called *a bishopric*,[1] for it was no longer thought possible to separate the Episcopal office from the temporal benefice, or that the spiritual power could exist without it. The ordinary forms of speech in that period, shaped by public opinion, confirm this. They confuse everything together. Instead of saying that the king bestowed the temporal possessions annexed to an Episcopal see, they speak of the king as "giving, conferring a Bishopric, or the Episcopal dignity," as "commanding, ordaining that such a one shall be a Bishop;" or they say that "by the royal command so-and-so has been consecrated."[2]

[1] [*Ital.* episcopato. —Ed.]
[2] Fulbert of Chartres, ep. 8 [ed. Migne. 35], writes of Frank,

forgotten amidst its temporal accessories.

Once more, these expressions did not convey, at the time when they were coined, all their real meaning; they foreshadowed what would come to be in the future. It is always thus; expressions are originated, worthless at first, mere concessions of truth to passion, mere falsehoods. But deeds soon follow words: there is a law which leads men to speak the truth, and which also leads them to treat words as real which may have been idly spoken. The forms of speech current in a nation show to those who look below the surface of human affairs, the path which it is treading, and its tendencies in the future. This identification in common speech of the Episcopal dignity with its temporal endowments, and this habit of attributing to the lay power

King Robert's Chancellor, that he was made Bishop, "eligente clero, suffragante populo, *dono regis.*" As I said above, these words were commonly used, and no one heeded their incorrectness. Among the formulas of Marculfus, that which contains the King's order says, addressing the Bishop designate : "*Pontificalem*, in Dei nomine *commisimus dignitatem*;" which form of speech demands some explanation even from a zealous advocate of the royal privilege, who adds as follows : " Quod saniori sensu et magis canonico intelligi non potest quam de regiorum jurium et feudorum investiturâ et concessione quæ Clodoveus ex ecclesiis manu liberali contulerat" (Hist. Eccl. sæc. xiii., xiv., Dissert. viii. art. 3). St. Gregory of Tours says of Cantinus, Bishop of Clermont (Lib. iv. c. 7) : " Tunc *jussu* regis *traditis* ei *clericis* et omnibus quæ hi de rebus ecclesiæ exhibuerant." And Clothaire II., in the edict by which he modifies the canon of the fifth Council of Paris, " ut si persona condigna fuerit, *per ordinationem principis ordinetur.*" We meet with such expressions continually in the writings of that period.

CHAP. IV. the distribution of Episcopal offices as of any other gifts which are naturally dependent on the will of the donor, showed but too plainly the subserviency and corruption of the clergy. They had already become the vassals of secular princes, preferring the good things of the world to the freedom of Christ. The popular language also showed the tendency of princes to grasp everything, to conquer the Church as they had conquered the soil. This tendency might for a time be restrained from its natural development by the personal piety of individuals; but in the long run it would infallibly follow the law of its natural gravitation, and bear the fruit of which it sowed the seed. Thus we see that at first, with the exception of some arbitrary acts concerning elections, the kings recognized the Church's right to choose her own Pastors. Even when they disposed arbitrarily of Episcopal sees, they accompanied acts of injustice with language which softened them and which breathed a pious spirit. They were unwilling abruptly to offend the feelings of Bishops and people, who were still strict and tenacious with regard to truth and Canon law, and had not yet become yielding and courtier-like.[1] Charlemagne's piety and recti-

[1] The formulas preserved by Marculfus show how the *Præceptum de Episcopatu* of the Frank kings was attempered: "Cognovimus

tude, as well as his policy, went still further, and restored to the Church some part of that liberty of which the Merovingian kings had robbed her. Louis the Pious followed the example of his magnanimous father.[1] But not so the kings their successors.

LXXXIII. It was but natural that at the death of any Bishop, his fief should return to the king, and that the king should enjoy the revenues of the vacant see, which were called "*regalia.*" This was of the very essence of the feudal system. But matters did not stop here. A covetous desire to appropriate this income led monarchs to

Antistitem illum ab hac luce migrasse, ob cujus successorum sollicitudinem congruam una cum Pontificibus (vel proceribus nostris plenius tractantes, *decrevimus* illustri viro illi Pontificalem in ipso urbe committere dignitatem."

[1] Pope Adrian I. had admonished Charlemagne that it was his duty to leave Episcopal elections unfettered ; and that great man received this admonition from the Head of the Church with that docility which is a far greater proof of a noble mind in princes, than is their resistance and disobedience. Charlemagne even set forth and sanctioned this liberty in the decree we find in his Capitularies of Aix-la-Chapelle, A.D. 803 (c. 2): "Not being unaware of the sacred Canons, we have given our assent to the ecclesiastical order (so that Holy Church may securely possess her due honour), that Bishops be elected by their own dioceses, by election of the clergy and people, according to the rules of the Canons, without any acceptance of persons or bribes, according to their personal merit and wisdom, so that they may always benefit those under them by their example and their teaching." In A.D. 806, Louis the Pious confirmed this law of Charlemagne in the Capitulary published after the Synod of Aix-la-Chapelle.

N

CHAP. IV. keep dioceses without Pastors for a length of time.[1] They delayed the elections by insisting that no Bishop could be elected without the royal permission.[2] Thus they made the Gospel and the

[1] This usurpation reached the culminating point in the eleventh century. Not to multiply instances, it will suffice to notice what happened to two Archbishops of Canterbury, Lanfranc and St. Anselm, under two English kings, William I. and William II. When Lanfranc demanded of William I. the property which his predecessors had held, the King answered fiercely, "Se velle omnes baculos pastorales Angliæ in manu suâ tenere." The historian who narrates this (Gervasius Dorobernensis, in Imaginationibus de discordiis inter monachos Dorobernenses et Baldeuinum Archiepisc.; see Historiæ Anglicanæ Scriptores Antiqui, p. 1329), says that the Prelate was amazed on hearing this, and remained silent out of prudence, fearing lest the King should do still greater injury to the Church. And the history of St. Anselm, Lanfranc's successor, still further shows the state to which the Church was reduced at that time. Eadmer relates (Lib. i. Hist. Novor.) that William II., having left Churches and Abbacies without Pastors in order to appropriate their revenues, Anselm thought it his duty as Primate to remonstrate with the King, setting forth all the evils which arose from the lack of Prelates, and humbly intreating the King to cease from thus injuring his own soul. The historian goes on to say that on hearing this remonstrance of the holy Archbishop, "non potuit amplius spiritum suum Rex cohibere, sed oppido turbatus cum iracundiâ dixit: 'Quid ad te? numquid Abbatiæ non sunt meæ? Hem, tu quod vis agis de villis tuis, et ego non agam quod volo de Abbatiis meis?'" To which the holy Prelate could do no less than answer respectfully, that the possessions of the Church were his only that he might protect and defend them, for that they were God's, and intended for the maintenance of God's ministers. To which the King wrathfully replied, "Pro certo noveris, mihi valde contraria esse quæ dicis. Non enim antecessor tuus auderet ullatenus patri meo dicere: et nihil faciam pro te." To such straits had the Church's freedom and possessions come in those days! such was the predominance and assumption of the lay power!

[2] The Church ever testified her reluctance to submit to such

salvation of souls dependent on the king's will, CHAP. IV.
his caprice, and above all, his covetousness. And
inasmuch as even presbyters had a share in the
Church's revenues, it was ordered that from henceforth the Church of God should be powerless to
dependence, and history is full of the struggle between the Church,
seeking freedom of action, and the secular power, seeking to subject
her to itself. Hence disputes were perpetually arising about elections which had been made without first obtaining the royal assent.
Richard I., in a letter to the Bishop of London about the year 1190,
complains loudly of an election as to which he had not been consulted : "Quod si ita est, regiam majestatem nostram non modicum
esse offensam." He declares, "Non enim aliquâ ratione sustinere-
mus quod a præfatis monachis vel ab aliis quidquam cum detrimento
honoris nostri in electione Episcopi fieret ; et si forte factum esset
quin in irritum revocaretur." In Richard's time the secular power
had made great progress in its invasion of the Church's rights, and
oppression of the Church's freedom ; while the power of resistance
on her part grew feebler, so that she would have succumbed, had
not God, taking care for her preservation, raised up Popes of extraordinary courage and devotion, who once more set her free. What
would the Church in her brighter days have thought of monarchs
who claimed the right of controlling her choice of her own Pastors,
and required that their consent should be sought before any election could be made ? What would the Chrysostoms and the
Augustines have said, could they have beheld a son of the Church
striving to fetter his Mother's hands, leaving her only such liberty
as a slave might receive at a master's pleasure ? With what noble
and holy wrath would they have answered such pretensions, maintaining the sacred rights of the Spouse of Christ ? Even in the
tenth century, and in the East, the Church bore witness that she
felt all the degradation to which she was brought by such oppression. Cedrenus relates that Phocas Nicephorus had forbidden
Episcopal elections to be made without his consent, and many as
were the crimes of that Emperor, the historian ranks this prohibition among the foremost of them : "Id omnium gravissimum, quod
legem tulit, cui et *episcopi quidam leves atque adulatores*" (here lay
the root of the evil), "*subscripserunt,* ne absque imperatoris sententiâ

CHAP. IV. ordain one of her humblest priests, save by royal concession and favour! [1]

LXXXIV. Again. The men of the law, who are to royal Courts what sophistical demagogues are to a corrupt populace, discovered the following singular argument:—

"The principal involves that which is accessory; but among the Church's possessions her

---

ac permissu Episcopus vel eligeretur vel ordinaretur." When Phocas' successor, John Zymisca, came to the throne, the then Patriarch of Constantinople, Polieuctes, refused to admit him or his followers into the Church, or to assist at his coronation, until he had made atonement for his crimes, and until he had abrogated the law of the last Emperor, which was fatal to the Church's freedom. The new monarch obeyed, and the law was torn up in the presence of all the people (Cedren. ad. ann. 969, p. 255).

[1] Among the formulas of Marculfus (19) we find one entitled "Præceptum de clericatu," which is the required licence given by the king to all candidates for the priesthood. It is called "præceptum," inasmuch as flattery assumed that whatever came from the royal lips was such. Would that princes could banish all this false courtier phraseology, and rest their power solely on the truth! How much stronger and more venerable their thrones would be! Yet the world mocks at such a proposal! The Bishops nevertheless continued to ordain priests regardless of this royal mandate. Among Gerbertus' Epistles we find one from an Archbishop of Rheims (Ep. 57), in which he speaks of himself as "accused of crime against the king's majesty by reason of having conferred ecclesiastical orders without his permission or license." The French kings even sought to contest the liberty of the faithful to quit the world, and devote themselves to God in the religious life. Hincmar, in a letter to Charles the Bald, tells that monarch emphatically that the Church has never acknowledged any such law. This letter is published by P. Cellotti with the Council of Douzi.

fiefs are the principal; hence all Church property must assume the character of fiefs, and be subject to the same legislation."[1]

By means of this singular argument all the Church's possessions had the honour of being considered "*noble things*";[2] possessions of the first rank, and thus, in a manner, royal.[3] Hence the king assumed feudal rights, not only over fiefs which were really his, but over all ecclesiastical property indifferently. From all he exacted his regalia, that is, the proceeds of vacant benefices,[4] which were destined to fall into his hands at the death of those who held them; and generally he disposed of them at his pleasure, as his personal property.[5] Thus the character of fiefs was ascribed

[1] See Natalis Alexander. In sæc. xiii. et xiv., dissert. viii. art. 1.
[2] [*Ital.* enti nobili.—ED.]
[3] These, they said, enjoyed a more powerful protection and defence; but is not the civil power bound to protect all property alike?
[4] The word *benefice*, which is universally retained in the Church, is derived from the early military benefices, and later, ecclesiastical benefices, assigned to their lieges by the mediæval monarchs. The very name reminds us how the clergy sold their liberty to those monarchs. They exchanged it for wealth.
[5] The Church was not silent, she sought to defend herself against such usurpations. But she could only set her Canons against military force. Already, in the year 451, the great Œcumenical Council of Chalcedon had framed this Canon (25): "Redditus vero viduatæ Ecclesiæ integros reservari apud œconomum ejusdem Ecclesiæ placuit."
The Council of Riez, A.D. 493, Can. 6, decrees, "Stabili de-

CHAP. IV. to the free possessions of the Church; thus the tithes were infeoffed;[1] and, advancing step by

finitione consultum est, ut de cætero observaretur, ne quis ad eam Ecclesiam, quæ Episcopum perdidisset, nisi vicinæ Ecclesiæ Episcopus exequiarum tempore accederet, qui visitatoris vice tamen ipsius curam districtissime gereret, ne quid ante ordinationem discordantium in novitatibus clericorum subversioni liceret. Itaque cum tale aliquid accidit, vicinis vicinarum Ecclesiarum inspectio, recensio, descriptioque mandatur."

In the Spanish Councils of Valentia and Ilerda, A.D. 524, 525, the discipline of the Council of Chalcedon is confirmed.

In the second Council of Orléans, A.D. 533 (c. 6), it is decreed, that in the event of the death of a Bishop, the neighbouring Prelate shall come to his burial, and, assembling his priests, shall make an exact inventory of the Church's properties, entrusting them to faithful and safe persons.

The fifth Council of Paris, A.D. 614 (c. 7), ordains that no one shall meddle with the property of any defunct Bishop or priest, and that no "royal precept" shall have any claim upon it, under pain of excommunication. It rules that "ab Archidiacono vel clero in omnibus defensentur et conserventur."

Hincmar, Archbishop of Rheims, wrote thus to his Bishops, in the ninth century (Ep. 9): "Et sicut Episcopus et suas et ecclesiasticas facultates sub debita discretione in vita sua dispensandi habet potestatem, ita facultates Ecclesiæ viduatæ post mortem Episcopi penes œconomum integræ conservari jubentur futuro successori ejus Episcopo; quoniam res et facultates ecclesiasticæ *non imperatorum atque regum potestate sunt* ad dispensandum vel invadendum, sive diripiendum, sed ad defensandum atque tuendum." Hincmar wrote in the same strain to King Charles the Bald (Ep. xxix., and in various other letters, xxi. xlv.).

Another Archbishop of Rheims, Gerbert, afterwards Pope Sylvester II., sets forth the same doctrine in his letter to his clergy and people (Ep. cxviii.).

These laws being so taught and reasserted by the Church, the princes of the ninth century could not seize upon the Church's rights without incurring public disapproval: thus the "Bertiniani Annales," A.D. 882, speak of the crime committed by Charles the Fat, who made over the possessions of the Church of Metz to

Laymen and soldiers, in Abbacies and Sees. 183

step, tithes, or other free property, were in this way granted in fief to laymen; as was often done with respect to real fiefs upon the death of the Bishops or Abbots who held them.[2] And inasmuch as the spiritualities were considered inseparable from the temporalities, the spectacle was witnessed of laymen, nay, of soldiers, reigning in abbacies over monks instead of their rightful Abbots, and in sees as Bishops over their clergy.[3]

Hugo, son of Lothaire the younger: " Quos sacri Canones futuro episcopo reservari præcipiunt."

[1] It is well known that the tithes were usurped by the laity, and conferred and given in fief by princes, as well as by Bishops and Rectors. This appears from the canon law. See Estravag. de Decim., c. 26, and Estravag. de iis quæ fiunt a Prælat. sine consensu, c. 17.

[2] For examples, see Nat. Alexan., sœc., xiii. and xiv. Dissert. viii. art. iii.

[3] The Council of Meaux, A.D. 845, did not fail to address Charles the Bald with Apostolic freedom, because he was guilty of this despotism, granting the Church's lands to laymen, " so that, contrary to all rule, contrary to the decrees of the Fathers, and to that which is becoming for the Christian religion, we find laymen presiding in monasteries as lords and masters among the priests and Levites and other religious, regulating their life and conversation, sitting in judgment upon them, as though they themselves were Abbots; granting dispensations and formally providing for the charge of souls and of the sacred tabernacles, not only without the Bishop's presence, but without knowledge on his part of what was being done " (Can. 10 and 42). Therefore these Fathers, addressing Charles the Bald, decreed, "ut præcepta illicita jure beneficiario de rebus ecclesiasticis facta a vobis, sine dilatione rescindantur, et ut de cætero ne fiant, a dignitate Vestri nominis regii caveatur" (Can. 18). Setting before him the enormity of thus rending the seamless garment of Christ, which was not done even by the soldiers

CHAP. IV. LXXXV. This identification of the temporalities with the spiritualities led necessarily to the usurpation of things spiritual as well as temporal. And thus we find princes granting investitures with the emblems of spiritual authority, the ring and pastoral staff. Hence it came to pass that Bishoprics remained vacant while the sovereign seized upon their revenues.[1] The

who crucified Him, they proceed: "Ante oculos reducentes tunicam Christi, Qui vos elegit et exaltavit, quam nec milites ausi fuerunt scindere, tempore vestro quantocitius reconsuite et resarcite : et nec violenta ablatione, nec illicitorum præceptorum confirmatione res ab Ecclesiis vobis ad tuendum et defensandum ac propagandum commissis auferre tentate ; sed ut sanctæ memoriæ avus et pater vester eas gubernandas vobis, fautore Deo, dimiserunt, redintegrate, præcepta regalia earundem Ecclesiarum conservate et confirmate " (Can. 2). It is to be observed that this Council distinguishes between lands given to the Church as freeholds, and those given in fief ; the King is rebuked chiefly for giving the former to laymen.

[1] In the Appendix to Flodoardus we find a "Notitia de Villa Novilliaco" thus expressed : "Defuncto Tispino Archiepiscopo, tenuit Dominus Rex Carolus Remense *Episcopium* in suo dominatu, et dedidit villam Novilliacum in beneficio Anschero Saxoni," etc. ; that is, to a soldier, where we see the confusion of the temporal benefice with the Bishopric. And since there is nothing which covetousness and power united will not attempt, the princes, when urged not to leave dioceses vacant, bethought them of sending commissaries called *Chorepiscopi*, instead of Bishops, retaining the revenues of the see meanwhile. These false pastors grievously afflicted the Church ; and thus we find numerous complaints and decrees against *Chorepiscopi* in the Councils of the eleventh century, until these anomalous officers, after damaging the Church for a long time, were done away with. Flodoardus (Lib. iii. Hist. Remensis, c. 10), writing of an epistle from Hincmar to Pope Leo IV. says, "In hac vero epistolâ, de his quos temeritas chorepiscopalis ordinare, vel

kings generally interfered with elections.¹ There was an unlawful trade in Episcopal sees. They were sold to the highest bidder. The high places of the Church were filled by unworthy men, possessing no other merit than that of their unworthiness; they were devoted to their prince, and truckled to his vices. Degradation and corruption abounded both among clergy and people, and a long train of evils was heaped upon the hapless Church, in consequence of this wretched state of things. And, although monarchs were blind to the fact, these evils reacted upon the State, disturbing and dividing it, and retarding that progress of civilization towards which, if the secular power be righteous, nature and Christ's religion, happily associated, of themselves guide the nations in their onward course.

LXXXVI. Under such oppression, the clergy grew daily more oblivious of their true dignity and freedom; willingly accepting an increase of

quod Spiritum Sanctum consignando tradere præsumebat, requisivit. Et quod terrena potestas hac materia sæpe offenderet, ut videlicet, Episcopo quolibet defuncto, per Chorepiscopum solis Pontificibus debitum ministerium perageretur, et res ac facultates Ecclesiæ sæcularium usibus expenderentur, sicut et in nostrâ Ecclesiâ jam secundo actum est," etc.

¹ For a statement of the steps by which princes usurped elections, beginning with intreaties and recommendations, and ending with commands and violence, see Tommassinus, Vet. et Nov. Eccl. Discipl., P. I. lib. i. c. 54.

CHAP. IV. wealth and temporal power in the place of those treasures, of which they no longer knew the value.[1]

[1] The abject words of Bishop Arturicus, quoted by Elmoldus (in Cronico Sclavorum, lib. i. c. 69 and 70) suffice to show how God's ministers had deteriorated under their increased temporal advantages. "*The investiture of Pontiffs,*" says that Prelate, "*is solely the right of the imperial dignity, which alone is excellent, and after God most sublime among the sons of men.*" (A Bishop thus to speak of the Emperor, forgetful that whatever his rank in the Church as a temporal sovereign, he is but her son and a layman !) "*This honour was acquired at a great price.*" (It is not a question of honour ; the power of appointing to Bishoprics is a most important office, a sacred and inalienable right of the Church. Can she sell that right ? Can princes buy it with earthly riches ? What else was the sin of Simon Magus ?) "*Nor was it in mere wantonness that our most worthy Emperors styled themselves* LORDS OF THE BISHOPS." (A Bishop praising such language !) "*But they compensated this inroad*" (It *was* an inroad then ?) "*with abundant wealth*" (Can the Church's freedom be compensated with money ? Can she cast aside the only true wealth of the Spouse of Christ in order to assume that bestowed by secular princes ?) "*whereby the Church was more plentifully adorned.*" (With virtues, or with an empty exterior magnificence ?) "*Nor does she now hold herself to be lowered by such subjection ; nor does she blush to bow down, in order that she may rule over many.*" (A singular opinion, truly worthy of a successor of the Apostles ! But the Church does not seek to *rule*, rather to *save* men ; the first is done through temporal power, the latter by the grace of God's Word and the Holy Spirit. If the Church became the slave of any one man, though through him she reigned over all the world, she would be repudiated by Christ.) The whole tenour of this Bishop's language is so extraordinary that I must quote some of the original words, lest it be thought I have misrepresented him : " Investituræ Pontificum imperatoriæ tantum dignitati permissæ sunt, quæ sola excellens, et post Deum in filiis hominum præeminens, hunc honorem non sine fænore multiplici conquistavit. Neque Imperatores dignissimi levitate usi sunt, ut Episcoporum domini vocarentur, sed compensaverunt noxam hanc amplissimis regni divitiis, quibus Ecclesia copiosius aucta, decentius honestata, jam non vile reputet ad

Not that from amidst these depths of humiliation the solemn voice of truth ever failed in the Church. That voice can never be silenced ; if the undying Church could cease to raise it, she would cease to be herself. But it was a plaintive solitary voice, rising up like the cry of a land of mourning.

It may suffice to quote a passage from Florus, a deacon of Lyons, who, in this tenth century, when the freedom of Episcopal elections was well-nigh lost, wrote a book on the subject, " in order to set forth what were the sacred laws of the Church, and to confute the opinion which was little by little asserting itself at Court, that the king's assent was necessary to the lawfulness and ratification of an Episcopal election." He begins by setting forth clearly the true doctrine on this matter : " It is plain to all who hold the priestly office in God's Church, that they are bound to obey all that is commanded by the authority of the sacred Canons, and by ecclesiastical custom, *according to the disposition of the Divine Laws, and Apostolic tradition*, with respect to the Ordination of Bishops. Accordingly, when a Pastor dies, and his see is vacant, the post of the departed

modicum cessisse subjectioni ; non erubescat uni inclinare per quem possit in multos dominari." Who would believe that after citing this passage Natalis Alexander should have added "*præclare dictum !*"

CHAP. IV. Prelate should be rightly filled by one of his clergy, elected by the general and unanimous consent of that clergy and people, solemnly and openly designated by public decree, and consecrated by the legitimate number of Bishops. There is no doubt that an appointment so made by the Church of God, is confirmed by justice and the Divine Law. These things have been established by the Councils of the Fathers, by the decrees of the Apostolic See, and by the Church of Christ from the beginning." In proof he quotes from St. Cyprian's epistle to Antoninus, concerning the election of St. Cornelius : " A man should be made Bishop by the judgment of God and of His Christ, by the witness of all the clergy, by the votes of the people, and by the consent of the venerable priests, and of good men" (*bonorum virorum*).

He then proceeds, " It appears from these words of the Blessed Cyprian, that from Apostolic times, and for something like three hundred years,[1] all Bishops of the Church of God were appointed by the Christian people, and lawfully governed them, without any interference of earthly power. When princes began to be Christian, we have one

[1] [*Ital.* anni quasi quattrocento. But if so, Florus made a mistake.—ED.]

plain proof that, speaking generally, the Church maintained her freedom in the appointment of her Bishops. It was not possible that an emperor, ruling all the world, could know and select all the Bishops who must needs be appointed in the widely spread countries of Asia, Europe and Africa. Nevertheless those appointments made by the Holy Church after the Apostolic tradition, and with due religious observances, were always validly completed. If in some countries a custom of consulting the sovereign concerning Episcopal appointments crept in, it was only out of brotherly love, and in order to preserve peace and harmony with the powers that be; not in any way to make the holy ordination more valid or authoritative; since that ordination cannot be conferred on any one by royal power, but only by God's will, and with the consent of the faithful. And this forasmuch as the Episcopate is no human office, but a gift of the Holy Spirit.... Whence it comes that any prince who believes himself able to confer as his benefice that which Divine Grace alone dispenses, sins grievously: in such concerns his power may follow in confirmation, but it may not take the lead."[1]

[1] "Cum ministerium suæ potestatis in hujus modi negotium peragendo adjungere debeat, non præferre." This is the true idea

LXXXVII. Nevertheless we must confess that the continued perseverance with which the lay power sought to reduce the Church to subjection, at one time by benefits conferred, at another by underhand dealings, was at last successful. The conquest was achieved. In the tenth century the Church herself seemed weary of struggling and protesting in vain against usurpation. She appeared to have lost voice and breath, to have become hoarse, so rarely and so feebly did she speak.

This was the most ill-starred of centuries. We find the clergy out of their rightful path, blinded by worldly wealth, and well-nigh accustomed to traffic with dignity and conscience. A further and noteworthy cause of the enslavement of the Church was the power of Otho I., who humbled the nobles, and strengthened his sovereign authority·by making it more absolute. Thereby society would have greatly benefited if the sovereign power had not strayed into usurpations of the Church's rights. But, with such precedents and vicious customs, every addition to the Imperial power did but tend to promote its usurpations.[1]

of the part princes should take on the Church's behalf ; not constituting themselves legislators, but lending their aid in order that all her laws and arrangements may be carried out strictly according to her mind.

[1] This did not occur at once. Otho I. was a religious prince, and

The Church in England and France. 191

Thus in the beginning of the eleventh century the freedom of election was altogether extinct.

In England the Abbot Ingulfus, in the time of William the Conqueror, writes thus: "For many years past we have not had any really free and Canonical election of Prelates; but every dignity, whether of Bishop or Abbot, has been conferred with ring and staff by the royal Court, according to its pleasure."[1] Respecting France under Philip I., the Pope complains to Procleus, Bishop of Chalons, thus: "Among the other

ranks third with Alfred the Great and Charlemagne. Several facts are recorded of him which prove his respect for the Church and her authority. One of his nobles having applied for the revenues of a certain monastery in order to maintain troops, he answered indignantly, that "were he to give the Church's revenues to the laity, he should fear to sin against Christ's precept, 'Give not that which is holy to the dogs.'" He did much for the Roman Church, confirming the free election of the Pope. Otho was not the man to end by destroying ecclesiastical liberty, but it owed its extinction to the increased power left by Otho as an inheritance to his successors, who were not so upright as he was, or so generous and large-hearted. It may even be added that one thing which forwarded that total ruin of the liberty of the Church which took place in the first half of the eleventh century was the very religious zeal of pious princes, especially of the first and third Othos, and of the saintly Emperor Henry. They meddled with the Church solely with a view to her benefit, of which she was so fully conscious that she offered no opposition; but by this means their successors obtained a power which they used to their own ends.

[1] "A multis annis retroactis nulla electio Prælatorum erat mere libera et canonica; sed omnes dignitates tam Episcoporum quam Abbatum per annulum et baculum regis Curia pro sua complacentia conferebat."

CHAP. IV. princes who in our time .... have trampled upon their Mother as though she were a bondslave, we know on good authority that Philip of France has so oppressed the Gallican Churches, as to have reached the climax of this detestable crime. The which thing grieves us the more, forasmuch as it is known how prudent and religious and energetic and faithful to the Roman Church that kingdom has been heretofore."[1]

Of Germany, St. Anselm, Bishop of Lucca, a contemporaneous writer, says, "Thy King" (he addresses the Anti-pope Guibert) "continually sells Bishoprics, publishing edicts forbidding that he should be Bishop who is elected of the clergy, or required of the people, unless the royal will has first chosen him; as though the monarch were the porter of that door of which the Truth hath said, 'To him the porter openeth.' You tear asunder the limbs of the Catholic Church, which you have invaded, throughout the kingdom, and which, after reducing her to servitude, you retain in your

[1] "Inter cæteros nostri hujus temporis principes, qui Ecclesiam Dei perversa cupiditate venumdando dissipaverunt, et matrem suam ancillari subjectione penitus conculcârunt, Philippum regem Francorum Gallicanas Ecclesias in tantum oppressisse certa relatione didicimus, ut ad summum tam detestandi hujus facinoris cumulum pervenisse videatur. Quam rem de regno illo tanto profecto tulimus molestius, quanto et prudentia et religione et viribus noscitur fuisse potentius, et erga Romanam Ecclesiam multo devotius."—Gregory VII., Ep. i. 35, ad Rodericum (Rodenum) Cabilonensem Episcopum.

Gregory VII. becomes Pope. 193

keeping as a miserable slave. You exchange the CHAP. IV. freedom of God's service for a degrading subservience to the Emperor, when you say that Bishoprics, Abbacies, all Churches, without exception, are subject to the imperial jurisdiction; whereas the Lord says, '*My* Church, *My* Dove, *My* Sheep;' and St. Paul, 'No man taketh this honour unto himself, but he that is called of God, as was Aaron.'"[1]

LXXXVIII. But in these most unhappy times, when the Church of God seemed hopelessly lost, Christ did not forget His promise. He raised up an extraordinary man, who, with an enormous moral power, which was certainly not of this world, braved all, dared all, and remained triumphant over all. He avenged the Church, repaired her losses, and, we may say, strengthened the kingdom of God upon earth. No one will doubt who was the messenger of God in the age re-

---

[1] The flatterers of the Emperor used such boasting language, and the Bishop of Lucca strove to refute them by an opportune, frank and generous work, breathing that spirit of primitive times, which, as I have said, was never wholly wanting in the Church. He introduces the argument of the second book thus : "Opitulante Domini nostri clementia, qui nos et sermones nostros Suo mirabili nutu regit atque disponit, accingimur respondere his qui dicunt, regali potestati Christi Ecclesiam subjacere, et ei pro suo libito, vel prece, vel pretio, vel gratis, liceat Pastores imponere, ejusque possessiones vel in sua vel in cujus libuerit jura transferre." This answer of the holy Bishop is full of learning and vigour.

O

ferred to; it will be felt that we are describing Gregory VII. This most remarkable man was raised to St. Peter's Chair, A.D. 1073. Complaints of Henry IV.'s unbounded dissoluteness, his unparalleled tyranny towards his Christian subjects, and the havoc which he had wrought in the Church had already been laid before Gregory's predecessor. But death had prevented Alexander II. from doing anything to heal the deep and deadly wounds in the Body of Christ.[1] It was for the lonely monk Hildebrand that God in His Providence had reserved the hard task of curing the ancient and cankered sore by sharp steel. All gentler means of cure had failed.[2] Gregory at first declined the Pontificate.

[1] The year before his death (A. D. 1073) that Pope had summoned Henry to Rome to give satisfaction to the Church for the crimes of which he was accused by the Saxons. Thus when Gregory VII. was raised to the Apostolic See he found the case already begun by his predecessor, who had bestowed all his energies in stemming the overflowing tide of evil in the Church, and in repressing simoniacal elections and restoring liberty. Otho of Frisinga says of him, "Ecclesiam jamdiu ancillatam in pristinam reduxit libertatem" (Lib. vi. c. 34).

[2] The witness of contemporaries is rarely disinterested, and for this reason I am careful to test their assertions, before quoting from such a mass of confused accounts given by partisans. The following is the story as told by Marianus Scotus (in Cronic. ad. an. 1075): "He (the Emperor Henry) did not scruple to tarnish and eclipse Christ's only and beloved Spouse, by means of concubines, that is heretics; treating the spiritual offices of the Church, which are the free gifts of the Holy Spirit, as mere merchandise, accord-

Having accepted it for conscience sake as the will CHAP. IV. of God, he saw clearly that in such sad times any Pope who was resolved to do his duty must fall a victim to it. Kindled with the spirit of self-sacrifice, he soon showed the world that he shared in that noble conception of the Episcopate which had inspired the primitive Bishops. Writing to his colleagues, he says, "Considering duly, that

ing to the sin of Simon, with vile bargains, contrary to the Catholic Faith. For which cause, certain of the Church, beholding and hearing these and other such misdeeds of the King Henry, were filled with zeal for Israel's sake, even as was the prophet Elias; and making loud lamentations, as well as written complaints, they sent messengers to Rome, who set before Alexander, Bishop of the Apostolic See, those numberless things which were said and done in the German empire by the mad simoniacal heretics, the King Henry being the leader and patron of all. Meanwhile, the Apostolical Lord Alexander departing this life, Gregory, also called Hildebrand, a monk, undertook the government of the Apostolic See. Gregory hearing the lamentations and just complaints of Catholics against Henry, and the impunity of his misdeeds, was kindled with zeal for God, and pronounced sentence of excommunication upon the King, chiefly on account of his simony." Contemporaneous writers agree in describing Henry as given to every kind of disorder in his private life, as well as guilty of tyranny over his subjects, and of profane insolence towards the Church. Yet the writers of the last century have undertaken his defence! While the righteous, noble Gregory, who set aside his ease and his life in order to restrain this brutal tyrant, to protect an oppressed people, and to save Christendom from ruin, is treated as an ambitious man who deserves the hatred and execrations of mankind ! But, thank God, even Protestants can see in Gregory VII. the true champion, not of the Church only, but of mankind, the author of modern civilization. (See the German work called "Hildebrand and his Times.") Of a truth the times of Gregory will supply abundant material for the reflections of future ages.

by reason of the shortness of this life, and the frivolous nature of earthly governments, no one is more worthy of the title of Bishop than he who suffers persecution for righteousness' sake, we have determined rather to incur the enmity of wicked men by obeying the commandments of the Lord, than to provoke the wrath of Heaven by an unworthy compliance with their wishes" (Lib. ix. ep. ii.).

LXXXIX. He tried, however, to prevail with Henry by fatherly gentleness and patience. It was all in vain. The Pope's nuncios, his letters, his affectionate efforts were all alike despised and mocked. Then he summoned his Cardinals and Bishops in synod, and took counsel with them. He set before them the steps which he had taken to recall the wanderer. He described the insults, and the bolder wrong-doing with which Henry had met his efforts. He noted the attempt which Henry had made to create a schism in the Church by means of certain corrupt Bishops his minions in Lombardy and Germany. The imperial letters, brought by ambassadors who attended the Synod, were read. They were full of sacrilegious vituperation. The ambassadors themselves were allowed to speak. In full Council they addressed the Pope as follows: " Our Lord the King desires that thou quit the Apostolic See and the Papacy, CHAP. IV. forasmuch as they are his, and that thou infest no longer this sacred place."[1] All the circumstances were duly weighed; the strange times, the evil which seemed to be irremediable without a drastic remedy. Then the fathers unanimously counselled the Pope, that if ever severity was expedient, it was expedient now. It was a last resource; the Church owed to herself as well as to posterity, a solemn example of ecclesiastical faithfulness. Moreover, they said, the Emperor had not received his crown unconditionally. He had sworn to observe terms and conditions. A valid contract between himself and the Christian people had been made, upon his election. Both parties had incurred reciprocal obligations. The people had taken their oath of fidelity con-

[1] A contemporary records this fact as follows: "Cum igitur dissimulare amplius tanti facinoris malitiam non posset, Apostolicus excommunicavit tam ipsum, quam omnes ejus fautores, atque omnem sibi regiam dignitatem interdixit, et obligatos sibi sacramentis ab omni debito fidelitatis absolvit: quia quod verecundum etiam est dicere, præter hæreticam quam prælibavimus culpam, aderant in sancto concilio nuntii illius sic audentes latrare: 'Præcipit Dominus noster Rex, ut Sedem Apostolicam et Papatum, ut pote suum, dimittas, nec locum hunc sanctum ultra impedias.' . . . Igitur quem sui solius judicio Dominus reservavit, hic non solum judicare, verum etiam 'suum' dicere, et quantum in ipso est, audet damnare: quam ob causam omnis illa sancta Synodus, jure indignata, anathema illi conclamat atque confirmat."—S. Anselmi Lucensis Pænitentiarius, in ejus Vita., c. iii. (Migne cxlviii. col. 913.).

ditionally on Henry's observance of certain terms, chiefly touching the liberty and maintenance of religion. The Church was the mother and guardian of all Christians; she had received the imperial oath in her own name, and that of the people. Inasmuch as the people could not set themselves free from their oaths, they had a right to expect that the Primate of the Church, as the interpreter and judge of oaths, would provide for her well-being and for their religion. Consequently, the Pope was now bound, as well for the Church's sake as for that of the faithful people, to pronounce sentence. He must declare the Emperor to have broken his faith, and thereby to have set the people free from their engagements to him. Such is the substance of the counsel unanimously given to Pope Gregory VII. by the Synod.[1] Thereupon

[1] Such a doctrine concerning the popular right was common among Christians at that time, and no one denied it. Kings were then really *constitutional*, although as yet that word was not invented. The Council assumed this fact. Paulus Bernr. in his Life of Gregory VII., quotes the words used : " Tua, sanctissime Pater, censura, quem ad regendum nostri temporis sæculum Divina peperit clementia, contra blasphemum, invasorem, tyrannum, desertorem, talem sententiam proferat, quæ hunc conterat, *et futuris sœculis transgressionis cautelam* conferat. . . . Tandem omnibus acclamantibus definitum est, ut honore regio privaretur, et anathematis vinculis tam prænominatus Rex, quam omnes assentanei sui colligarentur. Accepta itaque fiducia, Dominus Papa, *ex totius Synodi consensu, et judicio*, protulit anathema " (S. Greg. VII. Vita, auctore Paulo Benriedensi, §§ 62, 63).

Gregory, constrained by his conscience, excommunicated Henry IV., and declared his subjects to be loosed from their oaths of fidelity, A.D. 1076.

XC. This great event, as I have already said, marks an epoch; it was a period of renovation in the Church. It was the sign for a fierce battle. After many years of oppression beneath an ignominious yoke, the Church now raised herself anew. A violent struggle between the oppressed and the oppressor was inevitable. Nor did she triumph until three centuries of strife had passed. Scarcely had she forcibly cast aside her subjection to the secular power, when she was torn asunder by the great Western schism. This was hardly extinct, when the heresies of the North began to distract her; nor did she begin to find rest until the Council of Trent.[1] Meanwhile, the two great objects which Gregory had in view, were permanently established; to wit, the freedom of the ecclesiastical power, and the good conduct of the clergy. The first bore immediate fruit. It enabled the Church to triumph over her enemies, and it was the true motive power of the Council of Trent. From the date of that Council the second began to yield results in the reformation of ecclesiastical discipline and morals.

[1] [Did she then ? or afterwards ?—ED.]

XCI. This threefold and terrible struggle, with the civil power, with schism and with heresy, was inevitable. The two latter were born of the former, and outlived their mother. When Gregory VII. came to the throne, the seeds of these evils were quickening. The remedy was effective and at hand. But it could not be applied in time to prevent the outbreak of evils which were already imminent. If it could not prevent them, at least it successfully subdued them. The Church which Gregory came to rule might be compared to the dawn of a winter day, when nature is still dark and frozen. But the sun will presently be in the sky, and his warm rays will melt the frost, and will kindle new life where all was numbed and sterile.

XCII. We must, however, dwell yet a while upon this resolution of the Roman Council and of Gregory to dissolve the oath of fealty which his subjects had taken to the Emperor Henry. It has given rise to much idle talk and calumny directed against the Apostolic See.

Divine Providence had endowed the Church with wealth and temporal power. This began with the conversion of the Roman emperors. But it dated chiefly from the invasion of the barbarians who destroyed the empire, and founded the modern kingdoms. The object was to hallow society as well as the individual, and to make the influence of the Gospel felt in the laws and government of the world at large. If at first this good influence was visible in the increase of justice and equity in all branches of public administration, it was also found at a later period to have no less affected the very essence of the supreme power. The nature of this power was changed. But this change had been so gradual, that it was accomplished before men discovered the silent work of the Gospel, nor was it easy to trace the steps by which Christ's religion had produced an effect of such importance. Heathen, or natural sovereignty, had been *absolute*; Christianity made it *constitutional*. Let no one take offence at this word: I fully grant that in modern times it has been profaned. But if I may be allowed to set forth what I mean, before judgment is passed, it will be seen that I am far from entering on the perilous questions of these days, in which men seek after what is good without clearly recognizing it. A celebrated author and statesman, who cannot be suspected of favouring popular insubordination, writes thus: "The Popes have educated monarchy as we find it in modern Europe;" and "the nature of this monarchy, and that which raises it so far above the governments of earlier times, is that fundamental law by which monarchs, inspired by the Gospel spirit of justice and charity, lodge the right of punishment in the hands of duly constituted tribunals." Thus this eminent writer, who frankly states that a political constitution cannot be framed by man, has recognized the fact that when monarchy became Christian it received its fundamental laws. So be it clearly understood that, when I speak of a Constitution, I mean something very different from that which political parties seek to thrust upon either peoples or sovereigns; very different from the theories of ingenious or well-meaning men. I do not mean a constitution framed by man, but one that has arisen spontaneously in the course of time, and from the hidden force of circumstances. Such a constitution is framed by God Himself: since it is the natural result of a religious doctrine prevailing by its intrinsic evidence, taking possession of convictions, both of kings and subjects, and leading to tangible and practical results. I maintain that the powerful, unchangeable doctrine, which thus won acceptance in all European society, was the Gospel. And the result of this doctrine upon the opinions of monarchs and of peoples was that they "ceased to be arbitrary, and began to proceed upon unchanging principles."

In other words, princes submitted to the *Constitution* imposed on them by the Gospel, and they thereby accepted and recognized the principle and the imperishable source of all civil reforms.

Undoubtedly such a constitution did not at once come to light when the Emperors became Christians. We are now speaking of an actual Constitution. It was necessary for the Gospel to be first known and embraced by people and sovereigns, and then to penetrate their hearts, and rule their opinions. This was the work of time. Then it followed that the inevitable consequences of Gospel principles should be drawn out, and applied to the existing governments. This likewise was no speedy operation. Lastly, Christianity had to obtain such a hold over the temper of monarchs, as to force them to declare, " We are Christians ; we will be consistent; the Gospel law shall control our power, and master our personal passions." This was the important matter; and little by little it was realized. Until the power of religion was displayed in princes, they did not bow their proud heads, or become, instead of *absolute*, *Constitutional* monarchs, out of obedience to God Who had deigned to become the Brother of all mankind. Now I affirm, that when this constitution was formed, it was not confined to the single point touched upon by the illustrious writer quoted above. There were other points; indeed all which the Gospel temper has dictated and will dictate to mankind.

XCIII. We may distinguish three several conditions of Christianity, with respect to the political world: (1) before rulers had entered the Church; (2) when, having entered it, they were still not subject to the influence of the Gospel; and (3) when this influence had produced its happiest effects upon them.

So long as the Church possessed the people only, and the rulers were yet without her, she could only proclaim her heaven-sent teaching to the people. "Do you," she said, " O faithful people, who groan under the yoke of tyrants, and of worshippers of false gods, bear patiently their oppressions. Believe that all is ordered by God's good Providence. He watches over you, nor would unbelieving princes have such power, unless the Almighty Father so willed it for your good. Sin only is evil; virtue only is the true good. Seek after this, and leave all else to your Heavenly Father. When He shall see that a different order of things better enables you to gain life eternal, He will change the outward course of events, and your princes will be joined to you. Meanwhile, respect those who are set over you, obey them in all save that which is contrary to God's law; fight, die for them. Do this not from fear, but for conscience' sake, honouring in them God, Who orders all human events."

When, later on, the emperors were converted to the Faith, the Church still held the same language to the people. But she also undertook to teach the rulers, and since at first their knowledge of the Gospel was but superficial, she took them, so to say, aside, and while bidding the people never to rebel against their sovereign, whatever his faults, since humility, submission and sacrifice are the marks of a Christian people; she held this language to sovereigns: "Remember that you, too, are but men, and that in the sight of God all men are equal. You will be judged by Christ with the same judgment as the lowest and feeblest of your subjects; perhaps all the more sternly, since it is written, 'Judgment must begin at the House of God.' Know that your position is one to be feared, and not to be desired by a faithful heart. It is through righteousness and charity alone that you can escape eternal perdition, and save your souls. Beware of setting your hearts upon your earthly grandeur, all of which will drop off from you at the hour of death. Providence has placed you as rulers over the

Christian people not for your own, but for their advantage. Your dignity is but a ministry, a service; and in order to be greatest of all, you must make yourselves least of all." Such were the sublime and most human truths which the Church set before sovereigns who became her sons. They listened respectfully, marvelling to find a new glory, which they could not win through earthly power, or regal state, but only by the lowliness of the Redeemer's Cross. What was the result? These truths penetrated men's hearts, and prevailed. Almost every European throne boasted of heroes who lived according to the Gospel precepts. They administered and fought for justice with one hand, while with the other they succoured their newly found brethren, the poor, even ministering in person to them. They saw, in His poor, Christ Himself; and in aiding the poor they relieved His needs.

When the Church had thus taught the Gospel theoretically and practically to both parties, she addressed them in common, after this fashion: "O my sons, ye princes, who are now enlightened by the Gospel, will ye in all things conform yourselves to it?" "We will." "If so, bear in mind that ye are taught by that Gospel that ye have been made heads over God's people, not by chance, but by His Divine Will, in order that ye might keep peace, administer justice, and above all protect and defend His best gift, Religion. Are ye willing?" "Certainly, we are willing; it shall be our glory to govern God's people righteously and peacefully, and to defend our Mother, Christ's Church." "Then swear to it, in my hands, before your people." "We swear." "What surety do you give for your oaths? Is it not right and just, in order that your people may have full confidence in you, as in the representatives of Christ, that they should receive some pledge of that which you promise; so that the Christian people may never be ruled by unbelieving or rebellious princes?" "It is right; may God visit us with every calamity, if we are wanting to our oaths." "Say, then, are you ready to quit your thrones, should you stray from the Church's obedience? do you declare yourselves unworthy to wear a Christian Crown, which marks whoso wears it as the vicar of Christ, the King of Kings, if ye should become enemies of His Church? and are you willing to own that the oaths of fidelity taken by your subjects would become null and void in the case of such enormity?" "We own it; we agree to all this; we agree that the sons of the Church should be governed by faithful sons of that same Church; forasmuch as a prince who ceases to be Christ's minister for the good of the faithful, is as an enemy to Christ Himself." "Then, princes and people, my children, take with pure hands this sacred Gospel; may the mutual oaths by which ye now bind yourselves, ever remind you of the fundamental and immutable laws of all Christian kingdoms; they will be sources of endless happiness, if ye observe them religiously, and of tribulation and malediction to him who first breaks them."

This is no dream, but sober reality; this is the constitution of Christian kingdoms which arose in the Middle Ages, when the spirit of the Gospel had absorbed and subjected the highest ranks in human society. Those princes were penetrated with the teaching of Christ, and would have endured all things rather than renounce it. Confident in their intentions, they did not shrink from oaths which seemed to them just and right. They were willing to bind their descendants with the same generous bonds of justice and charity to their people, whom, as baptized with the same Baptism as themselves, they deemed their brethren,—a sacred trust committed to them by the King of Kings. Thus zeal for the Faith prevailed over ambition and the love of power. For the sake of the Faith, for the real good of the people, princes were content to transmit to their successors an empire which was externally less *absolute*, but which was in truth nobler, because more just, more religious. Thus they gave substance and stability to the sceptres that bowed before those eternal laws of love and righteousness, in obeying which man truly reigns. This Christian constitution was partly written, partly traditional, but it was agreed to by all; and of old neither princes nor people cast a doubt upon it. While men were at peace, and religious, there was no cause for doubt. It was a common possession, every one had an interest in its maintenance. Later on it was reduced to more formal and exact laws, such as governed the Roman Empire and the kingdom of Germany; we may see this as we follow Henry's history.

XCIV. Henry, finding himself threatened with deposition by the German nobles assembled at Tribur, came to the Pope at Canossa, to seek release from excommunication. He alleged, as a reason for his immediate release, that a year had almost expired since the sentence, while the Palatine laws pronounced a king who remained a year and a day out of communion with the Church to be unworthy of the throne, and to be *ipso facto* deposed, without possibility of restoration.[1] This

[1] Lambertus Scafnaburgensis, A.D. 1076, says, " Ut si ante hanc diem excommunicatione non absolvatur, deinceps *juxta Palatinas*

CHAP. IV. argument induced the Pope to grant absolution. He was deceived by the outward show of repentance which the unhappy Henry assumed. Just as in Germany the period of a year and a day of excommunication was fixed as depriving a monarch of his throne, so almost every Christian monarchy was held by an understanding between the interested parties, that heresy and infidelity were equivalent to deposition, and the oath of fidelity was only taken by subjects on condition that the prince was faithful to the Christian and Catholic faith.[1]

leges indignus regis honore habeatur, nec ultra pro asserenda innocentia sua audientiam mereatur : proinde enixe patere, ut solo interim anathemate absolvatur," etc. Were not these Palatine laws practically a constitution ?

[1] Henry acknowledged that this condition had its rise in the Church's traditions, in a letter addressed to Gregory VII. : " Me quoque, licet indignus inter Christianos sum, ad regnum vocatus, te teste, quem sanctorum Patrum traditio soli Deo judicandum docuit, nec pro aliquo crimine *nisi a fide* (quod absit) exorbitaverim, deponendum asseruit." St. Thomas, who has collected ecclesiastical tradition more surely and more extensively than any one else, and whose decisions are considered as the voice of the Church, maintains that this "constituent law" of Christian kingdoms, by which a Catholic king loses his throne on falling into heresy, proceeds from the constitution of the Church as framed by Christ Himself, and is not merely an expressed or understood convention between princes and their subjects, with the Church's mediation (Sum. II. ii. 13, 2). It is certain that until this convention was carried out, until this doctrine was received as just and good both by people and princes, the time had not come when the chiefs of the Church could exercise their right over the faithful; a fact which has not been sufficiently regarded by those who infer that this power was an abuse, because it was not exercised in the primitive ages of the

XCV. From this it is clear that the deposi- CHAP. IV. tion of a Christian prince depended upon a suit, the decision of which appertained to the Church's tribunal. All decisions concerning the Faith appertain to her, as well as the power of retaining in or rejecting from her bosom the faithful of every rank. Moreover it was fitting that the Church, who as a common Mother had drawn princes and people into a loving union, of which she had received the pledge, should have the power to judge between the parties in case of any violation of it, before either side proceeded to vindicate its rights by force. Before the creation of this Christian understanding between nations and their rulers, the royal power was, as we have said, absolute, by divine right.[1] It

Church. The Church had first to effect the reform of individuals, and then that of society in general ; when that was achieved, she was able to apply the laws sanctioned by Christianity. [The fatal objection to the theory is that it requires *moral inerrancy* in the Pope. Rosmini's argument would hold good of an assembly really representative of the whole Church of Christ.—ED.]

[1] It is in this sense that St. Paul said, " *Omnis potestas a Deo ;* " and St. Peter, " *Subditi estote* OMNI HUMANÆ CREATURÆ *propter Deum.*" Thus St. Thomas expressly teaches, that to withdraw from obedience to an unbelieving prince is contrary to the Divine right. " Est ergo contra jus divinum prohibere quod ejus judicio non stetur, SI SIT INFIDELIS " (Expos. in ep. i. ad Cor. c. vi. sec. 1). But on the other hand the holy Doctor recognizes the possibility of a case, in which the prince being Christian, the Church's authority may loose his subjects from their oath of fidelity. " Et ideo quam cito aliquis per sententiam denuntiatur excommunicatus propter

was established as such by God's Providence. While this condition of things lasted the Church did not recognize the possibility of Christian subjects casting off their obedience to their sovereign. But when the sovereigns themselves, giving heed to the voice of justice and charity, added to the lustre of their crowns by submitting to the Gospel and to its maxims; when they rejoiced to be the ministers and viceregents of Christ over free men, instead of being masters of slaves; when they voluntarily incurred the blessed obligations of dutiful sons of the Church of Christ, thenceforward monarchy existed, so to say, by "human-ecclesiastical right," and the Church recognized the possibility of a case in which subjects might be loosed from their oaths of fidelity.

This great change in human society did not come to pass all at once, but insensibly and without attracting notice. We therefore cannot wonder if, when an occasion arose for the first time for pronouncing so grave a judgment, in the days of Gregory VII., the Pope's act startled many men and gave rise to much calumny. The Church had long exercised a jurisdiction issuing from the same principles of public Christian right without

apostasiam a fide, ipso facto ejus subditi sunt absoluti a dominio ejus et juramento fidelitatis, quo ei tenebantur" (Sum. II. ii. xii. 2).

encountering the slightest opposition, or causing the least surprise, because as yet her acts had all been acts of indulgence, not of severity, not such as ran counter to stubborn and powerful vice.

XCVI. Moreover, those who object to the line of conduct pursued by the Church towards Henry IV., make great account of the evils to society which for so long a time arose out of the struggle between the Church and the Empire. I would beg such objectors to bear in mind, first, that for this very reason the Church held back from extreme measures until the reign of Gregory VII.[1] It is not quite fair to make use of her long forbearance as an argument against her jurisdiction, when the excessive corruption of the eleventh century forced her at last to sterner action. Further, I would beg them to consider calmly, whether "the step taken by Gregory was of such a nature as of necessity to cause all the evils that ensued."

XCVII. In truth this fearful struggle was not, as is commonly supposed, between the priest-

[1] Henry himself, in a letter to the Pope, speaks of Julian the Apostate as not having been deposed, through the *prudence* of the Church, not from any want of right on her part. "Cum etiam Julianum Apostatam *prudentia* sanctorum Episcoporum non sibi, sed soli Deo deponendum commiserit." And this was the ordinary opinion of those times. Whence do the modern views of public Christian right arise? It is an important question.

hood and the Empire; it was a struggle entered on "in the name of the priesthood and of the Empire." It was occasioned by a division of the priesthood into two sections, one of which fought for the Church, and *was* the Church; while the other fought for itself against the Church, sheltering itself under the semblance of zeal for the imperial rights. The nobles and the people were on the Pope's side,[1] but there were many rich and

[1] The German Princes appealed to the Pope against Henry. Not the Saxons only, as some modern historians seek to make out, but the Suabians and other German nations, as is shown by Bruno in his "De Bello Saxonico." After describing Henry's tyranny and his vice, Bruno proceeds: " Gens vero Suevorum, audita Saxonum calamitate, clam legatos suos ad illos misit, et fœdus cum eis fecit, ut neuter populus ad alterius oppressionem regi ferret auxilium : . . . Eamdem querimoniam fecerunt ad invicem *omnes pene regni Teutonici principes*, sed tamen palam nullus audebat fateri" (Ep. 18). Later, when Gregory VII. sent a letter breathing a truly evangelical spirit of peace to the princes assembled at Gerstenge, dissuading them from electing another emperor, the princes who meant to do this were " pars longe maxima." Some years later the princes again met at Tribur with the same object. They finally referred the matter to the Pope, sending envoys to Henry, who was now humbled and ready to accept any conditions, with this message, " Tametsi nec in bello nec in pace ulla unquam ei justitiæ vel legum cura fuerit, se *legibus* cum eo agere velle " (What were these laws according to which the German princes dealt with Henry, if not *fundamental laws;* in a word, the *Christian constitution* of the State?) "'et cum crimina quæ ei objiciuntur omnibus constent luce clariora, se tamen rem integram Romani Pontificis cognitioni reservare," etc. From which it is evident that those very German nobles who were about to elect the Emperor referred the cause to the Pope ; and also that this electoral body considered themselves *bonâ fide* to possess the right of electing another

No wish to tamper with Imperial rights. 215

powerful Bishops against the Pope. The cause is Chap. IV. evident. The Pope had in no sense made war upon the Emperor, whom he treated with paternal kindness, much less upon his crown or any of his rights, which no one ever wished to take from him. But the Pope *had* made war upon a dissolute and simoniacal clergy. He held himself bound in conscience to attempt, even at the price of his own blood, to exterminate vices, which had attained such proportions that they would have exterminated the Church, had they been any longer left unchecked.[1]

Emperor, if Henry persisted in his crimes. For after prescribing what he must do to give satisfaction to the State, whose laws he had broken, they go on to say, " Porro si quid horum prævaricetur, tum se *omni culpa, omni jurisjurandi religione, omni perfidiæ infamia liberatos*, non expectato ulterius Romani Pontificis judicio, quid reipublicæ expediat, communi consilio visuros." Such was the *jus publicum* of those times. Nor was this language refuted by Henry, or rebuked by the Pope, or looked upon as strange or contrary to justice and equity. It was left for the philosophers of our times to be scandalized at it, and to call it rebellion.

[1] A certain Hugo Flaviniacensis thus describes the true cause of the so-called struggle between the priesthood and the Empire: " *Ob hanc igitur causam*, quia scilicet sanctam Dei Ecclesiam castam esse volebat (Gregorius), liberam, atque Catholicam ; quia de sanctuario Dei simoniacam, et Neophytorum hæresim, et fœdam libidinosæ contagionis pollutionem volebat expellere ; membra diaboli cœperunt in eum insurgere, et usque ad sanguinem præsumpserunt in eum manus injicere ; et ut eum morte vel exilio confunderent, multis eum modis conati sunt dejicere. *Sic* surrexit inter regnum et sacerdotium contentio, accrevit solito gravior sanctæ Dei Ecclesiæ tribulatio " (In Chron. Virdunensi, ad an. 1073).

Fleury says, "All those Bishops who were on the Emperor's side,

CHAP. IV. The integrity and holiness of this great man, thus raised by God to the Apostolic See for the deliverance of His people, alarmed all the vicious clergy, and those who had purchased their Bishoprics from Henry. They were powerful both by reason of their baronies and their influence in the government. They rose with one accord, joined in a formidable league out of hatred of righteousness, and put in motion every means of opposition which the most consummate malice could suggest.[1] Their watchword was the cry that "all men must defend the rights of their own sovereign." But what rights belonging to their sovereign did these Bishops affect to defend? Was it the right to be simoniacal, and the insolent defender of clerical concubinage? For what other of Henry's rights was invaded? Had Gregory VII. ever

and who urged him on against the Pope, had been previously excommunicated for simony, heresy, immorality or other crimes; men to whom Henry had himself sold ecclesiastical benefices. What courage did a Pope require, who had to govern a Church with such a clergy, still more a Pope who aimed at its reform ; the secular powers being involved in the same vices, and ruled chiefly by the most corrupt among the clergy !" (Lib. lxii. 12).

[1] These clergy employed not only brutal violence, but every conceivable form of lie, calumny, and sophistry against Gregory VII. The Archbishop Guibert of Ravenna, who was later an Anti-Pope, did not scruple to falsify Nicholas II.'s decretal so as to make it appear that the Papal election had always been in the Emperor's hands. By such inventions many were deceived, and the whole question was complicated.

propounded the slightest infringement of any other right save that the Emperor should cease to treat Episcopal sees as marketable goods, or to prostitute them by improper appointments? It was solely to prevent a total and imminent ruin of the Church, that, other means having failed, and the Emperor growing worse and worse under the perfidious guidance of the Prelates who were his boon companions, Gregory finally excommunicated him.

Nor did the corrupt clergy rest content with having dragged Henry into this depth of evil;[1] they kept him there, and prevented the struggle from being put an end to. It was natural. War

[1] From his earliest youth Henry had been the tool of disreputable ecclesiastics, and several saintly men had been sent away from his Court because they would not pander to his evil ways. Bruno attributes Henry's excessive profligacy to his intimacy with Adalbert, Bishop of Bremen. He says, "Hac, igitur, Episcopi non Episcopali doctrina, rex in nequitia confortatus ivit per libidinum præcipitia sicut equus et mulus, et qui multorum rex erat populorum, thronum posuit in se libidini cunctorum reginæ vitiorum," etc. Henry himself, in a moment of repentance, true or feigned, writing a confession of his errors to Gregory, attributes many of them to his evil counsellors: "Heu criminosi nos, et infelices! partim pueritiæ blandientis instinctione, partim protestativæ nostræ et imperiosæ potentiæ libertate, partim eorum, quorum seductiles nimium secuti sumus consilia, seductoria deceptione, peccavimus in cœlum et coram vobis, et jam digni non sumus vocatione vestræ filiationis. Non solum enim nos res ecclesiasticas invasimus, verum quoque indignis quibuslibet et simoniaco felle amaricatis et non per ostium sed aliunde ingredientibus ecclesias ipsas vendidimus, et non eas, ut oportuit, defendimus," etc. (Vid. t. i. Constitut. Imperial. Goldasti).

cannot cease, until the enemy is vanquished. And in this case the only enemy was the corruption of these clerical courtiers. If Henry had but listened to the paternal warnings of the ruler of the Church, or if, after his first reconciliation with the Pope at the Castle of Canossa, he had not been drawn back into his old ways by the wicked Bishops, who made him a screen for their own vices, all the storm would have been laid. The Emperor, loosed from the bonds of excommunication, would have been at peace with the Church. He would have preserved his dominions, and the pious heart of the venerable Pope would have joyed over him with a father's joy. But if the pretended struggle between the priesthood and the Empire had thus come to a speedy end, as should have been the case, what would have become of all the simoniacal, dissolute Prelates, and of the men who had been forced upon their sees? They were well aware what would be the consequences. They knew how fatal such peace would be to their vices and pleasures, to the rich benefices they had purchased at enormous cost, and to their favour with the prince who was now their accomplice. What marvel, then, if such men were in despair at any prospect of reconciliation between Henry and the Pope, or if they made use of every means to precipitate the Emperor into fresh sins, CHAP. IV. and thus again to secure his rupture with the Church.[1]

XCVIII. Is any further proof required to show that the rights of the Empire were not really the object of this long and disastrous contest? Let us look on to what took place half a century later between Henry V. and Pascal II. No Bishop of primitive days could have held more saintly or dignified language, or could have proved more nobly that St. Peter's mind still governed his see, and that the Gospel of Christ knows neither yesterday nor to-day, but is of all time. I will quote the very words addressed by this great Pope to Henry V., because they are a clear proof that, even in the darkest times, the Church never lost that unworldly tone which

[1] When Henry obtained release from his sentence of excommunication at Canossa, the Bishops of his party were in despair at finding their cause abandoned by the Emperor. Robert of Bamberg, Udalric of Costreim, and others foremost among his evil counsellors were to be dismissed from court by express condition; and these men, together with sundry Lombard Bishops of the same stamp, raised so great an outcry, threatening rebellion, all out of pretended anger at Henry's loss of dignity, that they drew the Emperor from his better mind, and he returned to his evil ways. Certainly their logic was peculiar! The royal dignity, forsooth, was dishonoured because Henry had submitted to the Pope's correction of his vices; but they on their side proposed to punish the Emperor in a very practical way indeed!

ought to raise the Christian priesthood above all earthly and transitory aims, and to brace it with the might of God's word. At the same time the passage shows how clearly the Popes saw the truth of what I have been urging, namely, that the servitude and corruption of the clergy arose from their entanglement in worldly affairs. Pope Pascal magnanimously proposed that the clergy should renounce all their fiefs and secular dignities, in lieu of which entire liberty should be restored to them. Surely this was a grand proposal, considering the condition of the Church. Ecclesiastical historians have not dealt with it as it deserves. Future times, however, will do it justice, and will reckon it one of the brightest facts in the Church's history. But this high-minded proposal of the Pope, worthy as it was of the Apostles, appeared strange and preposterous to his contemporaries. The German clergy took fright, rebelled against the Pope, and induced the Emperor, who had already received and accepted the proposal, to reject it. What else could be expected? Thus for the third time the fascination which worldly wealth had for the clergy was fatal to peace between the priesthood and the Empire. The Empire withdrew from obedience to the Church to make itself the slave of a corrupt clergy; it was coaxed and intoxicated by the adulation which will always effect its purpose when employed by a class of clergy who have neither dignity nor self-respect to lose. Thus the Empire was a mere pretext and accessory in the great struggle. The profligate clergy cunningly involved it in their own quarrel; they fought for themselves while talking of the Emperor's rights and making use of his assistance. But let us hear Pascal himself. He wrote thus to the Emperor :—

"According to the tenor of the law of God, the sacred Canons have forbidden priests to occupy themselves with secular cares, or to attend the Court, save to intercede for those who are condemned, or who suffer injustice. But in parts of your kingdom Bishops and Abbots are so occupied with secular cares, that they cannot but assiduously frequent the Court, and are compelled to render military service. Ministers of the Altar have become ministers of the State, having received from Monarchs, cities, duchies, marquisates, money, castles, and other things appertaining to the service of the country. Hence arose a custom in the Church, that Bishops elect should not any longer receive consecration until they were invested by the royal hand.[1] Thus some have received in-

[1] Here was the real origin of investitures—fiefs.

Chap. IV. vestiture while the Bishop of the see was still living. These and numerous other evils which often arose by reason of investitures, moved our blessed predecessors, Gregory VII. and Urban II., who frequently assembled the Bishops in Council, and condemned these investitures by laymen. They pronounced clergymen who held Churches on such tenure to be deposed, and those who had invested them to be excommunicate, according to the Apostolic Canon which says, 'If a Bishop make use of the secular power to obtain a Church, let him be deposed, and let those who communicate with him be excommunicate.' Wherefore we will, O King Henry, our beloved son, that those royal rights which clearly appertained to the State in the times of Charles, of Louis, of Otho, and of other thy predecessors, be restored to thee. And we prohibit and interdict under pain of anathema, any Bishop or Abbot, present or future, from trespassing hereafter on the royal rights, that is to say, on cities, duchies, marches, counties, moneys, tribute, advocacies, military rights, or, in short, anything appertaining to the State, the army, or the camp. We further decree that the Churches with their oblations, and their hereditary possessions, which clearly never belonged to the State, shall remain free, as on thy coronation day thou didst promise to the Lord Almighty, in the face CHAP. IV. of the whole Church."[1]

Is this the language of a usurper? Is such generosity, such readiness to give up temporal power lawfully earned by the Church in earlier

---

[1] "Divinæ legis institutionibus sancitum est, et sacris Canonibus interdictum, ne sacerdotes curis sæcularibus occupentur, neve ad comitatum, nisi pro damnatis eruendis, atque pro aliis qui injuriam patiuntur, accedant. In vestri autem regni partibus, Episcopi vel Abbates adeo curis sæcularibus occupantur, ut comitatum assidue frequentare, et militiam exercere cogantur. Ministri vero Altaris, ministri Curiæ facti sunt, quia civitates, ducatus, marchionatus, monetas, turres, et cætera ad regni servitium pertinentia, a regibus acceperunt. Unde etiam mos Ecclesiæ inolevit, ut electi Episcopi nullo modo consecrationem acciperent, nisi per manum regiam investirentur. Aliquando etiam vivis Episcopis investiti sunt. His et aliis plurimis malis, quæ per investituram plerumque contigerant, prædecessores nostri Gregorius VII. et Urbanus II. felicis recordationis Pontifices excitati, collectis frequenter episcopalibus Conciliis, investituras illas manu laica damnaverunt, et si qui clericorum per eam tenuissent Ecclesias, deponendos, datores quoque communione privandos percensuerunt, juxta illud Apostolicorum Canonum Capitulum, quod ita se habet: 'si quis Episcopus sæculi potestatibus usus, Ecclesiam per ipsas obtineat, deponatur, et segregentur omnes qui illi communicant.' Tibi itaque, fili carissime Henrice Rex, et regno regalia illa dimittenda præcipimus, quæ ad regnum manifeste pertinebant tempore Caroli, Ludovici, Ottonis, et cætororum prædecessorum tuorum. Interdicimus etiam et sub anathematis districtione prohibemus, ne qui Episcoporum seu Abbatorum, præsentium vel futurorum, eadem regalia invadent, id est civitates, ducatus, marchias, comitatus, monetas, teloneum, advocatias, jura centurionum, et curtes quæ regni erant, cum pertinentiis suis, militiam et castra. Porro Ecclesias cum oblationibus et hæreditariis possessionibus, quæ ad regnum manifeste non pertinebant, liberas manere decrevimus, sicut in die coronationis tuæ omnipotenti Domino in conspectu totius Ecclesiæ promisisti."—Ep. xxii. (Migne's edition, Ep. 314, vol. clxiii. col. 283).

times, by her services to the State, a proof of Papal ambition and covetousness?[1] And what was

[1] Pope Pascal has been blamed by some for not maintaining the rights of the Church, when thus ready to give up her temporal riches to others. To these I would reply, It seems as though the acquisition of riches and power had not only actively demoralized the clergy, but had also given rise generally to an overweaning trust in human means for the protection of religion. Later on, this temporal wealth was but too vigorously defended, as we shall see hereafter. The ancient ecclesiastical maxim was that "It is better to give up, than to assert rights when such assertion is likely to produce spiritual evil;" inasmuch as temporal possessions are not indispensable to the Church, as are her liberty and her holiness, and therefore they do not deserve an absolute, unqualified defence. We may learn from St. Augustine's sermons, and especially Serm. cccxvi., what were his views as to the possessions of the Church. He says, "If any one thinks to despoil his children in order to endow the Church, let him seek another than Augustine to receive the gift, or rather, I hope it may please God that he may not find such an one;" thereby implying that his opinion was common among the Bishops of that period. He adds, "How worthy was the deed of Aurelius, Bishop of Carthage! There was a man who, being childless, and without any hope of offspring, left all his goods to the Church, reserving the income to himself. But later he had children, and the Bishop restored all the gift to him, when he little looked for it. The Bishop might have retained it according to worldly laws, but not according to God's Law."

St. Ambrose also writes: "Quid igitur non humiliter responsum a nobis est? Si tributum petit (imperator) non negamus. Agri Ecclesiæ solvunt tributum: si agros desiderat imperator, potestatem habet vindicandorum, nemo nostrum intervenit" (De Basilicis tradendis, n. 33). And with regard to this matter of tribute there has been too much eagerness to exempt ecclesiastical property from taxation. Where the Church's possessions are large, this exemption seems unjust and odious. Nay more, it was rather injurious than profitable to the Church in temporal things, since therefrom chiefly arose the great evil of mortmain, so that, as Barbosa says, "Regnorum utilitas postulat ut bona stabilia sint in commercio hominum non privilegiatorum *et exemptorum*" (Lib. ii. de Pensionibus., vol. xxvi. n. 19). The just arrangement would

asked of the secular power in exchange for the renunciation of such extensive rights? Did any deep design lurk beneath? Was it a political trick on the part of the Roman Court? Let God judge between those who would say so, and Rome. The Popes demanded nothing in return save *Liberty* for the Church, already oppressed well-nigh to extinction. I dare to say that they never demanded anything more : their ambition and their covetousness went no further.[1] But it is just this very

have been, " Let the State renounce all regalia with respect to property not originally bestowed by it, and let the Church pay tribute like the rest of the community."

[1] Pascal II. knew well that the question was complicated by the suggestions of bad men, and consequently he wrote thus to the King of England : " Amid all these contradictions we implore thee, O King, not to let any one suggest to thy mind, that we seek to diminish anything of thy power, or that we only seek to vindicate our greater influence in the promotion of Bishops. Do thou for the love of God give up pretensions which are manifestly contrary to God, and not to be acted on with His approval, and which, for our own soul's sake and thine, we cannot concede. For the rest, we will concede to thee whatsoever thou shalt ask according to God's will, with hearty good pleasure, gladly promoting all that can redound to thine honour and exaltation. Think not that thou weakenest thy power in desisting from this profane usurpation. Rather wilt thou reign with greater safety, efficiency, and honour, inasmuch as Divine Authority will reign with thee." These last remarkable words of Pascal indicate a fact which has been dwelt on by a profound writer of our own times, namely, that "although the Popes opposed sovereigns who sought to oppress the Church, they never abased them. The submission of kings to the Church's authority conferred upon sovereignty a sacred element, a kind of reflection of Divine splendour." Pascal's words to the English King exactly tally with this: "Nec existimes quod potestatis

liberty, this life of the Church which gives offence. The one unpardonable offence of the Popes throughout the struggle was, that they asserted and demanded it. Then the world cries out that thrones are insulted, and their rights usurped by Papal ambition. Such is the unjust and untrue motive power of the declamations made against the Roman Pontiffs; declamations which are characteristic of the last century. Such, too, is the real mainspring of that affected zeal for monarchical rights in times which are really doing all in their power to sweep kings from the face of the earth, while kings alone are blind to the fact.

XCIX. The proposition which I maintain is that the real cause of the struggle between the priesthood and the Empire was a depraved clergy, who resisted the reform which the Church sought to enforce. This fact becomes more and more self-evident at each step of the history of the contest. If we open any of the chronicles of the period, whatever may be the party or opinion which they represent and whatever page we glance at, fresh proofs will appear of the truth

tuæ columen infirmetur si ab hac profana usurpatione desistas. Imo tunc validius, tunc robustius, tunc honorabilius regnabis, *cum in regno tuo Divina regnabit auctoritas*" (Eadmer, lib. iii. Hist. Nov.; Paschal II., ep. xlix.) We might add that he alone truly reigns who obeys God, justice, and truth.

which I affirm. It is astonishing that modern historians should shut their eyes to so patent a fact, too often written in characters of blood. It were useless to bring additional proofs of that which history continuously demonstrates. But the truth has been so disguised and obliterated, that to many it sounds like novelty, and therefore it deserves a new and careful proof out of respect for popular opinion. For this reason, and in order to show how that which has been here maintained applies generally to the contest between Popes and princes, I shall leave the German Emperors, and shall briefly refer to what passed between Pascal II. and Henry I. of England.

Like his contemporaries, Henry appointed Bishops in all directions. The Pope warned him that the office was sacred, and not to be treated as merchandise; that it belonged to the Church to fill vacant sees; and that the successors of the Apostles should be duly called of Christ by means of Canonical election. The King resisted. Letters and embassies followed;[1] Pascal remained

[1] On the occasion of a first embassy sent by Henry I. to Rome in order to obtain from Pascal II. the right of investing Bishops, that Pope made this dignified answer: "Thou askest of the Church of Rome right and faculty to appoint Bishops and Abbots by investiture, and that the regal power may be enabled to do what our Almighty Lord has declared can only be done through

CHAP. IV. firm as a rock; St. Anselm the Primate of England supported him. This holy Archbishop had already

> Himself. He hath said, 'I am the Door; by Me if any man enter in, he shall be saved.' But when kings arrogate to themselves to be the Church's door, they are not shepherds, but thieves and robbers; as saith the Lord, 'He that entereth not by the door into the sheepfold, but climbeth up some other way, the same is a thief and a robber.' Verily, if thou askedst of us anything which we could righteously and in the sight of God grant to thee, willingly we would do so. But that which thou askest is so grave, so unworthy a request, that the Catholic Church can in no way receive or admit it. The blessed Ambrose let himself be driven to extremities without yielding the government of the Church to the Emperor. He said, 'Do not wrong thyself, O Emperor, by supposing that thou hast any imperial right over Divine things. Be not wroth, but if thou wouldst enjoy a long reign, submit thyself to God. It is written, "Render unto God the things which be God's, and to Cæsar the things which be Cæsar's." Palaces appertain to emperors, churches to ecclesiastics: thou hast right over the secular, not the sacred buildings. What wouldst thou with an adulteress? Yet she who is not united in lawful marriage is an adulteress.' Hearest thou, O King, that Church styled adulteress which has not contracted legitimate marriage? And the Bishop is the spouse of his Church. If, then, thou art a son of the Church, let thy Mother contract lawful marriage, not by means of man, but by Christ, God and Man. For the Apostle shows that Bishops were chosen of God if they be canonically elected, when he says, 'No man taketh this honour to himself, but he that is called of God, as was Aaron.' And the blessed Ambrose: 'I believe that he is chosen of the Divine judgment, who is demanded by all;' and again: 'Where universal consent demands any one, we cannot doubt that the Lord Jesus Christ is Author of the will, and Ruler of the demand, President of the ordination, and Giver of grace.' Thus, too, the Prophet David saith, 'Instead of thy fathers, thou shalt have children, whom thou mayest make princes in all lands.' Here we see the Church generating sons, and making them princes. In truth it were monstrous to say that the son generated the father, and that man can make a God! It is plain that Holy Writ calls the

suffered persecution and exile for the Church's CHAP. IV.
freedom under Henry's predecessor, William.
Henry had recalled him, from political motives,
and had received him honourably. But the Archbishop was incorruptible, and never would make
the concession of allowing him to invest Bishops
with his royal hand. In order to bring the dispute with Anselm to an end, a fresh embassy was
sent to the Pope ; three Bishops on the King's
part, two monks on that of the Primate. They
returned without having effected anything. The
Pope's firm and dignified letters[1] to Anselm were
read before an assembly of Bishops and nobles,
convened by the King. The matter seemed to be
decided and the King to be yielding. But at that

clergy gods, as being the vicars of God. Hence the Holy Roman and Apostolic Church did not hesitate by means of our predecessors to oppose the usurpations of kings, and the abominable investitures they sought to give ; nor could the persecutions of tyrants, with which she has been oppressed till now, move her. But we trust in the Lord, and Peter, Prince of the Church and first of Bishops, shall not lose the might of his faith so far as we are concerned " (Eadmer, lib. iii. Hist. Nov.).

[1] " Thy wisdom will remember with what efficacy, vigour, and severity our Fathers in past times fought against that *poisonous root of simoniacal depravity*, investiture. In the time of our revered predecessor in Christ, Urban, a venerable Council of Bishops and Abbots was gathered together near Bari, at which both your holiness and we ourselves assisted, as those who accompanied us will remember, when sentence of excommunication was published against that plague. We also, of the like mind with our fathers, feel the same, and testify the same." Pascal to Anselm. This letter is dated Dec. 12, A.D. 1102.

230 Bad conduct of three English Bishops.

CHAP. IV. very moment, when peace was apparently won, and the rights of the Church restored to her, everything was thrown back again by those very three Bishops who had been sent to the Pope. By means of a bold and insolent lie they won the King back to his evil resolve, and perpetuated the Church's slavery. Their imposture was speedily exposed, and punished with excommunication. They affirmed that in a private interview with them the Pope had conceded to the King that which he had refused in his letters, on the ground that if it were committed to writing other princes would demand similar concessions.[1]

---

[1] To this discreditable lie of the three courtier Bishops, Pascal replied, " We call to witness Jesus, Who tries the hearts and reins, that never from the moment we undertook the Holy See did we even imagine so cruel a sin. And may God ever preserve us from having one thing on our lips, and another in our hearts, remembering the imprecation, 'Lying lips are an abomination unto the Lord.' If we were silently to allow the Church to be damaged by the gall of bitterness, and the bond of iniquity, how could we clear ourselves before the Eternal Judge, inasmuch as the Lord hath said of His priests through the Prophet, 'I have made thee a watchman unto the house of Israel'? He does not well guard the city who, while he watcheth not, letteth the city be taken of the enemy. And if a secular hand gives the sign of pastoral office, the staff, and that of faith, the ring, what is the use of Pontiffs in the Church? The Church's honour would be overthrown, the vigour of her discipline dissolved, all Christian religion spurned, were we to permit audacious laymen to do that which none but ecclesiastics should do. No, the laity must not betray the Church, nor sons stain their Mother with adultery; the laity's part is to defend the Church, not to betray her. When Uzziah stretched forth his hand to the priest's

In vain the two monks who had also been of the embassy denied the story; they were insulted and silenced. Thus all hope of peace was lost, and that not through any obstinacy on the King's part, but through the misconduct of these time-serving, simoniacal Bishops.

Thus we see that it is an obvious injustice on the part of modern historians, to leave on one side the real point of the question, in order to bring forward a mere accessory. They lose sight of the cause, to consider the combatants. No doubt the Popes and sovereigns were the chief combatants. But the cause of strife was the clergy. The Popes sought to restore them to their ancient virtue and dignity, while the sovereigns sought to retain them in vice. So that in fact princes became merely captains[1] in the pay of the dregs of the ecclesiastical order, who sought for impunity under the royal shield.

C. What, then? Was it fitting that the Chief of the Church should let himself be frightened by mere brute force wielded by a corrupt clergy?

office, he was smitten with leprosy; and when the sons of Aaron offered strange fire upon the altar, they were consumed by the fire of the Lord." He goes on to prove that no prince can lawfully give Bishoprics at his will, and ends with excommunicating the impostors, and those who had meanwhile received Episcopal investiture from the King.

[1] [*Ital.* condottieri.—ED.]

or that the successors of St. Peter should flinch before the difficulty of the undertaking? Could they neglect to provide for the safety of God's Church solemnly committed to them, from fear of recusant and unfaithful ecclesiastics, in that her hour of trial? Would such poverty of spirit have been worthy of the Popes? Were they not bound to gird themselves up in a self-sacrificing temper to the noble work; their faith in the promises of Christ filling them with sure hope of success? On the other hand, was any great reform ever effected without much confusion? When were inveterate and widespread abuses ever overcome without opposition and hindrance? Did any people ever regain their lost dignity without sacrifices? or did any nation ever attain to prosperity, save through trial and hardship? And could we expect the Catholic Church, formed out of so many combined nations, when she had been degraded and enslaved, to rise up from the depths of degradation and become free, without a mighty effort and great social agitation? Of a truth men of petty minds know not what they say when they sit in judgment on great men raised up by Providence to lead the Christian nations, and to undertake the reformation of mankind.

CI. Consult the historians who are most

opposed to the Papacy, Protestant authors such as Hume and Robertson. They fully recognize the fact that "the restoration of society as well as of the Church, which both had reached the lowest point of degradation, coincides with the period of Gregory VII.'s Pontificate."[1] It only needs an unprejudiced eye to see that this coincidence was not casual, and that it is explained by the noble conduct of the Pope who is so abused by the historians. His acts, if attentively studied, will be seen to have benefited civil society no less than the Church, as indeed the interests of the two are indissolubly bound up together. But we are only treating of the Church's liberty in Episcopal elections,[2] and to that subject we will confine ourselves.

[1] The disorders in the feudal system, together with the corruption of taste and manners consequent upon these, which had gone on increasing during a long course of years, seem to have attained their utmost point of excess towards the close of the eleventh century. From that era, we may date the return of government and manners in a contrary direction, and can trace a succession of causes and events which contributed, some with a nearer and more conspicuous, others with a more remote and less perceptible influence, to abolish confusion and barbarism, and to introduce order, regularity, and refinement (Robertson, View of the State of Europe, Wks. IV. p. 25. Hume, Hist. Engl., ii. p. 441.)

[2] It would be a serious and useful study to trace out the work of Gregory VII. in a barbarous society, by setting forth principles of justice, equity, and humanity, as well as their results. For instance, at one Roman Council he established laws in favour of the shipwrecked, ordaining that "on whatsoever shore they may be cast, their calamity be respected, and that no one hurt either their

234 *Revived earnestness in the Church*

CHAP. IV. CII. The whole Church of God was roused from the lethargy into which she had fallen, by the cry of liberty which Gregory raised. It was a new, welcome, useful cry. The dying embers of faith, justice, and respect for the Church, were rekindled in every breast. All the Bishops of particular Churches, who remained true, answered to the appeal.[1] They enrolled themselves under the common standard. They repeated the ancient protests of Canons and treatises against secular usurpation. These had scarcely been heard of during the preceding century.[2]

persons or their goods." " Ut quicumque naufragum quemlibet et illius bona invenerit, secure tam eum quam omnia sua dimittat" (Concil. iv. Rom. sub. Gregor. VII.). This is one of those humane enactments which passed into the public law of Europe.

[1] Witness some of the Canons confirmed by Councils after Pope Gregory raised the standard of reform and liberty, before the end of the eleventh century. The Council of Clermont, A.D. 1095, decreed, " Nullus ecclesiasticum aliquem honorem a manu laicorum accipiat" (Can. 15). " Nullus presbyter cappellanus alicujus laici esse possit, nisi concessione sui Episcopi" (Can. 18).

Council of Nîmes, A.D. 1096. " Clericus vel monacus, qui ecclesiasticum de manu laici susceperit beneficium, quia non intravit per ostium, sed ascendit aliunde sicut fur et latro, ab eodem separetur officio" (Can. 8).

Council of Tours, A.D. 1096. " Nullus laicus det vel adimat presbyterum Ecclesiæ sine consensu Præsulis" (Can. 6).

[2] Time would fail to recount all that was done and suffered on behalf of the Church's liberty, in consequence of the stimulus given by Gregory, by such men as St. Peter Damian, St. Anselm of Canterbury, St. Anselm of Lucca, St. Ivo of Chartres ; and later, St. Bernard, and many other great Prelates.

The work was manifestly of God. For indeed what earthly counsel could have saved the Church in her extremity? Whence could have arisen so remarkable a man to fill the Apostolic Chair; a man who dared to attempt a thorough reformation of an old and corrupt world; to confront all external powers, all internal foes: a man who, within the space of a few years, in eleven councils, dealt with all the rankest and most inveterate evils of the time, purged the Church of them, and finally left to his successors instructions so clear and precise as to be of themselves sufficient to uphold the Church's rule? What save God's Providence ordered that long series of Pontiffs, who succeeded Gregory VII., among whom were Victor III., Urban II., Pascal II., Gelasius II., Calixtus II., who all partook of the strength and uprightness of their predecessor; who all looked upon him as their father and teacher,[1] and all, without exception or swerving, continued his great work of setting Episcopal

---

[1] In the profession of faith made by Pascal II. at the Lateran Council, A.D. 1112, he says that he embraced the decrees of the Popes his predecessors, "et præcipue decreta Domini mei Papæ Gregorii VII. et beatæ memoriæ Papæ Urbani: quæ ipsi laudaverunt, laudo; quæ ipsi tenuerunt, teneo; quæ confirmaverunt, confirmo; quæ damnaverunt, damno; quæ repulerunt, repello; quæ interdixerunt, interdico; quæ prohibuerunt, prohibeo in omnibus, et per omnia, et in his semper perseverabo."

CHAP. IV. elections free, and of purifying the morals of the age?[1] And most needful it was that so it should

[1] All these Popes, even those whose reigns were brief, fought bravely for the freedom of elections, all held Councils, and issued decretals. To recount all their efforts is impossible, but I will select some of their most important decretals. Victor III., who only lived two years, held a Council at Benevento, A.D. 1087, where he published the following decretal : "We decree, that if henceforth any one shall receive an episcopate or an abbacy from any layman, he shall not be held to be a Bishop or Abbot, nor receive the respect due to such office. Moreover, we reject such a one from the bosom of the Blessed Peter, and all entrance to the Church until he hath repented and given up the office he received by so great a crime of ambition and disobedience, which is idolatrous wickedness. And likewise of inferior ranks and offices in the Church. Again, if any emperor, king, duke, prince, count, or any other secular power whatsoever, presume to confer the Episcopal or other ecclesiastical dignity, let him be bound by the same sentence. And this forasmuch as the 318 Fathers of the Nicene Council excommunicated all such buyers and sellers, pronouncing anathema both on those who give, and those who receive." Urban II. vindicated the same liberties in three Councils which he held at Melfi, Clermont, and Rome, A.D. 1089, 1095, and 1099. In the second of these Councils the two following Canons were set forth : I. " The Catholic Church is pure in the faith, and free from all secular bondage." II. "Bishops, Abbots, and others of the clergy shall not receive any ecclesiastical dignity from princes or any layman whatsoever."

Pascal II. withstood the same abuse in eight Councils, of which five were held in Rome, in the years 1102, 1105, 1110, 1112, 1116, and the other three at Guastalla, A.D. 1106, Troyes, 1107, and Benevento, 1108, where he strove for ecclesiastical rights with marvellous wisdom and gentleness. The Council of Guastalla proves that the reform of the Church was beginning to bear fruit. " For long " (so it said), " evil men, clergy as well as laymen, damaged the Church, whence in our times many schisms and heresies arose. Now, by Divine grace, those evildoers being discomfited, she regains her liberty. Wherefore it is fitting that we provide for the thorough destruction of the causes of such schisms. To which end we con-

be. For the struggle was continual. It demanded persevering loyalty to those principles for a much longer period than any one man's life. It needed an indefatigable, courageous assertion of the truth, with Apostolical tenderness and by many Popes in succession. They thus seemed to represent only one undying Pontiff, just as it was one and the same Papacy which could overcome prejudices, subdue passions, and cause the slow power of truth to penetrate the minds of sovereigns, and subject

firm the constitutions of our fathers, and prohibit all lay investitures. And if any violate this decree, if he be a clerk thus guilty of insult to his Mother, he shall be thrust out of his office ; if a layman, he shall be put without the Church's bounds."

Gelasius II., harassed, driven out of Rome, and persecuted, fought manfully for the same cause.

Calixtus II., who after much difficulty concluded a peace, when Henry V. gave up investitures, had previously pronounced a solemn condemnation of the abuse in the Council of Rheims, supported by 420 fathers. We will quote the words of the Bishop of Châlons, who was sent as the Pope's ambassador to the Emperor. Having convicted the Emperor of breach of faith by his own handwriting, he thus clearly set the matter before him : " Sire, as regards us, thou wilt find us punctually faithful to all our promises. Nor does our Lord the Pope aim at impairing in any way the condition of the kingdom or of the crown, as some mischief-makers have affirmed. On the contrary, he teaches publicly that all men should serve thee by military service, and by all such services as were of old rendered to thee and to thy predecessors. But if thou thinkest that thy kingdom is improverished because henceforth thou mayest not sell Bishoprics, that is an error. It is for the benefit of thy kingdom that thou shouldst give up such claims as are contrary to the law of God." Such was the universal language ; we may defy modern sophistry to prove that the Popes sought anything further.

them ultimately to Christ. This was at last done when they solemnly renounced their usurpations at Worms, A.D. 1122, and the following year at the Œcumenical[1] Lateran Council, forty-nine years after Gregory VII. had first anathematized the abuse of investitures ! And who but Divine Providence finally perfected the great work, when unforeseen events led Otho IV., A.D. 1209, Frederic II., A.D. 1213 and 1220, and Rudolf I., A.D. 1275, to renounce the abused rights of regalia, of sequestration, and of deprivation, which greatly curtailed the liberties of the Church ?

CIII. The Church, under the guidance of the Holy See, may be said to have fully triumphed when Rudolf took the oaths at Lausanne. Everything implied that freedom of election was established for ever, and that the Flock of Christ might be expected to enter on a period of renewed life.

But at this very moment the enemy of souls invented a new and subtle method of troubling the peace and prosperity of the Church. This— ought I to say it ?—lay in the *unlimited reserves*. The position which the Holy See had obtained by its lawful and just triumph over the secular powers, secured for it great confidence. Its needs

[1] [So-called.—ED.]

almost constrained it. Other causes more to be deplored helped forward this serious change in its discipline. Not that the Holy See has not a right to reserve elections to itself, when any extraordinary cause requires it. The right to save the Church from peril must always exist. But it was the system of ordinary and universal reserves which raised all classes against the Papacy. The dispute arose simultaneously with the reserves. As early as the thirteenth century Gregory IX., in order to pacify the English, conceded the point respecting benefices which had lay patrons.[1] Soon after, a provision was demanded of the Council of Lyons.[2] When this was refused, the Mother of all the Churches lost in public consideration. She was the object of hostile demonstrations. In England Edward III. annulled the Papal provisions.[3] In France the Gallican Clergy issued decrees on their own account, by which they imposed laws on the Pope. In A.D. 1406, Charles VI. adopted these decrees as laws of the State. The Council of Constance was urged on all sides to seize the Pontifical reserves. Although that Council was restrained by some lingering reverence for the Chief of the clergy, the Council of Basle, which followed speedily, was at once more

[1] Ep. xiii. (ap. Mansi).   [2] A.D. 1245.   [3] A.D. 1343.

CHAP. IV. impatient and more daring. It laid hands on them without scruple. The decrees of this Council against reserves, expected bounties, and annates were received as providential interferences by France, which had demanded their enactment. In the year 1438 they were embodied in the too famous Pragmatic Sanction. In the following year Germany imitated the example thus set; the Popes yielded more and more, and at last the dispute was arranged by means of Concordats granted by Eugenius IV. and Nicholas V. in the years 1446 and 1448.[1] This time the abuse was on the Church's side; we are bound to acknowledge it candidly, as the Popes themselves have done. And thus this affair of reserves ended in humbling the Apostolic See, as much as it had been raised in public estimation by the results of the dispute about investitures.

CIV. The worst evil, however, lay in the fatal consequences which accrued to the Church after this matter was practically at an end. Doubtless the battle concerning investitures had been fiercer. But it was of a less damaging character, and the strife was more easily healed. In that struggle, Rome shone forth with the splendour of justice,

[1] The first of these Concordats was agreed on at Frankfort, the second at Aschaffenburg, under Frederic III.

and disinterested generosity; brute force, depravity and falsehood were her only antagonists.[1] But with the question of reserves it was otherwise. In this matter nations, Churches, princes attributed to Rome no motive save a low self-interest. Men were more disgusted than angry. And contempt is more damaging than anger,

CHAP. IV.

---

[1] I have already observed that as the Popes never interfered in Episcopal elections, unless in cases of obvious necessity, they were able to take a high tone when they exhorted princes likewise to abstain from interference. Pope Adrian could write forcibly to Charlemagne, " Nunquam nos in qualibet electione invenimus, nec invenire habemus." And with what weight he continues, "Sed neque vestram excellentiam optamus in talem rem incumbere. Sed qualis a clero et plebe . . . electus canonice fuerit, et nihil sit quod sacro obsit ordini, solita traditione illum ordinamus" (Tom. ii. Conc. Gall., pp. 95 and 120. See Car. Mag., op. Pt. I. Sect. iii. p. 518).

All through the discussion the Popes could assure the princes that, in sustaining the Church's liberties, they had no personal object or desire of influence in the matter. Pascal II. wrote to Henry I. of England, " Inter ista, Rex, nullius tibi persuasio profana surripiat, quasi aut potestati tuæ aliquid diminuere, aut *nos in Episcoporum promotione aliquid nobis velimus amplius vindicare*" (Eadmer, lib. iii. Hist. Novor.; Paschal, ep. 49). In the twelfth century, Alexander III. having founded the city of Alessandria and appointed a first Bishop, announced with great delicacy that he had no intention by that appointment to assert any wish to interfere with the free election of its future Bishops: "De novitate et necessitate processit, quod nulla præcedente electione, auctoritate nostra, vobis et Ecclesiæ vestræ electum providimus. Statuimus ut non præjudicetur in posterum quominus electionem liberam habeatis, sicut canonici Ecclesiarum Cathedralium, quæ Mediolanensi Ecclesiæ subjacent." So delicate and high-minded were the Papal proceedings, in those days, respecting elections.

R

just as the loss of temporal goods from violence and persecution is much less serious than the loss of moral dignity. Divine Providence saw fit to purge the Papacy of covetousness, and to that end it was permitted to undergo a severe and bitter trial. Covetousness, which never yields save to overwhelming force, was conquered by means of violence, hatred, and contempt. But Rome's discomfiture left traces on the minds of men, which have permanently weakened the Church of Christ. This circumstance especially favoured the heresies of the sixteenth century. Those heresies found the princes of Europe cold and languid in their love and esteem for the Holy See, and ill disposed to uphold it, in consequence of the scandal it had given. Perhaps some even rejoiced to see rebellion stirred up against the Popes amid the clergy themselves, who sought to throw off an old and galling yoke. And the liberty thus sought, speedily became license. It was more pregnant with consequences than the sovereigns of that period understood. It was really the assertion of the independence of natural reason in presence of revelation. It was a fatal rationalism which, like a deadly germ, developed in course of years into the mighty tree of unbelief, overran the world, changed social manners, shook thrones, and caused the more thoughtful part of mankind to have misgivings as to their future destiny. The revolutions of France and of Europe may be traced back to this distant source.

CV. A further disastrous result of this matter of reserves was, as we have already said, that the nomination of Bishops was ceded to the secular princes.[1] Thus that liberty of elections which had cost such efforts, such risks, and such weary toil to Gregory VII. and his indomitable successors, was impaired. Must we admit that Rome ceded part of that precious liberty in the Concordat of Bologna, A.D. 1516, in order to preserve certain temporal advantages? We will never affirm it, or let drop one word of blame concerning that which was done by Leo X. after most deliberate reflection, and with the concurrence of a General Council.[2] But we must lament the

[1] In England, shortly before Leo X.'s Concordat with Francis I., the nomination of Bishops had been ceded to the King as a Papal indulgence. Can it be true that Leo's successor, Adrian VI., ceded to Charles V. and the future kings of Spain the nomination of Spanish Bishops, as a proof of gratitude to his royal pupil for many benefits conferred on the Papal See? Is it possible that the Church's liberty could have been thus used in payment for personal obligations? Such liberality would indeed be deplorable!

[2] One cannot but smile at the words used by Natalis Alexander with respect to the elections : " Jus plebis in Reges Christianissimos *Ecclesiæ Gallicanæ libertatibus* et antiquo more ab Ecclesia tacite saltem approbato transfusum est " (Hist. Eccles. in § i. Dissert. viii.).

CHAP. IV. unhappy circumstances which made so burdensome a convention necessary, as a lesser evil; and the hard fate which awaited the combined wisdom of such a Pope and of such a Council who were constrained to abandon once more to the lay power a large share of that precious freedom of elections, to secure which whole centuries of agitation and discord in the Church and the world were supposed to have been worthily employed.

CVI. If, as has been said, the actual power of the Papacy had reached its climax at the time when the question of investitures was settled, the power of temporal princes, on the other hand, declined from that hour. The nobles, taking advantage of the strife, had risen against them. Here and there they shook off all allegiance, and established in Europe new and smaller principalities. But from the epoch of restored peace, the Papal power, having attained its climax, declined through those very means which, as human short-sightedness imagined, were to strengthen it. These were the reserves and other advantages which it appropriated, and which brought it a great deal of wealth. The secular princes profited

Truly it is an odd liberty which subjects God's Church to temporal princes! It might well be called the *servitude* of the Gallican Church.

by a season of repose to repair their losses; they missed no opportunity of enlarging their power and authority. At last, in the fifteenth century, a cruel French prince—Louis XI.—utterly unrestrained by principle, taught all the sovereigns of Europe how the nobles might be overthrown by violence, so as to give the monarch absolute power. This policy was practically adopted by all the Courts of Europe, though not always with equal boldness and undisguised tyranny. It was persevered in until Francis I. and Charles V. had completed the foundations of the great work, which gave a new form and character to European sovereignties. The Popes of the sixteenth century had to treat with these monarchs. The result was that they were forced to give up yet more of the Church's liberty, namely, Episcopal nominations, retaining only the right of confirmation. What was this style of discipline in substance but a division of the *reserves* themselves between the sovereigns and the Pope? And to this day the arrangement lasts, constantly widening one of the sorest and most pitiable wounds of the crucified Spouse of Christ.

CVII. Yet all men do not perceive it. They say that if only the nomination is conceded to the temporal power, while the Pope retains the right

CHAP. IV. of confirmation, there is no great interference with ecclesiastical liberty.

But this reasoning in favour of the existing discipline would have been treated, in better times, as a veil thrown over a wound which it does not heal, nay, without healing it, and if I may say so, as a mere diplomatic *ruse*. What was the Church's mind on this subject before the last period referred to? Let us infer from it what the ancient Prelates would have said, could they have beheld the nomination of Bishops abandoned to the lay power.

In the ninth century the lay power was constantly interfering with the elections, and thus with the Church's liberty. In the following century this aggression reached its climax. It was first of all required that no election should be made until leave had been asked and obtained of the prince. Diplomatists would say that this did not hinder a free election. But the Church of that time held all such pretensions to be a violation of her liberties. We have seen how Archbishop Hincmar and others of his period withstood the imposition of such bonds upon the Church. They declared that "an obligation on the part of a diocese to ask leave from a sovereign to elect a Bishop, was practically the same thing as constraint to elect whomsoever the sovereign pleased." That was the opinion then held of this aggression. What would those Prelates have said, if, instead of their asking for power to elect, the sovereign himself had nominated as of right the person to be elected? Would they not have feared as an inevitable result that there would be no Bishops save those whom it pleased the ruling princes to place over the Churches; and that the Papal confirmation would degenerate into a mere form, which would never be refused so long as the person nominated was not notoriously guilty of great crimes? But is this immunity from flagrant crime sufficient of itself to insure fit Bishops for our dioceses? And if the Church's wishes are not consulted, not even hearkened to, what ecclesiastical liberty remains —or, at least, to what purpose?

CVIII. The lay power made another step in advance during this century, with respect to its influence upon these elections, by means of " royal petitions." What more harmless than a simple petition? It constrains no one; the electors need not heed it. What said the Church? The celebrated St. Ivo of Chartres, a most ardent advocate of harmony between Church and State,[1] looked

[1] It will suffice to read St. Ivo's letter (ccxxxviii.) to Pascal II. in order to see how ardently he sought peace and concord, and

248 *Papal confirmation of slight practical value.*

CHAP. IV. upon the *royal petition* as virtually annulling ecclesiastical freedom.[1] The holiest and most intelligent Prelates of the ninth century concurred with him in protesting against it. But let it be considered, whether it be worse to express a wish, as was then done by the prince to the electors, with respect to some individual; or at once, and as of right, to nominate a person to be elected. If the royal wish was held to interfere with due Canonical election, what became of such elections, when the sovereign nominated the Bishop, and all that was left to the Pope was a possible refusal of confirmation? Could the Pope always and freely withhold this confirmation? Certainly not. First of all, he could only refuse it in event of the nominee being guilty of some serious crime. This crime must have come to his ears, and he must be able to prove the fact of guilt. Nor was this all. The Pope had good

how by every means in his power he strove to keep a good understanding between the State and the Church. In that letter the following words occur : " Novit enim Paternitas vestra, quia, cum Regnum et Sacerdotium inter se conveniunt, bene regitur mundus, floret et fructificat Ecclesia. Cum vero inter se discordant, non solum parvæ res non crescunt, sed etiam magnæ res miserabiliter dilabuntur."

[1] See Epist. lxvii., lxviii., and cxxvi. of this great Bishop. In Epist. cii. he says, "Non licet regibus, sicut sanxit octava Synodus, quam Romana Ecclesia commendat et veneratur, *electionibus Episcoporum se immiscere.*"

reason to beware, lest by a refusal he should irritate the sovereign, and involve the Church in some greater evil. This matter depended on the prince's individual character, on his religion, and on the ministers who ruled him. What could be easier for any prince than to instil such a fear into the Pope's mind, above all in times of incredulity, lukewarmness, and general hostility to the Apostolic See? What, then, remains to us of true liberty, as distinct from its form, in the election of Bishops? What would the ancient Church have said of such a state of things as our own?

CIX. Observe, too, that I do not measure these remnants of the Church's liberty by the maxims of primitive times, but only by those of the Bishops of the ninth century. That was an age of torpor, in which an enervated clergy was already pretty well inured to the royal yoke. Yet even then men had not forgotten wherein liberty consisted. Let us examine the mind of a succeeding century, when the Church shook off the yoke, and ecclesiastical liberty was once more restored by holy and vigorous Popes. Let us see what such Popes would think of our present condition, when through the chief part of Catholic Christendom, all Episcopal appointments proceed from the sovereign; and whether they would think appointments so made likely to turn out well or otherwise. Two facts will suffice. During Henry V.'s fierce persecution of Pascal II., what did he succeed in winning from the Pope, by dint of imprisonment, ignominy, want, fear of death, the desolation of Rome and its territories, violence, robbery, and the general dismay caused by the invasion of a wild soldiery, incited by the perjured Emperor himself? The privilege of investing Bishops with Episcopal revenues by means of the staff and ring. This was on condition that they were first elected canonically, freely, without simony, without " violence."[1] There were other conditions limiting the privilege. And Henry thought himself victorious when he had won such a privilege from the oppressed Pontiff. Yet it gave him no pretence for meddling with either elections or consecrations. All that he obtained was the privilege of giving his consent, and of installing the person elected in his Bishopric. But what followed? The whole Church rose against Pascal. The cry was that he had lessened her freedom. A schism seemed imminent. This was merely because he had allowed the monarch to invest with staff and ring, the symbols of a Bishop's

[1] ". . . ut regni tui Episcopis et Abbatibus *libere præter violentiam et simoniam electis* investituram virgæ et annuli conferas" (William of Malmesbury, De Gestis Regum Anglorum, lib. v. p. 660).

jurisdiction. In vain did the Emperor assert that he intended by this ceremony to claim no more than the right to invest a new Bishop with his temporal possessions.[1] The Church would not be satisfied, for in truth the staff and ring meant more than this. Moreover, investiture involved the royal assent before the person elected could enter upon his Episcopate. On all sides, Councils, Prelates, assemblies of Cardinals protested against the concession thus extorted from the Pope. Many threatened to renounce obedience to him in consequence. Nothing but the Pope's courageous humility could have appeased the commotion. He confessed that he had exceeded the lines of duty. He summoned a Council at the Lateran Basilica. He presented himself before it as a criminal. He accused himself. He laid down the insignia of his office. He declared himself ready to resign the Papacy by way of satisfaction to the Church, and to submit to the judgment of the assembled fathers. "This document," he said, "I executed without the counsel or subscription of my brethren, under the pressure of urgent necessity, not for my life, my welfare, or my fame, but by reason of the necessities of the Church. Under such circum-

[1] "Non Ecclesiæ jura, non officia quælibet, sed regalia sola se dare assereret" (Henricus). Peter Diaconus, lib. iv. Chronici Cassinensis, c. xl.

stances no conditions or promises are obligatory. And as I recognize that it was ill advised, so I confess the act to be wrong, and I desire with the Divine aid to correct it. The mode of such correction I refer to the counsel and judgment of my brethren here assembled, to the end that no mischief may thereby accrue to the Church, and no hurt to my soul." The Council having investigated the matter, gave sentence as follows: "We, assembled in this Council with our Lord the Pope, pronounce that this so-called privilege is null, having been extorted through violence by King Henry from the Lord Pope Pascal; and we condemn it with Canonical censure, and with ecclesiastical authority, by the judgment of the Holy Spirit, declaring it void and cancelled; and under pain of excommunication we pronounce it to have no authority or force, more or less." And the following reason is given for a similar sentence: "It is condemned, inasmuch as this privilege implies that whosoever is canonically elected by the clergy and people, shall not be consecrated until he be invested by the King; which is contrary to the Holy Spirit, and the institutions of the Canons."[1]

[1] "Et hoc ideo damnatum est, quod in eo Privilegio continetur quod Electus canonice a Clero et populo, a nemine consecretur nisi

Thus the fathers and the whole Church de- CHAP. IV.
cided it to be intolerable that a Bishop, lawfully
elected by the clergy and people, should require
the royal assent or investiture before he could be
consecrated. What would they have said had
Pascal utterly destroyed all free canonical election,
by yielding to the Emperor the yet greater privilege, that only his nominee could be consecrated?
Would they not have thought the circumstances of

prius a rege investiatur. Quod est contra Spiritum Sanctum et
canonicam institutionem." There were two flaws in this privilege.
1. The Bishop could not assume the government of his diocese without the royal assent, which might be refused either from caprice or
with intention to damage the Church; while the Church was hampered
in the exercise of her ministry, which she has received authority
from Jesus Christ to exercise freely throughout the world ; for which
reason Innocent II. decided that the King's dissent should only be
heeded when it was founded on fair reasons, lawfully proved. 2. The
word "investiture" was equivocal ; since to speak of "investing a
Bishop," appeared to imply conferring on him Episcopal jurisdiction,
which it was heresy and contrary to the Holy Spirit to attribute to
the secular power. To these we might add, 3. That it is injustice
and fraud if the King proposes to invest a Bishop with the free
estates of the Bishopric, as by his royal authority, and not as by
virtue of a privilege granted him by the Church who has power
over her own property. It was fair that the King should by his
own authority invest Bishops with feudal estates, inasmuch as these
always pertain to the prince, the feudatory only holding the usu-
fruct. But in those times the two kinds of property were confused,
and all the Church's estates were treated as feudatory, which came
to pass, not so much from the personal covetousness of rulers, as
from the nature of those governments, under which all property
was not defended alike, but the royal estates were best defended.
From this advantage of feudal estates over others, arose the
"feudi oblati."

Pascal's time less deplorable than those of the sixteenth century, when a Pope was reduced to thinking it a less evil to the Church of God to concede the nomination of Bishops to a temporal prince, than to encounter the consequences of a refusal?[1] I refrain from enlarging on this topic. But surely it is most suggestive.

CX. We may further conceive what the Church of the twelfth century would have thought of royal nominations, from another incident. It occurred under Innocent II. The Archbishop of Bourges had died, and Louis VII. left full liberty to the clergy and people of that Church to elect its own pastor. He made one condition. They must not elect Peter de Castra. Peter, he swore,

[1] Pascal condemned himself in another Lateran Council, A.D. 1116. The description he gives of how he was led on to make the concession is touching, from its humility and dignity. "When the Lord had worked His will, with His own, and had given me and the Roman people into the Emperor's hand, I saw daily and without intermission rapine, incendiarism, wars, adulteries. I desired to put away such miseries from the Church and the people of God, and that which I did, I did in order to free God's people. I did it as a man, inasmuch as I am but dust and ashes. I confess that I did wrong, and do ye all raise your prayers for me to God, that He would pardon me. As for that unhappy document, which was made in the tents of the soldiers, and which to its shame contains a sacrilege, I condemn it with perpetual anathema, so that no one may be willing to remember it, and I pray ye all that ye do the like." Then all cried out, "Be it so. Be it so." Such were the trying circumstances which extorted from Pascal a concession, which seems to me as a mere trifle compared with the right of royal nomination conceded four centuries later.

should not be a Bishop. Nevertheless, Peter was elected. He was at Rome. The Pope consecrated him without heeding the exception made by King Louis. The Pope ruled that "there could be no true liberty in an election where a prince might make any exceptions that he pleased, unless he could prove before an ecclesiastical judge that the person elected was deficient in the necessary qualifications. In that case the King was to be heard, like any other of the faithful."[1] Now here it was merely a question of allowing the King to exclude an individual. Yet this was treated by popes of high authority as a violation of ecclesiastical liberty. Liberty is a delicate thing, and will not bear to be trifled with. But what would Innocent II. have said had the question been, not whether the King should have power to exclude one man, in one single case, in one diocese; but whether he should permanently appropriate the nomination of all Bishops throughout his kingdom? Would he not have thought that the Church's liberties were indeed hopelessly lost under such a state of things? Nor may we say, as the ignorant and covetous are ever prone to do, that

[1] . . . "judicante veram non esse electionis libertatem ubi quis excipitur a Principe, nisi forte docuerit coram ecclesiastico judice illum non esse eligendum : tunc enim auditur ut alius."

256 St. Bernard agrees in principle with Innocent;

CHAP. IV. the extended views which these popes held concerning the liberty of Christ's Church were exaggerated.[1] I would appeal to the holiest and most thoughtful men of those ages; to St. Bernard, whose Catholicity was held up as an example by Napoleon himself. The wise Abbot of Clairvaux viewed the subject precisely as did Innocent II. When entreating Innocent for once to indulge Louis VII. by consenting to an appointment to the see of Bourges of some other person than Peter de Castra, he in no way differed from the opinions expressed by the Pope. St. Bernard was both loyal and frank in the terms of his letter to Rome; although he undertook to intercede for the King. He wrote thus to the Cardinals: "In two matters we make no excuse for the King; for his *illicit oath*, and for persevering *unjustly* in that oath. But this he did not willingly, but out of shame. As thou knowest, he

[1] Such views have never ceased, and never can cease to exist in the Church: they are as eternal as truth. It is sufficient proof that the Roman Pontiffs in the sixteenth century did not think otherwise than their predecessors, when we find Julius II., the predecessor of Leo X., appointing Bishops in opposition to the King, as, in the century before, Innocent VIII. had done with respect to the See of Angers. Without entering upon the question of right and wrong (which does not at this moment concern us), such a line of action on the part of the popes proves how clear and unchangeable were the views which were held concerning the liberty of the Church.

thinks it ignominious not to maintain his oath before the Franks, although he swore publicly to what was evil, and every one knows that illegal oaths are null. We confess that we cannot excuse him herein, nor do we seek to do so. We only ask forgiveness for him. Consider whether you can in any way find excuse for his anger, his youth, his royal position. You may, if you will, esteem mercy above judgment. Reflect that he is but a boy and a King; forgive him this time, on the condition that in future he shall not again so presume. And I would beg you to pardon him if possible, retaining the while all the Church's liberty, and all the veneration due to an Archbishop consecrated by Apostolic hands. This is what the King himself humbly asks. This is what our afflicted Church earnestly prays for."[1] Thus St. Bernard saw no excuse for a King who interfered so far as to exclude a single man from election. He held such interference to be a blow to ecclesiastical liberty. According to these principles, which are immutable in the Church, what will become of royal nominations? Was the period of their introduction one of freedom or of slavery? and should the sons of the Church rejoice or weep over them?

[1] Ep. ccxix.

CHAP. IV. CXI. To understand the malignant character of this Wound of the Church, we must bear in mind that when the system of royal nominations came in, it involved the abandonment of the Church's most cherished principles concerning elections. These principles had guided her for ages. Hitherto she had jealously guarded them. Let us examine these principles one by one. They were lost to the Church, so far as their effect is concerned, in the year 1516. But they live in the pious longings of the faithful.

It was an inviolable maxim of the Church that " the best man attainable should be elected Bishop." This plain, just principle implies a high idea of the Episcopate. The Church does not hold that there is a certain standard of teaching-power, goodness, and wisdom which will suffice for that office. She maintains that the highest and best gifts of any man are insufficient for a charge, which was said to be a " weighty burden for angel's shoulders." But if there were none really fitted for so great a dignity, at least the Church would have the best man possible elected to it.[1] But the

[1] All antiquity sets forth this principle. Let us see how Origen taught it in the second century. Describing how, under the ancient law, Aaron was made High Priest, he shows therein the foreshadowing of a due appointment of Bishops under the new Law. " Let us see how the High Priest was appointed. Moses gathered together

The best man should be the Bishop. 259

Concordat which sanctioned royal nominations was forced to substitute a new maxim for the old one. The nominee, it ruled, must be "a serious man, a master in theology or law, and at least twenty-seven years of age."[1] We hear no more about the best man; only about one sufficiently good. Certainly the prince who takes upon himself the nomination, is not released from an obligation to choose the best. But what guarantee has the Church that he will do so? The Church can only

---

the Synagogue, read the sacred text, and said, 'This hath the Lord commanded.' Ye see that although the Lord Himself had commanded the institution of the High Priest, and elected him, yet he convened the Synagogue likewise. And thus in the ordination of any priest, the presence of the people is required, in order that all may know and testify that he who is elected is *the most excellent, the most learned, the holiest, and the most eminent for virtue among all the people;*—ut sciant omnes et certi sint quia qui præstantior est ex omni populo, qui doctior, qui sanctior, qui in omni virtute eminentior, ille eligatur ad sacerdotium" (Hom. vi. in Levit. § 3). This has been the unbroken tradition of the Church. In the ninth century the Visitor, that is, the Bishop sent by the Metropolitan and by the prince to preside over an election, was wont to address the electors as follows: "We bid you by the royal command, and by that faith ye have sworn to preserve towards God, and our Lord the Emperor Louis, to the end that ye fall not under the heavy sentence of condemnation, and that terrible anathema which calls us all before the tribunal of the Judge, that ye hide not from us which among this congregation ye know to be *the best, the most learned, and the most remarkable for a pure life.*" "Ut eum quem meliorem et doctiorem et bonis moribus ornatiorem in ista Congregatione conversari noveritis, nobis eum non celare dignemini."

[1] These are the words of the Concordat.

CHAP. IV. reject the royal nominee, in case he be not "a serious man, a master in theology, and of the requisite age." What guarantee has the diocese to which he is appointed? When he was elected by the diocese, it could take its own precautions. When the provincial Bishops or the Pope appointed, it was in order that the Catholic Church might make the choice. She knew who would meet her wants. If a wrong choice was made, she only injured herself. No one else wronged her. But when a nominee is thrust upon her, she is obliged to accept him, provided that he is equal to the office. And what is the "seriousness" or the degree in theology worth? or the twenty-seven years? Even supposing an examination before confirmation by the Holy See, what guarantee does that afford to the diocese? It guarantees that the new Bishop is a serious man, and a graduate. But is that enough for the diocese? Will any "serious graduate" supply all that is wanted? What latitude the words suggest! How many shades of "seriousness" there are! what differences in doctrine among men who have taken their degree! Can we stop short at such words? or must we not also look at the facts? Do we trust our Universities, or does the doctrine they teach come down straight from heaven? Is it the wisdom of

Solomon, altogether good and sure? Are we CHAP. IV. not, in short, reduced to accepting Bishops whose merits are negative, men to whom no serious public blame is attached? The inspection of the Holy See can go no further. If it could and would, the struggles with royalty would be incessant. Thus a Bishop is at last elected, not because he unites in himself the largest share of deserts, but because there is no crime, or, more accurately, no proved accusation laid against him. But is such negative goodness sufficient to make a good Christian, not to speak of a good Bishop?

CXII. Another of the Church's inviolable maxims was that the Bishop to be elected should be " a priest, known, loved, and desired by all those whom he was to rule ; "[1] that is to say, by the clergy and people of his future diocese. Thus a man might possess very great merit, and yet not satisfy the ancient requirements of the Church for the Bishop of a diocese. He might be unknown to the diocese. He might not suit the

---

[1] See above. A Bishop not known to his diocese was held to be illegitimate, and an intruder. In a letter of Julius I. to the Orientals (ad Antiochenos, apud Athan. Apol. 2), he says that Gregory, who had been placed in the see of Alexandria, was an intruder, "quia nec multis notus, nec a presbyteris, nec ab Episcopis, nec a populo postulatus fuerat." And St. Celestine I. : "Nullus invitis detur Episcopus" (Ep. iv. § 5). St. Leo: "Qui præfuturus est omnibus, ab omnibus eligatur " (Ep. x.).

special needs of his intended flock. He might be unacceptable to them. Churches, like individuals, have more confidence in one minister of the altar than in another. The wish to have as father and Pastor a man in whom most confidence is placed is itself good and just. It ought to be satisfied. But if the prince nominates the Bishop, this wish will seldom be gratified, and the wise and charitable maxim of the Church is thus set aside.

CXIII. A third invariable principle in the Church was that " the Bishop to be elected should be a priest long known to the clergy of his future diocese, and not a stranger from a distant country."[1] He must have lived, and so to say grown old in the diocese. He must know the circumstances and the people; their wants, and how best to meet them. He must be known and valued for his long services : if he is already a father to the people, and a brother to the clergy, all will be attached to him, and ready to respect him. But this plain, evangelical principle is inevitably disregarded by royal nominations. It is a natural result. A monarch cannot, will not, or, at all

---

[1] All antiquity solemnly affirmed this : "*Ex presbyteris ejusdem ecclesiæ, vel ex diaconis optimus eligatur*" (St. Leo, ep. xiv. § 6). And Innocent I., in his Epistle to the Synod of Toledo (Ep. iii. cp. 2), condemns the affair of Rufinus, "qui contra populi voluntatem et disciplinæ rationem Episcopum *locis abditis* ordinaverat."

events, does not give heed to such details. He CHAP. IV.
sends the men whom he desires to promote from
any place whatever; possibly not merely from
without the diocese, but from without the province,
or even natives of a foreign country. Here is a
stranger, who perhaps speaks a different language,
perhaps offends national prejudices. His only
reputation is that he is a royal favourite, an able
man, and a courtier. How can he become the
confidant, the friend, the father of his people?
How can such a father preserve or promote the
regenerate life of his flock? I do not say that
a saintly flock might not prosper under such a
Bishop. Perhaps if the flock consists of saints,
the Bishop is not wanted! But we are talking of
Christian people as they really are. And to lead
men to live up to the Gospel precepts another
class of Bishops is required. The system under
discussion is well fitted to un-Christianize the
world; and when that is once accomplished, how
long will princes be able to govern it?

CXIV. It may be said that a good sovereign
could of his own will maintain these principles of
antiquity, which can never be renounced by the
Church. Certainly. But to that end, it should
be inserted in the compact that all princes are to
be born good! Suppose, however, that the sove-

reign is good. Can it be expected that a layman, immersed in the cares and pleasures of temporal government and of Court life, will be a profound theologian? Will he be familiar with the principles of ecclesiastical discipline, or appreciate their full importance? Will he be kindled with such an Apostolic zeal as to prefer these principles to all self-interest, to maintain them against the seductions of flattery, the evil passions, and the intrigues of those around him, on whose counsels he depends? Surely it is too much to expect of mortal man!

But even taking so improbable a state of things for granted, it would not suffice. The prince must not only know, and seek to uphold the unalterable principles of the Church's discipline. He must be able to uphold them. But to this end, he must personally know each individual Church as well as it knows itself, and having identified himself with the Universal Church, he ought to identify himself with each single Church. Who does not feel that this is impossible? But, in truth, one consideration, confirmed by general experience, and resulting from the nature of things and of mankind, settles the question. "Generally speaking, every person or corporation is the sole true judge of its own necessities." It sees things with the keen and watchful eyes of self-interest. There may be exceptions. But this is in the main a governing law of corporations and associations. Especially is it applicable to the Church, whose interest is spiritual and moral, and for that reason straightforward, simple, consistent, clear as daylight. Hence it follows, that if the Pastors of Churches are appointed by others, they will never be chosen with the faultless judgment which the Church would exert on her own behalf, and which was exercised in her behalf for so many ages. Thus, if a good Prince nominates, the Church's rights are still damaged, for who can deny the claim of the faithful to have the best possible Pastor?

The Church has one interest in electing her Pastors; she is concerned for souls. A prince has many interests. Is it likely that amid all his own interests, and all those of his adherents, he should think of nothing save the Church's interests in the nomination of Bishops? Is it possible that the study of her welfare should be ever uppermost in his mind, overruling all other considerations? Such a sovereign would indeed be a hero or an apostle. A sovereign should be content if a Bishop be a consistently faithful subject; and this every holy man, whose heart is full of the spirit of the Gospel and the Church, must inevitably be.

But a sovereign should exact no more. He should not require a Bishop to be his secret agent, or, if I may venture to say it, a police officer. This destroys the Episcopal character. It violates the fundamental principles of the Episcopate. "No man that warreth entangleth himself with the affairs of this life," is a maxim so delicate that even a thought might violate it. There is a wide difference between the evangelical loyalty which springs from conscientious motives, and which is founded on justice and uprightness, and a political fidelity dictated by human interests, and founded on utilitarian motives without regard to justice. A Bishop is a man of justice. He ought to be such of his free will. A Christian prince should not build any political or worldly speculations on a Bishop's sacred character. But speaking frankly, and of the generality, what is the chief guide of princes save policy? Indeed in all things, Religion excepted, it must necessarily be so. How, then, can such a matter as the nomination of Bishops, in which policy should have no part, but which should be altogether regulated by pure and spiritual motives, be safely entrusted to a man whose position, education, habits and precedents all force him to act from a political point of view? Can we rest in full assurance that the interests of religion will be considered before those of policy? And what is policy? Is it not ever on the watch to turn everything to its own advantage, and to appropriate for that object whatever it can lay hands on? What, then, will a Bishop be who is appointed for political reasons? Surely the Church does not need that her sons should be the offspring of political astuteness.

CXV. There was a time when the Church waged unsparing war against simony. It was held to be the most disgraceful and fatal of vices. But is secret simony not simony? Is simony less vile and lamentable because it is disguised under a political veil? Is a painless gangrene less fatal than a wound which causes the patient acute distress? And what but simony is the pursuit of secular ends when making Episcopal nominations? what else are the adroit means used to obtain vacant sees from princes? A refined, decent, nay modest simony it may be; not barefaced or externally offensive. But none the less there is the gangrene. Nothing but the knife can remove it.

Why is a sovereign so eager to appropriate the nomination of Bishops? Is it solely with a view to the Church's welfare? If so, he would assuredly let her choose her own Bishops. He cannot pretend to choose better than she could.

CHAP. IV. Is it that the Bishops may be his faithful subjects, according to the precepts of the Gospel, and the spirit of the Church? If so, for that very reason he should let the Church choose them. The more worthy a man is to be a Bishop, the more holy, the more Apostolic he will be, and consequently the more loyal, with true Christian loyalty. But remember, I say loyal, even at the cost of life. I do not say he will be a flatterer, a courtier, a party man. I do not say that he will be the servile minister of the royal or the ruling will, which it is his duty to enlighten and guide by the Gospel Law, of which he is the interpreter.[1] If, then, these

[1] Well were it, if all, princes and subjects alike, knew wherein lies true fidelity! It does not consist in unworthy actions, in bargaining with conscience. It always goes hand in hand with justice and sincerity. Thus I offer this very work as a proof, not only of my faithful attachment to the Church, but also of my fidelity to my sovereign. May it be received as it is meant! May the purest intentions not be perverted and calumniously interpreted! The conception of evangelical fidelity, of which I speak, is continually found in ecclesiastical tradition. I will quote one instance which has reference to our special subject, the election of Bishops. In the eleventh century the King of France imposed an ignorant and unworthy Bishop upon the Church of Chartres. The canons of that Church sought to persuade the Archbishop of Tours and the Bishops of Orleans and Beauvais to apply to the King, with the object of inducing him to remedy the damage done to ecclesiastical discipline. They added these words: "Neither be ye slow to do this, out of respect due to the King, as though not to do it proved your *fidelity* towards him. For ye will be really *most faithful* to him, if ye correct those matters in his kingdom which need correction, and if ye lead him to will their correction" (See Fulbert, Bishop of Chartres, ep. 132).

are not the reasons which make a sovereign so CHAP. IV. desirous of retaining Episcopal nominations, it is evident that he seeks in them a support which is not moral, but material, as being by its very nature political; not of God, but of man. He does not seek it only for the purposes of justice. And is not this simony? and, therefore, is not simony at the root of royal nominations? Is not the Church's character thereby changed, and the Episcopal office degraded and injured? Indeed, if the sovereign honestly aimed at nothing but the spiritual good of the Church, and found himself in a position to nominate Bishops, he would not trust either himself or his ministers; he would rather take the Church herself as his counsellor, and would give faithful heed to her judgments.[1]

[1] One chief reason why the Church never liked sovereigns to dispose of Bishoprics, was that she foresaw simony to be, in such a case, inevitable. In the Council of Rheims, when it was a question of peace between the Church and Henry, Calixtus II. declared that nothing should be left undone to banish simony from the Church, "quæ maxime," he said, "per investituras contra Ecclesiam Dei innovata erat." Pope Pascal had already affirmed that the root of simony was to be found in lay influence over Episcopal appointments. And in the Lateran Council, A.D. 1102, he renewed the prohibition against receiving at the hands of the laity either Church appointments or ecclesiastical property. "Hoc est enim," he says, "simoniaca pravitatis *radix*, dum ad percipiendos honores Ecclesiæ, sæcularibus personis insipienter homines placere desiderant." This is self-evident. The best Prelates of the Church

270 *What a prince would do, if well advised.*

Chap. IV. CXVI. But further, I maintain that it is the true temporal interest of a prince to leave the Church free to choose her own Pastors. This may at first seem a paradox. Ordinary politicians have treated it as being one. But considering the question from a higher point of view, and taking a wide and deep view of a prince's interests, we shall see the practical truth of this fair principle, "That which is just and conformable to the spirit of the Christian Religion, is also generally most useful to a Christian prince." I say generally, supposing it to be accepted as a State maxim. Let us apply this principle to the subject before us.

A Bishop who is not appointed by the sovereign will be a mediator between prince and people. A monarch can entirely trust him. For the Catholic Church has always inculcated the

have never ceased to deplore it. St. Anselm of Lucca calls all such dependence on the royal will the seed of simony. He doubts if the Christian religion can long endure under such a system. "Quis enim non advertat," he says, "hanc pestem seminarium esse simoniacæ hæreseos, *et totius Christianæ religionis lamentabilem destructionem.* Nempe cum dignitas Episcopalis a principe adipisci posse speratur, contemptis suis Episcopis et clericis, Ecclesia Dei deseritur," etc. (Lib. ii.). They sought not only to extirpate simony from the Church, but its every root and seed; and are these to be left unheeded because they are out of sight? A corrupt jurisprudence would lead us to such an absurd conclusion. But so false a theory cannot last, because the Church of Christ will endure while the world exists.

doctrine that "subjects may not rebel against their sovereign for any cause whatsoever." Thus the more he is endowed with the ecclesiastical spirit, the more entirely he is the Church's chosen servant, the more earnest will a Pastor be in teaching submission, obedience, endurance, even under the greatest oppression. The people will hang on the lips of one who inculcates gentleness and who sets an example of it. They will deem him an impartial man, a priest of Christ owning no law save the Gospel. But in Bishops appointed by the sovereign, the people see only so many State officers, who practically have the same interests as their princes. How will their words be received? They will be without moral weight. Thus the influence of religion, which should be so great, is rendered useless to a sovereign, inasmuch as no partisan can be a mediator. A sovereign may derive political support from the clergy, when they have become a section of the nobility, and hold large possessions, and thus have numerous adherents. But the unconquerable moral force which is peculiar to the Church and the Gospel; the power of righteousness in the human heart, which God gives, and which subdues the world, is not found in countries where the Bishops are appointed by the secular power.

272 The Church in the French Revolution.

CHAP. IV. Where sovereigns have grasped too much, they have lost more than they have gained. Moreover the result is hurtful to religion. Religion becomes odious to the people when she shares in the hatred stirred up against princes by political factions. So far is she from being able to support the throne that she can scarce hold her own ground. We have seen this come to pass in our own times in France. The French clergy could not rein in the frenzy of the rebellion of which, together with the King, it became the victim, precisely because it was identified with the royal policy, and was chosen by the sovereign himself. Truly it is a terrible lesson to us! The clergy who fell honourably beneath the guillotine were learned, pious, even heroic. Yet they had no weight with a nation which was not dead to the voice of Christianity, or to the generosity of virtue. The noblest endowments availed nothing. Gallicanism[1] was the ruin of the French clergy. It taught a State religion. Its original sin was that it was the sovereign's creation. That was enough to make it a mark for all the opprobrium and bitterness which was showered

[1] [This is surely inaccurate. The essential features of Gallicanism are independent of the question of the election of Bishops, and the French clergy "fell" because it had been enervated by wealth and to a certain extent, by worldliness.—ED.]

upon it. But that hatred was not hatred of the clergy. It was hatred of the King. It persecuted him as identified with the clergy, and so it persecuted religion itself.

CXVII. Again, it is easy to see that a conqueror or a usurping adventurer would find it useful to have Bishops who prefer temporal possessions to religion, and who are ready to sell their souls to him. But surely a Christian prince, recognized as legitimate, cannot ask for more than to be surrounded by disinterested men, who will speak the truth, even at the risk of his displeasure? Now I maintain that no greater service can be rendered to a Christian Prince than that of teaching him a true conception of justice and the real advantages of the Christian religion. There is no surer way of filling the Church's high places with such men, than by leaving their selection to the Church herself. She is guided by the Holy Spirit. Whereas no one assumes that the temporal government can know and have the Spirit of God better than the clergy and the Church. Thus it seems to me, that if a sovereign desires to have Bishops who are heartily loyal, and free teachers of truth, and yet seeks to appoint them himself, he should do it secretly. He should let no one know that the choice is his. Let it once be known, and he will be deceived. But who appreciates the modest, yet straightforward freedom of the Gospel, which essentially belongs to the Episcopal character? What sovereign, what policy is clearsighted enough to perceive that this evangelical liberty on the part of Bishops would save the State from excesses, would keep it back from the edge of the abyss towards which the passions or the heedlessness of rulers often drive it? How many revolutions, and what anarchy would have been averted, if this precious liberty, a balm which, wherever it exists, can preserve Christian states from corruption, had been appreciated as it deserves? But rulers, far from understanding the benefit which would accrue from such a check, so important to their safety, upon their injustice and passions, are swayed by worldly prudence. They obey nothing but a blind and unlimited desire for power; they deem any limit to it a hindrance to their policy. As if a government which has set aside every restraint, however lawful, and has thus come to be free to do whatsoever it will, just or unjust, could last! As if it was not sure to find its own destruction in the limitlessness of its power! No monarch, if really absolute, could retain his throne for many days. The checks upon his will which he might seek to destroy in the sphere of right would reappear aggravated and enhanced in the province of fact. It has been justly observed that, "when princes seek to shake off all subjection to the Church, they find themselves mere slaves to the people." This saying illustrates the political events of our own day. In spite of the mists raised by men who are at once the flatterers and the hidden enemies of royalty, and of the systematic prejudice of modern historians who have treated of the eleventh century, I wish here to make one reflection, and I appeal to all dispassionate and far-seeing men whether it be not just. The reflection is as follows:—Were not the free clergy, as represented by Gregory VII., of more advantage even in temporal things to Henry IV., although in seeming opposition to him, than his own clergy, who obeyed and fawned on him, and were the real causes of his downfall? Strange as the assertion may seem, it is easily proved. It is enough to recall the proceedings of the German barons. Indignant at the Emperor's irregularities and at his tyranny, the Saxon and German nobles rebelled against him. Complaining bitterly of the Pope's moderation and delay, they threatened to elect by themselves another Emperor, without awaiting his judgment. The Pope, on the contrary, held back. He sought to arrange matters. He acted as a true mediator between the sovereign and his nobles. He hoped that Henry would return to a better mind. In that case the Pope was ready to support him. But the German lords, impatient of further delay, made their choice without the Pope's consent. He still strove for conciliation. They elected Rudolph of Suabia, thus making the confusion hopeless, and wholly ruining Henry. But if Henry had held steadfastly to the Pope, he would have been one of the greatest of sovereigns. All dissensions would have been adjusted by the help of the free clergy, whose very independence enabled them to conduct such a mediation. Who, then, deprived Henry of this advantage, leading him on to his melancholy end, as a dethroned, poverty-stricken wanderer? Surely those very servile clergy to whom he had sold their Bishoprics. They blindly counselled him, not to maintain a rightful authority, but to claim obstinately an unbounded power; a vain assertion of power to work his will for good or evil without restraint; or, more truly, to work evil, since no one denied his right to do good. This servile clergy was the means of Henry's destruction. A clergy loyal to him, not from policy, but on true Christian principles, CHAP. IV. would have saved him.[1]

CXVIII. Now this attempt to find in the Episcopate a support *per fas et nefas*—a means, not of making due authority more esteemed by the people, but of enslaving the people to any authority,—this principle to which the secular power clings so closely, tends inevitably to the nomination of Bishops who are real enemies to the Church. Such men keep up an externally

[1] The truth of these conjectures is borne out by what occurred with respect to Henry IV. of France. The Pope had no personal hostility towards him, no political aspirations in the matter; he only desired that France might have a Catholic King. But the Catholic confederates in France did not share his views. In a letter addressed to the Pope's legate Gaetano, they urged the Pope to nominate another King for France, and the Sorbonne was of the same mind. "Sorbona, hujus sententiæ est, urgetque Pontificem ut ipse regem Galliæ pronuntiet, declaretque; alioquin Gallia conclamata est, expersque remedii, et esse hanc potestatem Pontifici regem declarandi, rationibus plane evidentibus, multisque exemplis ostendunt. Immo adjungunt, ubi Pontifex regem pronuntiaverit, isque in Gallia denuntiatus fuerit, continuo a clero et ab omnibus catholicis receptum iri" (Sub an. 1592, die 16 April). But what did the Pope do? He did not become a partisan of either side; he held the dignified place of mediator, and finally his mediation benefited Henry, who forsook his heresy, was reconciled to the Church, and thereupon was recognized as King of France by the Pope and by all France. But had he persisted in heresy, in spite of all his personal courage he would doubtless have been overthrown. A clergy who urged him on against the Pope and the Church, would have been a worse enemy than the Pope; the Pope's remonstrances helped him to regain the Church's favour and the affection of his subjects. It is thus that a free Church holds princes in or restores them to their true interests, and promotes even their temporal advantage.

venerable appearance which is indispensable in our day. But instead of being the free ministers of God, they are no more than royal ministers clothed in Episcopal vestments. The fidelity required of them having its source in earthly motives, they must be men who appreciate earthly aggrandizement. It is necessary carefully to avoid the choice of men who look for a higher prosperity, and who esteem the riches and dignities which they receive from the prince as an added weight which they accept without exultation, but with resignation and for the love of God. Such evangelical men, whom the " truth has made free," are feared by worldly politicians as hindrances to their shallow enterprises. Consequently now, in contrast with primitive times, the Church rarely sees such men filling her Episcopal sees. The world lacks honest preachers of the Gospel. God's eternal Justice lacks teachers and priests. Sovereigns lack faithful friends and counsellors.

The very fact that a Bishop should be capable of rendering loyal service to his prince by fully

[1] Cardinal Godfrey, Abbot of Vendôme, writing to Calixtus II. on Investitures, says, "Ex jure autem humano tantum illis debemus (to temporal princes), *quantum possessionem diligimus*, quibus ab ipsis vel a parentibus suis Ecclesia ditata et investita dignoscitur" (Opusc. iv.).

setting forth the truth, proves what I said before, CHAP. IV. that ordinary minds are unequal to the Episcopal office. It requires the greatest courage and discretion. He Who said, "The Good Shepherd giveth His life for the sheep,"[1] required no common generosity of spirit in His Bishops. These words are not counsels of perfection, but rules of duty. A man who is worthy enough in ordinary life, might when raised to an Episcopal Throne be no better than a "wolf," or a "dumb dog;" as Scripture styles those Pastors who can neither die for their flocks nor warn them of their danger. But what monarch makes it a point of conscience to appoint no Bishops save men of such vigour and earnestness as to be ready to die rather than keep back the truth when it should be spoken?

CXIX. There are yet further objections to royal nominations. Looking upon Bishops as so many political officers, sovereigns and their ministers select them on the principles which are followed in other departments of government; and naturally require in them the same political views as their own. Consequently Bishops cannot confine themselves to the study of eternal truth and justice. They cannot avoid taking a

[1] St. John x. 11.

part in politics. They cannot be content with promoting peace and love among mankind through the Gospel precepts. It follows inevitably that as the heads of Cabinets change, and with them the character of political government, Episcopal appointments will correspondingly vary. To-day a certain class of men will be selected, to-morrow another; instead of, as might be desired, always disinterested men, free from party spirit. Thus private interests and passions are considered and provided for, rather than the spiritual welfare of the people, and the preservation of the Church of our Lord Jesus Christ.

CXX. I will not attempt to follow out all that might occur to damage both Church and State from the nomination of Bishops in the unhappy case of a foolish or wicked King, an enemy of the Church, or surrounded by ministers of that character. We know too well what has occurred in such circumstances: It is unfortunately too notorious how easily, not only bad princes, but even good sovereigns who sincerely desire the Church's welfare, are deceived by false or plausible heretics, who always abound in Courts.[1] Heresy

---

[1] It was in this manner that Arianism was propagated, as indeed all heresies are spread abroad through Court favour, and by means of princes who have yielded to the artifice of heretics. How many heretical Bishops have been forced upon the Church by the secular

veils itself beneath a show of piety, and lay theology is not always quick to detect the fraud. Ambition and self-indulgence are fostered by smooth words; fraud and hypocrisy cost nothing. Thus really good princes have appointed decided heretics who feigned to hold Catholic truth, until such time as, having gained strength and poisoned the country, they have cast aside the mask, when they no longer cared to wear it. Such things have but too recently been witnessed by the Church. But I would speak of a yet more fearful, because more hidden danger, or rather of an existing evil.

CXXI. At the present time, and for a long while past, an indefatigable power has been at work in every corner of the world, with the object of scattering the poisonous seeds of schism in the Church of God. There exists a system of schism, but as yet it is unseen; it only becomes visible when it explodes. Meanwhile its agents,

arm! If the sixteenth century did not see a universal intrusion of such Prelates as arose in England, Sweden, etc., it was chiefly because too often the very Episcopate itself was overthrown and set aside by heresy. The secular power has no means of guarding against false systems of religion save a close adherence to the leaders of the Church, and trust in her government; inasmuch as there is no other living, supreme, enduring, guiding voice. Do they wait the Convocation of an Œcumenical Council? Is it always possible to summon this extraordinary tribunal? and meanwhile are they to let themselves be deceived? Let them turn to the Gospel, and read, "On this rock I build My Church;" and let them believe the Gospel. [This, of course, begs some important questions.—ED.]

many of whom are men of good faith, whisper seductive and insidious words into every royal ear in Europe. They persuade kings that such a system is a necessary bulwark to their authority and power. They denounce the Catholic system as a mere human invention, an evil imagination of Papal ambition. Who can wonder if monarchs are led astray? Can it be expected that they should have sufficient penetration and disinterested love of the truth to enable them to judge wisely between this schismatic system and the Church's true teaching? Surely not. Their only way to discover the truth is to turn a deaf ear to all private and unauthorized teaching, and to give heed to the Pastors of the Church, according to their rank in the hierarchy, resting finally on Christ's own words, that His Church is founded on Peter. Those words utterly condemn the princes who have chosen to follow any other teacher than the head of the Church.[1] But too often every prince has his own theologians, and thinks himself justified in the sight of God in following the counsels of some particular Bishop of his realm. Such a course must involve him in a vicious circle. How can he be sure that

[1] [The reader will remember that the writer takes the Roman Catholic interpretation of St. Matt. xvi. 18 for granted.—ED.]

A King's wishes reflected in his courtiers. 283

the voice of God is heard through private theologians? or that it is the Church who speaks? The Church whom he hears should be free, not enslaved. She should speak through her regular hierarchy, not through any one member who sets himself up in opposition to the rest. Otherwise there is no opinion, however wild, that may not be maintained on the authority of individual theologians, or of Bishops who are the vassals of their sovereigns. It is not thus that truth is attained. The sovereign will by this means only arrive at the reflection of his own wishes, or at the interests of those whom he consults. But meanwhile that schismatical system of which I speak is already too prevalent; it prevails almost universally. And nothing more tends to give it increased extension than the royal nomination of Bishops. Naturally, princes who are themselves attached to this false system nominate Bishops whose opinions are well known to them. Moreover, since the schism is concealed as fire beneath cinders, it is evident that not even the Pope's reserve of confirmation can obviate this secret mischief to the Church. All declarations and oaths are useless palliatives, powerless to bind men who are dead to the pleadings of conscience, since their very profession is deceit and seduction. Would that these lamentable truths were not proved by experience! But when throughout a kingdom there are only such Bishops as these to be found, the first trifling occasion will give rise to schism, and it will speedily assert itself unchecked. If but a minority of the French Church proved schismatical on the occasion of the Concordat between Napoleon I. and Pius VII., it was owing to a happy inconsistency in that singular clergy. While through national pride they had founded in Europe the schismatic system I allude to, they were in practice faithless to their hollow theory, by reason of their innate piety. And if that small schismatic Church did not succeed in disturbing and crushing the whole Church of France, or even the Universal Church, as might have happened under different circumstances, it was solely through the intervention of Divine Providence, which permitted that the policy of the great man who was master of France, ruling all things with a rod of iron, should attach him to the Church and the Pope, thereby rendering the schismatic faction powerless, though none the less arrogant.[1]

---

[1] Richelieu, whose testimony is unimpeachable, since he was so undoubted a supporter of an absolute policy, considered Gallicanism to be a schismatic system. He saw the spirit of schism in the pretension on the part of an individual Church to decide important questions which affect the interests of the Church and of all Christian

CXXII. Whatever abuses and irregularities CHAP. IV. may creep into elections when made by dioceses or provinces, they will always be only partial. Their evil consequences will not become national. They will not be the results of a system, or the first essays of a malignant attempt to control all elections and to pervert whole kingdoms. But once give up nominations to the sovereign, and what a terrible power for evil is intrusted to the will of an individual! Or surrender them to a Cabinet, and what an alarming power is created outside the Church! This power will outlast individual princes, and will endure as long as Cabinets exist with their maxims of worldly policy.

Alas, that this schism has already attained so much strength! Its foundations have been covertly laid throughout Europe. Of a truth they are strangely unlike the stones whereupon the temple of the Lord is raised!

States—questions which can only be decided by the Pope and by Œcumenical Councils. What, then, if the Church of any one nation, or an individual Bishop, counsellor, or professor of theology presume not merely to decide such questions, but to decide them contrary to Councils and Popes and their express decisions : are not such proceedings schismatical? Can any Christian prince conscientiously abide by such individual judgment? Can he affect to have rightly sought after the truth and the doctrine of the Holy Catholic Church? Can he in good faith believe that he is only seeking to maintain his own rights, and not to infringe on those of others? [These questions may at certain periods of Church history be answered in more ways than one.—ED.]

CHAP. IV. Yet men go quietly to sleep while the Catholic Church is surrounded with these fatal dangers! The worldly wise of our age think that all is well. Others, yet more prudent, hold that Catholics should not venture to protest, that they should maintain a rigid silence, lest uneasiness should be created and offence given. All disturbance they consider imprudent and rash. Such prudence fatally undermines the Church; it works secretly, and those who denounce its stealthy actions and disclose its treachery are branded as agitators and the enemies of society. Meanwhile the Church groans, and may but too justly utter the Prophet's saying that "in peace her bitterness became most bitter."[1] And if some faint whisper, breaking this deathlike stillness, is raised with a hope of restoring the Church's health, whence comes it? From among the lowly faithful, or at most from some poor but courageous priest. During the Revolution, when France renounced Catholicism for a State religion, two poor priests alone dared to present a petition to their Bishops, and to lay before them these reflections on nominations to the Episcopate.

"So long," they said, "as the Chiefs of our Religion are men chosen by herself, Religion has

[1] Isaiah xxxviii. 17. Vulg.

nothing to fear. The Churches of the East, of Germany, and of England were not destroyed by persecution or by starvation. They perished through the evil intervention of force in the appointment of their Bishops; either through a voluntary barter of independence on the Bishops' part, or through their ignorance of the limits within which free and faithful men are justified in resisting sacrilegious aggression. And now, O ye venerable remnant of our Episcopacy, your turn is come to encounter the covert onslaught of men in power. They have already considered your hairs, blanched by all that you have suffered; they have numbered your years; they rejoice over your advancing age, knowing that man's term of life is limited. As one by one you fail, they will fill up your sees with such priests as are honoured with their confidence. These Bishops will decimate your ranks without seeming to destroy unity. In time the lingering remains of shame will be cast aside. Secret ambition will form vile contracts. And when the last of you shall lie down to rest beneath the high altar of his Cathedral it will be with the conviction that his obsequies are the obsequies of the Church of France."

CXXIII. What, then? will the Church be forsaken? Is there no hope that Catholicism will shake off this oppression, and that Episcopal elections will once more be free, since otherwise the Church cannot subsist? No, none. All the strength is on the side of schism. The Church can boast of nothing but weakness. In the present state of things, neither Bishops nor Pope can remedy the evil: there is no human power equal to the emergency. But there is such a thing as persuasion. And there is the Word of God. This should be pressed upon the world although rejected by it. Thus the Lord's ambassadors will at least save their own souls, which they would imperil by silence. Nor is this state of things new to the Church. In other days she has seen no help in man. In truth, she never did see any. But she knows that Divine Providence is greater than man. God wills that all the glory shall be His alone. He wills that the sole Invisible Head of the Church, our Lord Jesus Christ, shall be exalted over all. He will triumph even when His enemies fondly imagine their victory to be complete, and when the faithful who trust in Him are bereft of all succour, save through Him alone. It is especially in the matter of free elections, without which the Church must perish, that, overruling all human thoughts, the Almighty Providence of Him Who has received of the Father " all power

Bases of a Christian constitution. 289

in heaven and in earth," has ever been conspicuous. CHAP. IV.

CXXIV. The Christian people, and Christian nations, as members of this people, have a constitution by right; by the right of existing facts; and this is truly Divine right. All facts are of Divine right; they are of God, Who alone rules all things. Woe to him who touches this constitution! Woe to the nation which breaks its laws! The evil consequences of doing so will overtake it, and it will be ceaselessly distracted and torn asunder until it retraces its steps, and once more restores the constitution in question. The laws of this constitution are simple, universal, and unchangeable.

The bases are essentially two : 1. A supreme right; 2. A general fact, which results from particular facts : namely, that there is, first, a supreme legislative power, or, if you will, a power which enunciates the highest laws; and, next, a power which sanctions them. And these two powers are never united in the same person, but always belong to different persons. Let me explain myself.

In the Christian people is ever heard a voice announcing the Gospel law, which is perfect righteousness. This office is committed to the Church ; and it is the power which makes and promulgates laws. But what sanction does it get?

U

I do not mean in the next life, but in this? The Church is defenceless so far as material weapons go, and her essential character is described in the words with which Christ gave their mission to the Apostles: "Behold, I send you forth as sheep in the midst of wolves."[1] It is not in the natural order of things that temporal authority should be in the hands of the Church. There is another power. God has kept law and its sanction apart. The promulgation of laws He has committed to His Church, reserving to Himself alone their temporal sanction; so that none should glorify himself, or tyrannize over his fellow-men. For the Church cannot wield this sanction by reason of her physical weakness. Still less can the temporal government wield it, since there is little cause for men to glory in brute force. Yet God does not ordinarily give His temporal sanction to the law of the Church by miracles. He has organized among His people the sanction of the law as announced by the Church; that is to say, He has so constituted the body of believers as to make them feel the happy necessity of themselves sanctioning the Divine law. Thus the Power which sanctions that law has given up its authority to His people. What I am going

[1] St. Matt. x. 16.

to say will throw light on this assertion, at which CHAP. IV. no one ought to take offence.

Among Christian peoples, that is to say, in every Christian nation, there are always, in fact, three powers: the supreme or governing power, the power of the nobles, and the power of the people. Wherever any one of these three powers is in fault, it meets with resistance and punishment from the other two, which join together to defend justice against the transgressing power. This is simply an historical fact; I abstain from entering upon any question of right. In order that each of the powers may be kept in the subjection which provides against its offending with impunity, it is evidently necessary that at all times any two of the powers should be stronger than the third, since it is only thus that their alliance on behalf of justice can afford her a practical sanction. But such sanction will be efficacious in proportion to the superior strength of the two allied powers; and justice will be defended and assured accordingly. And forasmuch as the aggression may proceed from any one of the three powers, the best division of strength in favour of justice is undoubtedly that "by which in any case the authority of justice against the aggressive power shall be most effective." Hence it follows that the division of strength which is most favourable to justice in a Christian people, is that which establishes a perfect equilibrium among the three powers, so that each should possess an equal strength, and in the event of any transgression the offending party should meet with an overwhelming opposition, in the proportion of two to one. But if one power alone becomes stronger than the two others put together, the result is a *tyranny*. And if two powers combine to maintain injustice, and to oppress the minority, the result is *conspiracy against the State*. But if all the three powers conspire together against justice, so that while they remain at liberty the Church become the victim of oppression, then indeed that nation will assuredly lose catholicity, and will ere long *forsake Christianity itself*. These are the three radical diseases of civil society in the Christian world. It would be hard to say what the destiny of a nation thus detached from the Church, and withdrawn from the rule of truth, will be. It ceases to belong to the people of God; it ranges itself among unbelieving nations. Such, at least, must be its end. Infidel nations are subject to their own peculiar ills. But it takes to itself something more dreadful than do infidel countries, namely, a law of degradation which will carry it to incalculable depths, unless intervening circumstances arise. History contains no example Chap. IV. of a nation which has undergone all the changes to which such a condition condemns it. A point has always been reached at which the downward course has been arrested, and the guilty nation has shrunk back in terror from the abyss before it, and has once more approached, or re-entered, the Catholic Church. Setting aside, then, the case of deadly apostasy, and speaking only of those other evils to which Christian nations are liable, tyranny and conspiracy against the State, I say that any Catholic nation which is labouring under either, will never regain its tranquillity until it has cast out the seed of its malady, and re-established the law of its Divine constitution; namely, that two powers shall always be stronger than the third alone, and ever ready to protect justice if that third power infringe it.

CXXV. It was this very constitution, peculiar to Christian States, that Providence employed to free Episcopal elections, when one of the three powers strove to usurp them. There was a time when the nobles obstructed this liberty, straining every nerve to exercise an arbitrary control over the elections. Then Divine Providence made use of the princes and people united, to preserve the rights of the Church, and to restore the freedom

CHAP. IV. of her elections.¹ At another time the aggression came from the people, and then the Church found her defenders in the sovereigns and the nobles.² Imperishable benefits were rendered to

¹ In the eighth century an armed and arrogant nobility invaded the Bishoprics on feudal grounds. Charlemagne and Pepin defended the Church, and for this reason Pope Zachary gave to the latter the privilege "*ad personam*" of nominating Bishops. The Abbot Lupo di Ferrara writes : "Pipinus a quo per maximum Carolum et religiosissimum Lodovicum imperatores duxit rex noster originem, exposita necessitate hujus regni Zachariæ Romano Papæ, in Synodo, cui Martyr Bonifacius interfuit, ejus accepit consensum, ut acerbitati temporis, industria sibi probatissimorum, decedentibus Episcopis, mederetur" (Ep. lxxxi.).
² There were two periods in which the nobles and the supreme power attempted to seize upon the elections—in the first by open assault, in the second by underhand arts ; and thus insensibly they attained their end. In France the supreme power combined with the people in opposition to the nobles and to the freedom of the Church, thus producing a conspiracy against the State. At the assembly of the Commons, A.D. 1615, the third order was for Gallicanism, and the Catholic system was defended by the clergy and the nobles, so that, as Barthol. Grammont, President of the Parliament of Toulouse, writes (Lib. i. Hist. ad ann. 1615), the Catholic party said, "Clerum et nobilitatem convenire in eandem sententiam, nec ideo contrariam opinionem valere quia ita populus censet : duorum vota et calculos uni prævalere."
In the year 1673 the clergy again set forth the same doctrine, but A.D. 1682 they contradicted their forefathers. The clergy of royal nomination under a despotic King like Louis XIV. were altogether royal ; and then Gallicanism took shape and achieved its triumph. But in what did this conspiracy on the part of the supreme power and the people against Church and State, result? In the King's ruin. The nobles being all but crushed, the King found himself face to face with the people, whom he had himself excited. Two opposed powers without a mediator cannot long go on without strife, and in this case the people dethroned and murdered their King. What a lesson ! Surely it is a false policy which only seeks

the Church by those pious monarchs, which she will commemorate to the end of time. Finally, the monarchs themselves became the aggressors and tyrannized over the elections. Hence the great struggle which began in the time of Gregory VII., when the nobles and people together maintained the Church's cause against the sovereign's usurpation. When the sovereigns were depressed, the nobles once more regained power; and they skilfully acquired a hold both over the elections and the Episcopal sees. They so contrived, that the people and the greater part of the clergy should be excluded from any voice in the matter, and that the elections should depend upon the Cathedral Chapters, which were filled, with some few exceptions, with the dregs of the nobility. But the sovereigns again got the better of a degenerate nobility, repressing, and at last altogether controlling it. Then, in their turn, the princes obtained the nomination of Bishops, or at all events the principal influence in elections. This

to render the supreme power unlimited! Extremes meet, and whoso is unduly exalted, will fall the more miserably.

It is a remarkable fact, that Cardinal Richelieu took part with the Church against Gallicanism, although he it was who paved the way for its triumph; for he was the great instrument of the depression of the nobles, and of absolute monarchy. That great man did not foresee the consequences of what he was doing; and how many who think they see, are in truth equally shortsighted!

influence was legalized under the form of protection; it was employed with caution, and with attention to outward form and to the gentle refinements of diplomacy. But meanwhile the schism becomes daily more irreparable. Who will save the Church from it? Who will save the world? Who will save the thrones which have laboured to prepare for themselves the most awful and strange calamities? Of which of these three powers will Divine Providence avail itself to enforce the law of justice, and to restore to the Church that complete liberty which no mortal hand may assail with impunity? A glance at the world enables us to answer the question. The awful judgment of Divine Providence is not veiled or doubtful. It has already begun, and resounds in various quarters of Europe and of the world. England and Ireland, the United States, and Belgium elect Bishops freely: and assuredly God will not delay the restoration of a similar liberty to all Christian nations; let the monarchs reckon upon that as a certainty. The people is the rod which He wields. Rebellions are execrable, and no one execrates or condemns them more than the Church. But that which is not done by the Church or by good men, will be done by the power of Jesus Christ, Who is Lord of both kings and people, Who makes all

of full liberty to the Church.

things bow before His Will, and Who is ever wont to bring good out of evil. He can use even the wicked to His own wise ends.[1]

CXXVI. Yes, I dare to assert boldly, that the general confusion of Europe is inevitable. One measure only could avert it; the restoration to the Church of her full liberty, with just and respectful treatment. But this measure is precisely the only one not contemplated, or it is obstinately rejected. All resources in turn are tried;-the force of arms and the persuasions of diplomacy. But all such means are only equivalent to the last succours rendered to a dying man. At best they only serve to prolong his mortal agony for some few moments. Is it intelligence that is wanting? No. It is faith, it is love of justice that are wanting. Men do not believe that Providence has an unchangeable rule in the government of events: they do not believe that the Church has a mission which must be fulfilled at any cost; they persuade themselves that they can do without her. Thus unbelief overpowers intelligence, and renders unintelligible the sacred and universal cry of Christian peoples for Liberty. The peoples

---

[1] [Our author is betrayed into an exaggeration by the strength of his convictions. Revolutions surely depend on other causes and have other results than those on which he insists.—ED.]

Chap. IV. give a false reason for their rebellions; they lie to themselves; because, although they have a profound instinctive apprehension of the true reason, they have no power of expressing it. Would that they might learn that Christians, who are essentially free, cannot obey man, unless in him they obey God's authority; cannot obey, save as they learn from the Church's teaching that Gospel law of humility and gentleness, which an enslaved and despisèd Church is no longer able to teach them! Would that these truths were appreciated! Even yet it might not be too late!

CHAPTER V.

Of the Wound in the Left Foot of the Holy Church, which is the Servitus (or Enforced Infringement of the Full Rights[1]) of Ecclesiastical Property.

CXXVII. From that which has thus far been set forth, we see that the fall of heathen Rome, foretold by Holy Scripture under the name of Babylon, was, in the course of Divine Providence, something more than an act of justice avenging the blood of the Martyrs and extirpating the last relics of idolatry. It was further designed by the Divine Wisdom with which the King of

[1] [*Ital. Servitu'*. Phillimore's International Law, I. 390. "The doctrine of *servitus* occupies an important place in the Roman Law; and in some shape, and under some application or other, exists of necessity in the jurisprudence of all nations. This obligation to service constitutes a right in the obligee, or the person to whom it is due, and it ranks among the *jura in re*, while it operates as a diminution and limitation of the right of the proprietor to the exclusive and full enjoyment (*libertas* rei) of his property." In the following pages the word is translated "servitus," with a meaning which will have to be borne in mind.—ED.]

kings governs human events, to secure that, when the old and decrepit society had gone to pieces, a new society, the daughter of the Church of the Incarnate God, should take its place. On her forehead is traced a sacred and indelible sign to make her, like her mother, undying, so that together they should continually advance towards a hitherto unknown civilization. But it was fitting that the glory which was thence destined to accrue to the Divine element in the Church of Christ should be attempered and almost counterbalanced by the humiliation which was to attend on the human element in her. It was thus intended that all good in her should be attributed to the Lord and His Christ, and not to man. Hence God permitted that the barbarian conquerors whom He used as His instruments for the destruction of the Roman Empire, and who were unconsciously moved to become disciples of the Church, should introduce Feudalism, which in course of time extinguished the Church's liberty. This was the source of all her ills. In truth, wealth alone would not have precipitated the clergy into the abyss which we have been exploring; nor would temporal dominions have had so fatal an effect if they had been independent. Indeed God employed temporal sovereignty to preserve the freedom of the Apostolic See, so that Chap. V. at least the Head of the Church might escape the universal servitude, and, being free, might in time set free its members likewise. This great work Rome must yet achieve.

CXXVIII. Feudalism was in fact the only, or at all events the principal source of all these evils. As a system combining profane and barbarous overlordship with servitude and vassalage to temporal princes, it, so far as it was overlordship, divided the clergy from the people (Wound i.). It split the clergy into two sections, invidiously styled superior and inferior clergy. It substituted the estranging relationship of overlord and vassal for the more binding tie of father and son. Hence the neglected education of the clergy (Wound ii.). Hence also the division among the higher clergy, namely, the Bishops, who forgot that they were brothers through jealousies, roused on their own account, or on that of princes whose vassals they were. Thus each Bishop became separated from the people, and stood apart from the Episcopate as a whole (Wound iii.). Moreover, Feudalism, so far as it was vassalage, by making the Bishops personally subject to their prince as his liegemen, chained the Church with all her possessions to the chariot of the lay power which dragged her over the rocks and precipices upon which in its irregular and headlong course it is often broken and ruined. Thus after countless degradations and disasters, the Church, deprived summarily of her endowments, finds herself so exhausted that she can no longer defend even the right of nominating her own Pastors (Wound iv.). And, I say, Feudalism enslaved the Church with all her possessions. For the barbarian rulers, accustomed to see vassals all around them, looked at ecclesiastical matters as at everything else; while time-serving lawyers aided to shape what was mere barbarous despotism into a theory of rights. They argued that "the principal involves the accessory," and they thence deduced the rule that, as the royal fiefs were principals, the freeholds of the Church were also to be considered feudal possessions. Thus feudalism absorbed everything, leaving neither the persons nor the property of Churchmen free.

CXXIX. I put aside the temporal sovereignty, which is peculiar to the see of Rome. It could have no reference to any other sees, at least for a long time past, and it saves the Papacy from ignominious servitude. But I affirm that the clergy are corrupted and debased, not by free but by "enslaved" property. The *servitus* of

Legacy of feudalism to our age. 303

ecclesiastical property was the unhappy cause which hindered the Church from maintaining her ancient rules concerning her possessions, and from regulating, as she would, their acquisition, their administration, and their disposal. And this loss of suitable provision for the administration and use of Church property, in accordance with the rules of antiquity and in the temper which befits Churchmen, is precisely the fifth Wound, which pierces and rends the Body mystical.

CXXX. Feudalism has well-nigh perished, and will soon altogether vanish before advancing civilization, as clouds disperse before the sun's rays. The Church no longer holds any fiefs. But the legal principles, the customs and the spirit of Feudalism survive. The policy of governments draws its life from this source, and modern codes inherit from the Middle Ages this luckless bequest. I point out the cause, with a view to studying the effects.

CXXXI. The Primitive Church was poor, but she was free. Persecution did not deprive her of free government, nor did the violent spoiling of her goods interfere with her true liberty. She was subject to no vassalage, to no " protection," still less to " tutelage " or " advocacy," there. Under these specious and treacherous names the *servitus* of ecclesiastical property was introduced. From the time of its introduction the Church could no longer maintain her ancient rules respecting the acquisition, the management, and the disposal of her material property; and the neglect of rules, which were a safeguard against the evil and corrupting influence of such possessions, led her into the greatest dangers. Let us survey the most important of these rules.

CXXXII. The first rule concerning the acquisition of property was, that all oblations should be spontaneous. Christ said to His Apostles, " Into whatsoever house ye enter, first say, Peace be to this house . . . And in the same house remain, eating and drinking such things as they give, for the labourer is worthy of his hire."[1] These last words became the rule of the Apostles, and are continually repeated by St. Paul.[2] By them Christ imposed on the faithful an obligation to maintain the Gospel labourers, and on these latter He conferred the right to be maintained by the faithful. It was really a precept, but this does not make the act of giving less spontaneous; because adhesion to the Gospel, and incorporation with the Body of believers was to be spontaneous. Spontaneity of human action does

[1] St. Luke x. 5-7.   [2] 1 Cor. iv. 4, 15; 1 Tim. v. 17, 18.

not cease until moral obligation is reinforced by Chap. V.
active coercion. But Christ added no more
stringent sanction than " And whosoever shall not
receive you nor hear your words, when ye depart
out of that house or city, shake off the dust of your
feet."[1] The punishment of such offenders is left to
Divine Justice, according to the gentle spirit of the
Heavenly Law-giver, Who nevertheless has promised that in His own good time He will visit
them.[2] The history of Ananias and Sapphira
proves the same thing. " Peter said, . . . Whiles
it remained, was it not thine own? and after it
was sold, was it not in thine own power?"[3]
And in like manner, the collections which
St. Paul enjoined the Churches of Galatia and
Corinth to make, in order to provide for the needy
Christians of Jerusalem, were to be left to the
discretion and charity of each believer : " Upon
the first day of the week let every one of you lay
by him in store, as God hath prospered him."[4]

CXXXIII. Again, the precept by which
Christ enjoined the faithful to maintain the clergy,
refers only to the necessaries of life. This is
shown by the words, which direct the evangelical labourers to " eat and drink " in " what-

[1] St. Matt. x. 14.
[2] St. Matt. x. 15.
[3] Acts v. 3, 4.
[4] 1 Cor. xvi. 2.

CHAP. V. soever house" they enter. "Edentes et bibentes quæ apud illos sunt." And St. Paul keeps close to our Lord's language when he writes to the Corinthians: "Have we not power to eat and to drink?"[1] If the supply of positive necessities for the primitive clergy was left to the voluntary exertions of the faithful, how much more would any offerings that exceeded these limits have been matters of free will?

CXXXIV. Tertullian bears witness that these spontaneous offerings were continued at the end of the second and beginning of the third centuries. In his "Apology" he says, "Each one lays by a little money every month, or when he can and will, for no one is constrained; all is given freely These are as it were the deposits of piety."[2]

We find the same maxim more or less set forth through all the brightest ages of the Church She willed and taught not only that the faithfu should not be constrained to make their oblations, but that they should not be induced to do so by any artifices or persuasions. And as late as the ninth century we find Canons published by the third Council of Châlons with a view to pro

[1] 1 Cor. ix. 4.
[2] "Modicam unusquisque stipem menstrua die, vel cum velit et si modo possit, apponit: nam nemo compellitur, sed spont confert. Hæc quasi deposita pietatis sunt" (Apol. c. xxix.).

tecting the gifts offered by the faithful to the Church from any such abuse.¹

CXXXV. The law of tithes, appointed by God under the old Levitical covenant, was not confirmed by Christ under the new Covenant. The reason I believe to be that the Author of Grace would not lay any burden upon His people beyond that which was required by the nature of things. And as this involved no more than the maintenance of the clergy by the faithful among whom they laboured, and as such maintenance would vary according to circumstances, any fixed contribution was liable to be at one time excessive, at another insufficient. But since our Lord in no way forbade such oblations, leaving them to the discretion of the faithful, many, especially those who came from the synagogue, from the earliest times voluntarily offered tithes according to the ancient custom.² And in the sixth century Justinian, at the instance of some Bishops, strong adherents of the old rules, forbade the use not only of force, but of ecclesiastical penalties in recovering them.³ The Church might easily reduce to a pre-

¹ Tommasin, P. iii. L. i. c. xxiii.
² Irenæus, lib. iv. c. xiii. ; Origen, Hom. in xi. Num. St. Cyprian, De Unitate Ecclesiæ, c. xxvi. "At nunc de patrimonio nec decimas damus" seemingly a reproof to those who were less zealous, and did not pay tithes. ³ L. 39, Cod. De Episcop. et cleric.

CHAP. V. cept what was thus established as a custom. This she did, first somewhere in the sixth century,[1] and later universally,—whenever she found this provision for the maintenance of the clergy to be convenient or necessary. But such offerings only ceased to be voluntary when the secular authority enforced them. This came to pass in the seventh century under the influence of feudalism.[2]

CXXXVI. And here we must bear in mind, that the Gospel introduced a new kind of rights to the world, which we may term *ecclesiastical rights*. At first men knew only of the rights of strict justice, and beneficent actions. The first might be enforced by outward violence, the second were altogether free. But the Divine Lawgiver Who reformed the world, introduced between these two laws of moral action, a third ; of which the right which He gave to the ministers of the altar to live by the altar is an instance. This right is protected solely by the threat of Divine displeasure, to which Canonical and spiritual penalties equally correspond. The greatest penalty which the Church can inflict is that of separating the disobedient and contumacious from the body of the faithful, and thus depriving them of the bene-

[1] Second Council of Macon, A.D. 585.
[2] In Capital. Ann. 779, 798, 801.

fits of communion. Such penalties, by means of CHAP. V. which the Church maintains her rule and her rights, are altogether strange to a secular government. This was taught by Christ in the words, "Ye know that the princes of the Gentiles exercise dominion over them, and they that are great exercise authority upon them, but it shall not be so among you."[1] What happened, then, when ecclesiastical property fell under the temporal yoke, thereby ceasing to be free in the Church's hands? That which should not have happened. The civil power endowed it with the sanction of coercion. The civil power possessed and knew of no other sanction. Moreover, it believed itself to be thus doing the clergy a signal benefit: "et qui potestatem habent super eos, benefici vocantur."

CXXXVII. It was undoubtedly just, and in no way opposed to the spirit of the Gospel, that such property as the Church had acquired through free gifts, should be protected, like any other property, by public authority. For all such donations carried with them rights according to strict justice. But the exercise of force in constraining the faithful to make offerings, such as tithes, firstfruits, and similar gifts, was contrary to the ancient principle. Nor could the originally spon-

[1] St. Matt. xx. 25, 26; St. Luke xxii. 25, 26.

taneous nature of such gifts be forfeited because it had become customary to offer them. It is a mere legal sophism to say that a free giver becomes a strict debtor, simply because he has continued his gifts during a long period of time.

CXXXVIII. This first degee of *servitus*, to which voluntary oblations were subjected, lessened goodwill between the faithful who offered them and the clergy. It abolished the kindly ties of benefactor and benefited, or more truly of mutual benefaction, since the one gave temporal, the other spiritual things, according to the Apostolic precept, " Si nos vobis spiritualia seminavimus, magnum est si nos carnalia vestra metamus ? "[1] For such primitive and natural relations the chilling and odious relations of debtor and creditor were substituted, depriving the gift of all merit and grace, and the giver of all gratitude; while the clergy, being assured of their living, saw no increase or diminution proportioned to their labours in the offerings made to them.

CXXXIX. But a yet more fatal step towards *servitus* was that which confounded all free property freely bestowed upon the Church with fiefs. All was gradually absorbed under the head of feudal tenure. Thus the idea gained ground

[1] 1 Cor. ix. 11.

2. *A common administration.*

that the possessions of the Church were the property of the feudal lord, to whom the Churchmen owed allegiance. To this day we retain the proof of this *servitus* in our language, calling the Churches " mainmort," which signifies a class of serfs.[1] This evil seed, after having secretly borne most mischievous fruits among the clergy, led finally to the modern spoliations of the Church; as, for instance, to the solemn decree of November 24, A.D. 1789, in which the National Assembly of France pronounced all ecclesiastical estates to be national property. It was thus that the Revolution in the name of civilization inherited the spoils of Feudalism.

CXL. The second maxim which shielded the Church from the corruption consequent on worldly possessions was, that " where she had such possessions, they should have a common administration and be dispensed in common to all." Thus the primitive Christians laid the price of their houses and fields which they had sold at the Apostles' feet, and it was dispensed to the faithful according to their several needs, " prout cuique opus erat."[2]

[1] The tenant could not call his land a property, "because the tenants or serfs of the glebe were styled 'mainmort,' inasmuch as they could hold no personal property " (Cibrario, Dell' economia del medio evo, L. iii. c. iii.).
[2] Acts iv. 35.

CHAP. V. Surely this community of goods greatly promoted love and unity, both between believers generally, and between the clergy and the faithful! "The multitude of them that believed were of one heart and of one soul: neither said any of them that ought of the things which he possessed was his own, but they had all things in common."[1] The pleasing spectacle of this fraternal love, hitherto unknown, led the Hebrew Philo of Alexandria, to write its eulogy. The saints always considered it as the best illustration of evangelical love. And history shows how St. Chrysostom desired to introduce it among his flock at Constantinople; while Horace describes a somewhat similar state of things as the perfection of Rome's happiest times, when he says that private expenditure was small, but that of the community large.[2]

CXLI. This principle was long observed among the clergy. The Bishops, as successors of the Apostles, were depositaries of all the Church's goods. These they distributed, for the most part, every month; according to the needs of their clergy. No one held any personal property. When, in the year 321, Constantine permitted the Church to inherit property by testamentary benefactions, he worded the permission thus: "Let

[1] Acts iv. 32. [2] Carm. ii. 15.

in the fourth and fifth centuries. 313

each one be free to leave at his death such property as he thinks fit to the holy and venerable Council of the Catholic Church."[1]

Later, as we see by a rescript of the fifth century, attributed to the holy Pope Gelasius, the Church expressly forbade any separate estate to be ceded to any individual ecclesiastic, in order that ecclesiastical property might be better administered and preserved.[2] The same spirit dictated a law of Valentinian, forbidding all legacies or inheritances to individuals among the secular or regular clergy.[3] Of this law the good men of that period, such as St. Ambrose or St. Jerome, did not complain. They did greatly complain of the clergy who to their shame had caused its enactment. " I do not lament the law," says Jerome, " but I lament that we deserve it. The cautery is excellent, but why is there the wound to need cauterizing ? Let there be an heir, but let it be the mother of the children, that is, the Church ; let her who brought forth the flock,

[1] Cod. Theod., lib. xvi. De Episcopis, Ecclesiis et clericis, tit. ii. § 4.
[2] Gratianus, Caus. xii., Quæst. ii. c. xxiii. " Nec cuiquam clerico pro portione sua aliquod solum Ecclesiæ putetis esse deputandum, ne per incuriam et negligentiam minuatur : sed omnis pensionis summam ex omnibus prædiis rusticis urbanisque collectum ad Antistitem deferatis."
[3] Cod. Theod., lib. xvi. tit. ii. § 20 (ed. Goth. vol. vi. p. 48).

Growth of separate benefices.

CHAP. V. who nourished and pastured it, be its heir.' Why should we interpose between the mother and the children?"[1] Nor would the saint permit individuals among the clergy or the monks to intervene between the Church as depositary of pious offerings, and her children, to whom she distributed them as need might require. It is hard to say to what extent this community of goods, administered by Episcopal wisdom with the counsel of the clergy,[2] contributed to preserve a wholesome unity, both among the clergy themselves, and between the clergy and the people.

CXLII. But as the Gospel spread into villages, and it became necessary to establish country churches at a distance from the Cathedrals, a separate maintenance was required for every such church.[3] This arrangement was at first excep-

[1] Ep. ad Nepotianum, §6. St. Ambrose alludes to this law when he says, "Quod, ego non ut querar, sed ut sciant quid non querar, comprehendi ; malo enim nos pecuniâ minores esse, quam gratiâ." He adds, "The Church's possessions belong to the poor. Count how many captives she has redeemed, how many poor she has fed, how many exiles she has pensioned" (Ep. Class i. Ep. xvii.).

[2] Berardi says, "Etenim ea ætate, quotiescumque negotium ecclesiasticum peragendum erat, Episcopus cleri consilium, convocata synodo, expetebat" (Gratiani Canones, etc., De Gelasio., c. xlvi.).

[3] "Postea vero primum factum, ut presbyteris ruralibus, quos parochos adpellabant, bonorum administrationem concederent, eorumdemque exemplo presbyteris illis, qui in civitatibus titulos, sive ecclesias tegere dicebantur. Id etiam totum constat ex

tional. Temporary incomes were allotted to monasteries, to deserving clergy, and to pilgrims, as Pope Symmachus had ordered in the sixth century.[1] Hence the name "precarii."[2] But the primitive customs as to the tenure, administration, and use of ecclesiastical property gradually died out. The clergy held separate benefices. As a consequence, the common life among the clergy gradually disappeared. Its loss was greatly regretted by the Church, and she repeatedly but ineffectually strove to restore it, by laws and canons. But the obstacle to her doing so was again the barbarous feudal system.

CXLIII. Feudalism involves personal service, which in itself is unsuited to a clergyman's character, since he ought to be his own master. But a vassal's property was further subject to a special *servitus*, in consequence of the personal service required of the usufructuary. This was another ground of intrinsic opposition to the

Concilio Agathensi, cui præfuit idem Cæsarius anno 506, præsertim vero Can. 32, et 33 (Gratiani Decreti Pars Secunda Caus. xii., Quæst. 2, c. 53 and Berardi, *ibid.*).

[1] Gratianus, Decreti Pars Secunda Caus. xvi., Quæst. i. c. 61.

[2] A recent author observes that at first the enjoyment of a special property was never conceded to individuals, except where no congregation of priests existed, "as their community life preserved the ancient state of things for some time" (Walter, Manual of Ecclesiastical Law, § 241).

spirit of the Church, and of the clerical office. For the personality of Christ's ministers altogether disappears in the Divine constitution which He left to His Church. They do not represent themselves, but the Church. The whole Church acts by their means, and in all their ministrations by the Power of her Head. They, as organs, have no more a distinct personality than the foot or the hand, or any other member of the human body. Thus a perfect mystical unity is the very foundation of this admirable constitution. And just as, if the members of the human body sought each to become independent, the body would lose its proportions and its beauty, and become a monster, or, more truly, would cease to exist, so is it with the Church. But it was precisely this which the feudal system attempted to effect. Each vassal can represent only himself and the person whose vassal he is, with his possessions. Thus this vassalage is a service rendered to a temporal lord, with an object and duty essentially temporal and secular. As long as it was a question of free possessions, they might be used for spiritual purposes, as, indeed, had always been the case with the free property of the Church. It was administered and dispensed both theoretically and practically for charitable purposes. By it Divine worship was maintained and the ministers of the sanctuary were supported. The hands of the poor, the the widow, leper, the slave, the pilgrim, and of all who suffered were the precious caskets wherein the Church stored her treasures, safe from human rapacity. In so doing the Mother of the faithful did not go beyond the requirements of the Church's ministry, which is one of maternal love and of Christian pity.[1] But the vassal, the servant who is constrained to consider his lord's service, and to employ his possessions for his benefit, sets out with an essentially different aim. His aim is no longer ecclesiastical ; he is no longer a " good soldier of Jesus Christ ; " he, despite the Apostolic precept, is " entangled [2] with the affairs of this life." He is no longer representative only of the Church ; he is an isolated individual ; he

[1] It will be desirable here to call the reader's attention to the opinion expressed upon this subject by an author of the fifth century, Julianus Pomerius ; he says, "Nunc autem quod Christiani temporis sacerdotes magis sustinent quam curant possessiones Ecclesiæ, etiam in hoc, Deo serviunt ; quia si Dei sunt ea quæ conferuntur Ecclesiæ, *Dei opus agit*, qui res Deo consecratas, non alicujus cupiditatis, sed fidelissimæ dispensationis intentione non deserit. Quapropter possessiones quas oblatas a populo suscipiunt sacerdotes, *non sunt inter res mundi deputari credendæ, sed Dei*" (De Vita Contemplativâ, L. ii. c. xvi. 4).

[2] "Thou therefore endure hardness, as a good soldier of Jesus Christ. No man that warreth entangleth himself with the affairs of this life" (2 Tim. ii. 3, 4).

is like any one else; he is a courtier, who, ever bearing in mind his lord's honour and interests, must hold his court, maintain a certain personal pomp and display, or even put himself at the head of his soldiers. He must, in short, play the count or the baron in his own and his lord's interests; he cannot be simply the Bishop, seeking only the welfare of the Church, and of his people, as intimately associated with him.

CXLIV. This unnatural transformation of Churchmen impressed the mediæval Bishops with a sense of their *individuality*. It weakened their sense of unity in the body of the Episcopate and of the clergy. It loosened the bonds which in happier times rendered the Church so glorious and so mighty through Christ for good. It divided dioceses like states and baronies. It divided and subdivided ecclesiastical possessions; and these, as they were united or divided, implied or caused the moral union or division of their possessors. At last these possessions were entirely cut up into individual tenures. Hence the origin of the word "benefice," which comes from the feudal vocabulary; the first benefices were lands granted by the prince to be held by his courtiers and comrades in guerdon for their services.

CXLV. It is to be observed that when an

idea or a form impresses itself powerfully on the intelligence and imagination of men, it becomes the norm or model by which are shaped those thoughts and actions that can take the impression; while those which cannot, still range themselves in a subordinate position, and group around it, as handmaids round their mistress. Thus in the Church's primitive times, the great idea of Unity was graven on every Christian mind; and the thoughts and words of the faithful and the clergy, the ecclesiastical arrangements and the disposition of property, all were influenced and illuminated by the ruling idea of the Unity of Christ. But feudalism was based upon an altogether opposite idea, namely, on the idea of division, which results from that of individuality, and on the specific idea of individuality which results from that of seigniory. And as the feudal system prevailed in temporal matters, it also impressed its leading idea on the mind of the clergy. Hence the woes of the Church.

CXLVI. The barbarians who conquered Europe had for their leading idea that of force, violence, personal bravery, dominion. Little by little the Church instilled her own antagonistic idea into their rude minds. Hence arose a struggle between the two ideas. And just as when two social bodies governed by opposing ideas are brought face to face, some among them fight openly, each using their own weapons, while others seek to conciliate and combine, yet secretly maintaining a hidden opposition, so was it with the barbarian rulers. On one hand they oppressed the Church, striving to subject her to their idea of overlordship, which was violent, selfish, earthly. On the other hand they almost insensibly received and appropriated the opposite idea, the ministerial, moral, unitive, spiritual idea of the Church. Thus their action was twofold and contradictory; it combined pious deeds and benefactions to the Church, with wicked deeds of despotism most injurious to her, according as one or the other idea prevailed. The same thing occurred among the clergy. One section subdued and taught these wild men by the Gospel message, instilling into their minds the unifying idea of charity; while another section suffered in the struggle and received into itself the opposite idea. So that in the action of the clergy saintly and heroic examples and efforts to maintain the unity of Christ are found in a like contradiction side by side with profanity and irregularity, unworthy complaisance, and selfish tendencies, destructive of unity and all Christian and ecclesiastical communion. The struggle between two ideas and the contradictory action that ensued, both in temporal and ecclesiastical matters, is characteristic of the Middle Ages; it fully explains the events of that period, especially the collisions of the Empire and the Church. The Church cannot perish; her ruling idea cannot be altogether extinguished; inasmuch as Heaven and earth will pass away, but the word of Christ will not pass away. And therefore each time that the ideas of worldly and violent dominion and disunion have asserted themselves in opposition to the Church, and have crept in among the clergy so as to compromise their very existence, the Church has arisen like a giant who awakes from sleep. With unexhausted vigour she has in her extreme peril found means to overthrow her enemy, to force him back from the ground which he had won, and to reassert for herself and for her ministers that principle on which her very life depends.[1]

[1] We have said that any reconciliation of the two ideas of individuality as peculiar to the barbarian rule, and of organic union as peculiar to the Church, is impossible, and that their passing fusion is only apparent; the first often bid fair to annihilate its opponent, but the Church ever rose anew with fresh strength and power. Dare we then predict that there will never be peace between the temporal and spiritual powers? God forbid so fatal a prediction. Peace may be had, and will be had, but on one condition only, namely, that the temporal power should banish the idea of *individuality*, a mere relic of barbarism and feudalism, and

Y

322 Church possessions treated as private property.

CHAP. V. CXLVII. Now this explains the sudden vicissitudes of ecclesiastical property. Mediæval suzerains, acting according to their principle of individuality, were not content with considering the freeholds of the Church as fiefs. They actually seized them, treated them as their own property, disposed of them to the laity, alienated them. These usurpations naturally fomented discord between them and the Church. She resisted the abuse with conciliar enactments, Papal laws, and canonical penalties.

Those Prelates who were lieges to the prince, and who had imbibed the principle of individuality with their fiefs, imitated their leaders, and disposed of ecclesiastical property as if it had been their own. They forgot that it was common property; they enfeoffed it, exchanged it, gave it to laymen, expended it in pomp, in luxury, in enjoyments, armies and contests. To this the Church

build itself up anew on the Church's principle which cannot fail—the principle of organic Christian unity among men. This is the only possible reconciliation ; not of the two principles which cannot be reconciled, but of the two orders—temporal and spiritual, which are perfectly reconcileable. Thus all temporal seigniorial governments should be changed into *Civil Societies.* After nearly a thousand years' struggle, is not this desirable change now approaching? All European society tends that way. Thus the long struggle which Providence permitted, and which assumed the form of a conflict between the lay and ecclesiastical powers (though not such really), will end in a perfect and finished work.

opposed numerous canons and decrees, which only riveted still closer the chains of alienation, administration and disposition of property; while they loosened the bond between the Prelates and the inferior clergy, whom the Church was forced to protect by many minute provisions, against the arbitrary dealings and cruelty of their superiors. Hence the struggle we so often witness now between Chapters and Bishops, and the difficulty of removing parish priests, which, to a great extent, deprives the Bishops of the power to apply a prompt remedy to the scandals and spiritual troubles of the people.

CXLVIII. But inasmuch as the Divine Founder of the Church willed that the principle of a common ecclesiastical property should not perish, either as regards its possession, its administration, or its enjoyment, He saw fit to raise up and multiply religious orders and monasticism, which made express and public profession of this wholesome principle. And the faithful, guided by that Christian instinct which never fails them, were from that hour more inclined to carry their gifts and oblations to the regular clergy, who preserved rigidly the ancient principle, than to the secular clergy. So that when the third Lateran Council, A.D. 1179, enforced the restitution of tithes alienated to the laity, these tithes were for the most part given up to monasteries, and not to the Churches to which they had belonged. This was practically permitted by the Popes themselves, provided it was done with Episcopal consent.[1]

CXLIX. A third and precious maxim of antiquity was that " the clergy should only use that which was really necessary for their maintenance, and that the rest of the Church's goods should be employed in pious works, especially in relieving the poor." Christ had founded the Apostolate on poverty, and on that trust in Providence which had moved the faithful to support their teachers in the gospel. He had Himself given a sublime example. " The foxes have holes, and the birds of the air have nests, but the Son of Man hath not where to lay His Head."[2] Such was the prospect He held out to those who would follow Him. And Peter had left even his humble nets to follow his Master. The Apostolic College had a common purse, wherein the oblations of the faithful were deposited; thus setting forth what the Church was to do, and what she did. When the paralytic asked alms, Peter was able to answer, " Silver and

---

[1] Decret., Greg., L. iii. tit. x. c. vii.; L. v. tit. xxxiii. c. iii. and vi.; L. iii. tit. xiii. c. ii. § 2.
[2] St. Matt. viii. 20; St. Luke ix. 58.

gold have I none."[1] But necessaries were insured to the Apostles by the right of living in the houses of the faithful who received them, and who, in so doing, received more than they gave. Thus St. Paul taught his disciple Timothy that "Godliness with contentment is great gain. For we brought nothing into this world, and it is certain we can carry nothing out. And having food and raiment, let us be therewith content."[2] Thus to enter the ranks of the clergy, in the better days of the Church, was equivalent to a profession of evangelical poverty.[3] In those days the expression, *secular* clergy, was not invented; it only appeared in that decay of ancient discipline, when apparently even the world might have its own clergy. For long the profession of poverty continued to be the ornament of the priesthood, so that those who were admitted into it generally resigned their own property, or gave it away among the poor, because, as says Isidore of Pelusium, "tum voluntariâ

---

[1] Acts iii. 6. [2] 1 Tim. vi. 6-8.
[3] We have it on the express authority of Julianus Pomerius, who writes, "Itaque sacerdos, cui dispensationis cura commissa est, non solum sine cupiditate, sed etiam cum laude pietatis, accipit a populo dispensanda et fideliter dispensat accepta; *qui omnia sua, aut pauperibus distribuit, aut ecclesiæ rebus adjungit, et se in numero pauperum, paupertatis amore, constituit; ita ut unde pauperibus subministrat, inde et ipse tamquam pauper voluntarius vivat*" (De Vita Contemplativa, lib. ii. c. xi.).

CHAP. V. paupertate gloriabantur."[1] The administration and dispensation of the Church's possessions came to be entrusted to these upright and disinterested men, as guardians of the treasures of the poor. Julianus Pomerius, after citing as instances of voluntary poverty two great Bishops, Paulinus of Nola and Hilary of Arles,—who being rich men had made themselves poor for Christ's sake,—goes on to say, "From which it is easy to see that such men—who that they might be Christ's disciples, renounced all that they possessed—convinced that the Church's riches are no other than the prayers of the faithful, the satisfaction for sins, and the patrimony of the poor, did not use property for private purposes, as though it was their own, but dispensed it to the poor, as being held only in trust. That which the Church has, she has in common with those who have nothing, and therefore she may not give to those who already have enough of their own, since to give it to any who already have is simply to throw it away."[2] Thus the clergy took their means of living from the common fund;

[1] Lib. v. ep. 21.
[2] De Vita Contemplativa, lib. ii. c. ix. The following sentence is worthy of note, " Quod habet Ecclesia cum omnibus nihil habentibus habet commune ; " as proving that at that time the Church's possessions were considered as belonging to the community, not to individuals.

as they formed a part of those poor to whom that fund appertained. The Bishop was first among the poor, and while he dispensed the common fund to the poor, it was but just that he should take a portion for himself[1] and for the clergy under him. This great principle was so deeply rooted in the public mind that it was not thought seemly for a priest who retained any possessions of his own to live by the Church's funds. Since he was not in need, he had no right to them; he would be encroaching on the rights of the poor. This is asserted by the fifth-century author already cited: "Those who, having possessions of their own, yet seek to receive something, cannot without great guilt receive any of that which of right belongs to the poor. Of a truth the Holy Spirit hath said of the priesthood:[2] 'They shall eat of the sins of My people.' Now those who have nothing of their own, do not receive sins, but the food which is needful for them; and so those who have possessions, do not receive food of which they have abundance, but they take other men's sins.

---

[1] This maxim is found also in a decree of Gratian, Can. xii. q. 1, cap. xxii., where an Apostolic Canon is quoted: "Ex his autem, quibus Episcopus indiget (*si tamen indiget*) ad suas necessitates et peregrinorum fratrum usus et ipse percipiat, ut nihil ei possit omnino deesse." [Cf. Labbé and Coss. III. Conc. i. pp. 34, 35.—Ed.]

[2] Hosea iv. 8.

CHAP. V. Thus even if the poor, by industry and labour, can avoid taking that which is chiefly due to the weak and sick, they should do so; since if all those who can dispense with assistance take the Church's alms, she cannot succour as she should those who have no other succour. Let those who serve the Church in too carnal a fashion, beware lest they be more anxious for worldly stipends[1] than for eternal rewards. If any minister of the Church has not wherewithal to live, the Church does not give him a reward, but lends him that which is needful; in order that he may receive hereafter that reward of his labours which even in this life, trusting in the promise of the Lord, he awaits with confidence. As for those who having possessions do not claim anything as due to them, and yet live at the Church's cost, it is not for me to describe how great their sin is, in taking the bread of the poor. They who ought to help the Church with their means, burden her with their expenses; they live in the congregation, not as though their duty was to feed the poor, or to lodge guests, but to save their private outlay."[2]

CL. Before the Middle Ages the abuses which were opposed to this generous principle could only

[1] How much less "benefices," a word which implies a gift of a (feudal) lord to whomsoever he will.
[2] De Vita Contempl., lib. ii. c. x.

be partial. For they originated with individuals, and not with Church authority which naturally repudiated them. But how was the principle to be generally maintained when the Church's possessions, losing their primitive character, became feudalized, and all the most eminent ecclesiastics so many feudatories? From that moment the disposal of property was subject to another law and took a new direction. Instead of any longer flowing continually into the hands of the poor, the stream either became stagnant, or flowed back into the hands of the feudal lord. The primitive idea was effaced, or rendered inoperative; the idea of absolute property was substituted for it: the sacred deposits were henceforth subject to depredation.

CLI. This dispersal of the common fund into benefices assigned to individual clergy, deprived the priesthood generally of a human stimulus to a fulfilment of their sacred duties. They no longer received a quota from the Bishop proportioned to their labours or their merits. At the same time they were separated from the Bishop, as they became independent of him in respect of their maintenance;[1] while the bright example of the Church

[1] We learn this from St. Cyprian, who distributes an equal portion to the readers Celerinus and Aurelius as to the priests, "ut et sportulis eisdem cum presbyteris honorentur" (Ep. xxxiv.), and St. Gregory the Great in various letters. Writing to a Bishop,

publicly and ministerially maintaining the poor was lost. With the temporal, the spiritual provision for the poor was also diminished. The Church had specially cared for those poor who depended on her. Through that care they were taught, and stimulated by gratitude to know, venerate, and love the Church, who became their mother in a twofold sense. Hence arose the secularization of charitable works, which, in the paucity of clergy, were undertaken by separate institutions. In these, little by little the laity came to take a chief part. In this state of things it doubtless pleased Divine Providence to ordain that many good Christians grew more fervent in good works. But the mischief was that, as these works were no longer animated by a Church spirit, or by the wisdom which religion inspires, they became more earthly; they lost the religious character which refined them and enabled them to promote the salvation of souls. Thus ancient is the origin of modern philanthropy. This loss, however, will be repaired when the clergy once more become generous and unselfish. When that wished-for time comes (and it seems to be

he says, "De reditibus Ecclesiæ, quartam in integro portionem Ecclesiæ tuæ clericis, secundum meritum vel officium, sive laborem suum, ut ipse unicuique dandum perspexeris, [dare prospexeris] sive aliqua præbere debeas tarditate" (Lib. xiii. ep. xliv. ad Joannem Panormitanum Episcopum).

4. Church property devoted to fixed purposes. 331

approaching), the laity will no longer be willingly estranged and divided from the clergy. By this division they forfeit spiritual understanding, and their material works are religiously barren. Whenever the laity and clergy put aside their divisions, and become once more one body in Christ, the co-operation of the laity will be most useful and precious, as the members of our human body are precious to the head. Thus we see that the creation of separate benefices hindered the spontaneous flow of the Church's wealth into the hands of the poor. The duty of almsgiving was divided amongst the holders of benefices, guided by their own wisdom alone and unaided by the Bishops; and thus the poor ceased to be what they had been, a sacred body, watched over by the Church as her special trust.

CLII. The fourth maxim which regulated ecclesiastical property, and prevented it from becoming injurious to the honesty of the clergy, was that " not only such property was to be used for pious and charitable ends, but also, to avoid all danger of arbitrary or selfish expenditure, it was to be portioned out for fixed purposes." As soon as the Church's property became considerable, and grave abuses arose, although they were but partial and accidental, the Church wisely intervened by in-

332 Ancient partition of Church property.

CHAP. V. sisting on an appropriation of her funds to certain defined objects. Thus arose the ancient division of her property into four parts. One was for the Bishop, another for the subordinate clergy, a third for the poor, and the fourth for the maintenance of Divine worship and of the Church's material fabric. This partition is prescribed by the Council of Agde, A.D. 506, and that of Orléans, A.D. 511; and they refer to more ancient Church rules. Gregory the Great frequently alludes to it in his letters.[1] Certainly nothing could be better calculated to obviate the corruption which might attend wealth, than to regulate its employment by precise laws;[2] inasmuch as abuse is inevitable where the use of large property is left to the arbitrary disposal of an individual holding it in trust. Many monasteries have apparently been demoralized and ruined by the fact of their pos-

[1] iv. 11, v. 12, viii. 7, xi. 64. In Spain the portion destined to the poor was united to those of the clergy and Bishop, so that the division was tripartite.

[2] It seems probable that the division was not always into four equal parts, but that the proportion of each part might be varied as necessary. C. Sebast. Berardi, in his work on the Decree of Gratian, refers to a Canon of Pope Gelasius, adding, "In quo sane illud observandum est quadripartitam illam ecclesiasticorum redituum distributionem non adeo rigide esse intelligendum, ut ad proportionem quandam, ut vocant, geometricam, non ad arithmeticam rationem exigatur" (Gratiani Canones, P. ii. c. 51; De Gelasio.)

sessing enormous wealth, without any definite laws as to the first claims on it, so that it has been spent according to the fancy of the Abbots or other superiors, into whose hands it may have fallen.

CLIII. But how could the old and sacred rule be kept up, when once feudalism had entered the Sanctuary? It was to the interest of the feudal lord, or rather of that fierce aristocracy which was the result of the feudal system, that property should accumulate in the hands of the great families, in the hands of the few. This accumulation was the very foundation of the secular power, which consequently opposed the scattering of riches, by an equitable and charitable distribution. The creation of separate benefices became necessary in order to insure the maintenance of the weaker portion of the clergy, who would have perished of hunger and misery if they had not been shielded from the rapacious grasp of the great nobles. Among these the Bishops must be reckoned; for they no longer belonged, as of old, to the people. The early Bishops, though often of noble and wealthy houses, made themselves one with the people, whose poverty they shared, by the fact of becoming Bishops. They now belonged to the class of invading and domineering aristocrats. From

334   5. *"More blessed to give than to receive."*

CHAP. V. that time, the abuse became law; the Church's Canons were evaded by endless verbal quibbles,[1] if not by open infraction and violence. The fourfold division, the fixed destination of Church revenues was considered intolerable. The old principle, together with the spirit which inspired it, had practically been wrecked.

CLIV. The fifth principle with which the Church counteracted the perils of riches in the ages preceding feudalism was, " A generous spirit, free to give, chary to receive." She ever proclaimed boldly the holy but little heeded precept of Christ, "It is more blessed to give than to receive."[2] She continually preached this doctrine as glad tidings to a world enslaved by selfishness; it shone forth in all her acts and proceedings. The Bishops esteemed temporal possessions and their administration as a burdensome weight, which they endured only for charity's sake.[3] There were as

[1] Among other deplorable verbal glosses, or more truly, positive lies, must be included *commendations*. In order to elude the law which forbade one person to accumulate several benefices, they were given *in commendam*, that is, the administration was entrusted to such a person. This was done even with Episcopal and conventual property, which was "commended" to laymen, who enjoyed its revenues undisturbed: much as though a lamb were given to the wolf's care, and specially recommended to his attention! All jurisprudence became perverted by similar iniquitous falsehoods.

[2] Acts xx. 35.

[3] St. Augustine wrote (Ep. cxxvi. § 9), "God is my witness,

yet no laws which threw great difficulties in the way of the alienation of Church possessions; wealth was received with great reserve, and distributed with corresponding freedom. St. Ambrose was wont to refuse such offerings or legacies as might injure the donor's poor relations. "Non quærit," so he wrote, "donum Deus de fame parentum;"[1] and he added, "Misericordia a domestico progredi debet pietatis officio." The Church could do this, in the days when she was free, not yet fettered by a thousand shackles, among which the chief was the so-called protection of the secular arm. One result of the Church's enforced *servitus*, is that she is no longer able to perform those generous acts, which were common among the earlier Bishops, and which made her shine with such moral beauty. I have already referred to St. Augustine and Aurelius on this topic. In one sermon by the great Bishop of Hippo, he defends himself against a current rumour to the effect that "Episcopus Augustinus de bonitate sua donat totum, non suscipit" (a strange accusation!); in consequence of which the people complained that

that I tolerate but do not love all the administration of these ecclesiastical matters with which we have to do, inasmuch as I owe my service to the love of the brethren and the fear of God; so that if I could set them aside without hurt to my office, I would gladly do so."

[1] In Luc. C. xviii.

CHAP. V. no one would give, or leave inheritances any more to the Church of Hippo. Possidius, in his Life of St. Augustine, relates how a certain magnate of Hippo, having formally given a possession to the Church, afterwards repented of his liberality, and asked for it again for his son. St. Augustine restored the gift, refusing even to retain a donation for the poor. But at the same time he set before the covetous man the guilt of his action. It is also told of St. Augustine that, perceiving certain of the subordinate clergy to be envious of the Bishop, in whose hands were the Church's means,[1] he discussed the subject with the people of God, to whom in those days the Bishops communicated everything; setting forth how " he would have preferred to live on the contributions of the people of God, rather than to bear the charge and government of these possessions; and that he was ready to give this charge up to them, so that all God's servants and ministers might live as we read in the Old Testament; they that serve the altar, partaking of the altar. But the laity would in no wise consent." [2]

[1] Human nature is always imperfect, but I wish to distinguish a partial and exceptional error from one that has become a universal custom, damaging the whole social body, and doing away with the principles which govern it.

[2] "Sed nunquam id laici suscipere voluerunt" (Possid. in Vita August., cp. xxiii.).

CLV. St. John Chrysostom tells his people why the Church no longer lived by the accidental collections of the faithful, while yet she accepted donations of permanent property. He says that the clergy were obliged to do this, not for their own sakes, but in order to provide for the poor. The primitive fervour of charity had been lessened among the faithful. "It is by reason of your niggardliness," he says, "that the Church requires what she now has. If every one acted according to the Apostolic laws, her revenue would be in your hearts, which would be a sure and safe deposit, and an inexhaustible treasure. But now that ye lay up treasure on earth, and shut up everything in your coffers, it behoves the Church to make expenditure for the widows, for the virgins, for guests, and for the needs of travellers, or of those who are in chains, as well as for the distress of others who are maimed or mutilated, and for many other purposes. What is she to do"?[1]

CLVI. Who would not lament that such a change should have supervened in the ages of destruction and barbarism which succeeded in the Church; and that a clergy, once of such a noble temper, so liberal and so full of charity, should

[1] Hom. xxi. in Ep. ad Cor.

have fallen so far below its early condition as to deserve the stigma of the words

"In cui usa avarizia il suo soperchio!"

Let us examine two causes of this. One is the deeds of barbarian princes; the other the measures which the Church was constrained to take in her own defence, in order to avert a still greater evil.

CLVII. Feudalism, as we have seen, had changed the character of ecclesiastical property, so that it was frequently alienated, and ceded to laymen by sovereigns, and even by feudal prelates themselves. The Church was obliged to oppose the abuse by means of her laws; and from that time forward her legislation began to take a direction altogether contrary to the ancient principle. It facilitated as much as possible the Church's acquisition and preservation of temporal property, and threw obstacles in the way of any alienation of it. Legislators are wont to propose measures of improvement when an abuse is greatest. In this case it was excessive. But it often happens that when an abuse has been remedied as far as possible, they do more than is wanted. Or they fail to weigh duly the mischief which may arise from the legislation itself, or the good which may be forfeited by an increased restriction of liberty. Thus abuse and good use are linked together; or, as it sometimes happens, the legislation whose rightful Chap. V. aim was the extermination of an abuse, survives the abuse after its suppression, and presses heavily on society when the cause which justified it has ceased to exist. In the case we are considering it was no doubt a great evil that ecclesiastical wealth should be diverted from its right destination, applied to profane uses, and bestowed as the reward of secular services. It thus failed to fulfil the pious intentions of those who had offered it to God. But at the same time it was a great gain that the Bishops with their clergy should be able to renounce, when it was desirable, offerings and inheritances bestowed on the Church; that they should be able, without excessive difficulty and formalities, to sell her property, and distribute it to such as had need, so that the Church might be able to relieve all the ills to which mankind is liable. The Church is rich enough, if she has the treasure of charity, and an ample flow of benevolence: she is happy enough when she can say with St. Ambrose, "Aurum Ecclesia habet, non ut servet, sed ut eroget, et subveniat in necessitatibus."[1] Surely, then, it is most grievous, and

[1] The "Corpus Juris Canonici" contains the grand doctrine, held by St. Ambrose and other Fathers, respecting the spirit of liberality with which the Church should be ready to break even her precious vessels in order to succour the living vessels which

very damaging to the Church's true interests, when room is given for the scandal that her clergy's hands are ever open to receive, but unready to give. Undoubtedly the thought that whatever flows into the Church's treasury will never again issue forth is saddening. It breeds contempt, excites envy, and extinguishes liberality among the faithful. It produces a suspicion that the Church is hoarding treasures which the people need in order to maintain their families, to extend commerce, and to defend the State. It gives ground for government interference with the disposal of ecclesiastical property, through the dishonourable laws of mortmain. It widens the breach between the people and the Church and clergy. It gives rise to unbelief, provokes the calumnies of bad men, and too often under their influence kindles the fury of the multitude, or the cupidity of the powerful, so that they violently break open the Church's treasuries in search of gold, and even tear down the gates of the Sanctuary to rob it of its wealth. I cannot but believe it to be much more desirable, much more useful for the Church of God not to give occasion for any such disasters, than to abound in temporal

are redeemed by the Blood of Christ. See Gratian, Caus. xii. Q. ii. C. lxx. lxxi.

wealth, or to prevent the possibility of alienating, even inconsiderately, some part of her possessions.

CLVIII. Little by little the Church succeeded in restraining her barbarian conquerors by means of admonitions, of Canons, and of penalties, so that they should not squander the ecclesiastical patrimony at their will. But it must be borne in mind that the secular power did not only injure the Church by violence and depredation. It inflicted a yet greater injury through its very bounties, and through its legislation, which extended a secular and profane guardianship and protection to the Church and her property. Civil government has not an ecclesiastical instinct, and whenever it puts forth a hand upon the Sanctuary, its touch chills and enfeebles. Charlemagne and Otho I. favoured the Church. But their unfortunate gift of fiefs was suggested to them not solely by devotion to the Church, but also by the policy which sought both to weaken the power of the nobles, and to subject the Bishops to themselves. It was a fatal bait by which the clergy were caught. From that hour the secular power continually concerned itself with the Church, until at last its favours and caresses deprived her of liberty, which is as necessary to her as the very air she breathes. How can a temporal government aid the Church except by material force, which is its only natural instrument of action? But violence is altogether opposed to the spirit of the Church; we shrink with horror from a picture of the Church armed with chains, fetters, and the axe. What a cruel misrepresentation, by which not bad men only, but the good are repelled! Moreover the temporal power neither knows nor respects the limits of its protection. Accustomed to command, it seeks to command wherever it can; incapable of appreciating the real good of the Church, it claims to be a judge of what that good is, and makes it consist solely in worldly advantages. It treats the administration of the Church's property on the same principle as its own, ignoring the wide difference which exists between them; it accumulates as much, and spends as little as it can; it enriches the Church, if necessary, even with privileges and immunities, extending to it an exceptional and exaggerated protection, sometimes opposed to justice, and to civil equality, and always odious to the people who have no share in it.[1] In this

[1] The immunity from taxation should be viewed from two different periods of history, since all European States have undergone a complete transmutation between their foundation and the present time. In the first period they were *seigniories*, and the tributes levied on the subjects were the private property of the prince

if the Church cannot control her property.

way the rule of readiness to give, and chariness to receive, which intrinsically belongs to the Church, becomes practically impossible, her possessions being no longer at her own disposal, but subject to the lay power.

who ruled and maintained the State on his own account; so that when he remitted tribute, he disposed of what was his own; and thus the nobles and ecclesiastics were exempt. But slowly, the secret influence of Christianity and of the Popes changed these European States into true *Civil Societies.* And now the question arises whether it is just that in a civil society the Church should be exempt from public charges. On the hypothesis that her property does not exceed that which is needed for the maintenance of the clergy, or that any surplus is given to the poor, such a privilege would not be unjust. But all property which exceeds these demands, and is not, as formerly, applied to benevolent purposes, should in all reason pay tribute like any other. Such a course would certainly be the most respectable; and even profitable to the Church herself. The formalities required for the alienation of ecclesiastical property were multiplied over and above those which were necessary in that of ordinary property; for instance, the years of prescription were prolonged: while, on the other hand, the ordinary proofs of validity required for wills were diminished when the heritage went to the Church. If these privileges are looked upon as a defence against the frauds employed more extensively against the Church than against private individuals, they cannot be blamed; and from another point of view, some such rules may even be praised as an emendation of the civil law, making way for a more equitable system for all men alike. The formalities required in proof of the validity of a will by the Roman law were excessive. The Church repealed these as concerned ecclesiastical property, and thus increased the general freedom. But the laws once amended, it is not desirable that the Church should be privileged in worldly matters; enough if she retains her privilege, or more truly her sacred and inviolable right of liberty— full liberty, not only to receive and administer the offerings, past or present, of the faithful, but also to dispose of her property in accordance with the spirit of charity which animates and rules her.

6. *Expenditure subject to public scrutiny.*

CLIX. The Church again exhibited her elevation of purpose in her sixth principle, which was " a desire that the disposal of her property should be known publicly." This principle was carried out in primitive times. We have already seen how the early Bishops took counsel in all things with their people and their clergy; and this they did with respect to temporal as well as spiritual matters. Furthermore, the priests and deacons who administered Church property were necessarily elected by the Christian people, according to Apostolic tradition, as persons known and trusted by the faithful.[1] With what delicacy St. Paul suggests to the Corinthians that they should themselves choose the bearers of their alms sent to the needy Christians of Jerusalem! " Upon the first day of the week let every one of you lay by him in store, as God hath prospered him, that there be no gatherings when I come. And when I come, whomsoever ye shall approve by your letters, them

---

[1] When the first Deacons were appointed, the Apostles called the multitude of disciples, and said, "Brethren, look ye out among you seven men of honest report, full of the Holy Ghost and of wisdom, whom we may appoint over this business" (Acts vi. 2, 3). They left the selection to the multitude, "look ye out," while they retained to themselves only the confirmation and ordination of those selected ; thus using as lightly as possible the ample powers which they had received from Christ. Surely such holy prudence should be a model to all Prelates !

will I send to bring your liberality unto Jerusalem. And if it be meet that I go also, they shall go with me."[1] He was both Apostle and Bishop; he had full powers; yet he would not select the almsbearers, but let the people choose for themselves. "All things are lawful unto me, but all things are not expedient."[2] Would they have mistrusted the Apostle? No; but that was not enough. The Apostle abstained as far as possible from interfering in temporal matters. Reserving his Apostolic powers for necessary occasions, he left the people free as to the rest. It is a natural and just satisfaction for the people that they should be able to do something; that they should see with their own eyes, use their judgment, share in the general interest, and help to forward it. In the same spirit St. Chrysostom did not shrink from offering to give account to his people of the employment which he made of the Church's revenues: "We are also ready to give an account to you."[3] The early Bishops acted generally in the same spirit.

CLX. It is not enough that Church property be conscientiously administered: nor will an account sent in only to her rulers satisfy Christians

---

[1] 1 Cor. xvi. 2–4.   [2] 1 Cor. vi. 12.
[3] In Ep. ad Cor., Hom. xxi.

who have piously given of their substance to the Church. It would be a great advantage to the Church, if the application of her property, and especially when held by religious orders, were determined, with all possible precision, by wise laws of her own making. A suitable amount, neither too large nor too small, would be assigned to each purpose ; and an annual account would be published, so that all the world might know clearly how much had been received and expended. Thus the faithful would be able to give expression to their approval or disapproval of the disposal of the Church's revenues. The government would also have all the information it needed. It is assuredly neither good nor expedient that the justice and charity with which the Church directs the administration of her property should remain hidden under a bushel; she should, on the contrary, shine as a light set on a candlestick. Such a measure would conciliate the minds of the faithful. Such an instructive example would influence the world. Her ministers, supported by public opinion, would not fail through weakness, when under temptation. Men are much less prone to open than to concealed sin ; and the necessity of rendering a public account to the faithful, and to the world in

7. *Faithful administration of Church property.* 347

general, would quicken the consciences of any who are inactive for want of stimulus, and would show the importance of filling all ecclesiastical offices with men of thorough rectitude and true piety.

CLXI. The seventh and last principle to be noticed was that "the Church should administer her own property with the utmost vigilance and faithfulness." This she has ever inculcated on those to whom she has entrusted any administration, on the ground that her substance belonged to God and His poor, and that to squander it by carelessness or sloth was sacrilege. This principle is of the more importance, since its neglect has given a pretext to governments for interfering, and thus perpetuating the *servitus* of the Church and her possessions.

CLXII. It is true that the Church, often persecuted and oppressed, always struggling with the temporal power whether it were friend or enemy, and burthened with the arduous care of souls, had never leisure to perfect the system of her administration, or to establish a well-organized system with respect to her property. If we consider how much she has received during the course of centuries, and how much she has lost from lack of a vigilant and economical administration, it is evident that she would be very differently circumstanced now, had her property always been wisely managed. But human strength is limited. It can never achieve two separate undertakings simultaneously, even although they may be closely allied. And the spiritual labours of the Church must necessarily have absorbed nearly all her attention. She could not therefore devote much care to the well-being of her temporal interests until the more important part of her discipline, which concerns the good of souls, was first, fully established; or until experience had demonstrated what great mischief might accrue to her spiritual interests through serious neglect of her temporal affairs. That attention to her temporal concerns was at first neither possible nor expedient, seems to be taught by the example of our Lord, Who permitted a faithless administrator to remain among His own Apostles, possibly as a warning that they were not to be distracted from spiritual interests, even by the danger of temporal loss.

And here I close my remarks with a conclusion which follows from the evidence produced; namely, that when Pascal II. magnanimously proposed to renounce feudal property, he put the axe to the root of the evil tree. But the times were too diseased to bear so strong a remedy.

CLXIII. This work, begun in the year 1832, and finished in the year following, was laid aside in the author's study, and all but forgotten. The times did not seem propitious for the publication of what had been written rather as a relief to his own soul, which groaned under the afflictions of the Church of God, than for any other object. But now (1846) that the Invisible Head of the Church has placed a Pope in St. Peter's Chair who seems destined to renew our failing life, and to give to the Church a fresh impulse which will lead her in a new and glorious course, the author calls to mind these forsaken papers, and no longer shrinks from entrusting them to the hands of friends who, in bygone days, shared his sorrows, as they now share his brighter hopes.

APPENDIX.

ON THE ELECTION OF BISHOPS BY CLERGY AND PEOPLE.

LETTER I.

Stresa, June 8, 1848.

REVEREND SIR,

I am desirous of thanking you for the honourable mention which you have made, in your valuable journal, of the little work published by me recently at Milan, under the title, "La Costituzione secondo la Giustizia sociale," etc. Instead of offering barren thanks, allow me to profit by this opportunity to explain more fully my opinion on the point to which you allude when you say that I should like to "restore the democratic element even to ecclesiastical government."

Everywhere I love union, and hate discord. For union is charity; or, more correctly, charity is real union. It was inculcated by our Divine Master upon individuals no less than upon all human societies. Loving the people most heartily, I specially love their union with the clergy. By this I do not mean that the people ought to have a direct share in the Church's government: that, I know full well, was entrusted by Jesus Christ to the Apostles and their successors the Bishops, who form a beautiful and united hierarchy, which centres in the Primacy left by St. Peter as an inheritance to the Popes. The people's share can only be that of charity and counsel, as when fathers and sons correspond.

It was to such a share as this that I alluded when, in the

APPENDIX. little work above-mentioned, I proposed as a healing, and indeed as a necessary, remedy for our evils, that we should return to the ancient custom of electing Bishops, by the clergy and people. This custom only gave the people an opportunity of expressing their wishes about the candidates, of honouring them by their testimony, and of accepting the elected Bishop with confidence. I added that this form of election, which is confirmed by innumerable Canons and Councils, is of Divine right. St. Cyprian says in his sixty-eighth Epistle, "Quod et ipsum videmus de divina auctoritate descendere, ut sacerdos, plebe præsente, sub omnium oculis deligatur, et dignus atque idoneus publico judicio ac testimonio comprobetur."

In order to make my meaning quite clear, I would add here that I am not speaking of a *Divine constitutive right*, but of a *Divine moral right*. These are two altogether different things. The infraction of the latter does not involve invalidity. Therefore those Bishops who are nominated by civil governments are legitimate Pastors, since they are confirmed and commissioned by the Pope, as is defined by the Council of Trent (Sess. xxiii. c. 8). This distinction between the Divine constitutive right and the Divine moral right will serve to reconcile the different opinions expressed on this question by various authors.

The essential element of Divine *constitutive* right in the institution of Bishops is to be found in their consecration and in the mission given them by the Church. These two things are altogether independent of the people and of all lay power, as the Council of Trent teaches: "Docet insuper sacrosancta Synodus in ordinatione Episcoporum, sacerdotum, et cæterorum ordinum, nec populi nec cujusvis sæcularis potestatis, et magistratus consensum, sive vocationem, sive auctoritatem ita requiri, ut sine ea irrita sit ordinatio: quin potius decernit, eos qui tantummodo a populo aut sæculari potestate ac magistratu vocati et instituti, ad hæc ministeria exercenda adscendunt, ut qui ea propria temeritate sibi sumunt, omnes non Ecclesiæ ministros, sed fures et latrones per ostium non ingressos, habendos esse" (Sess. xxiii. cap. iv.).

But let us turn to the Divine *moral* right, and let us see how at the present time this is injured by the continuance of the irregular election of Bishops. Such irregularity is no longer necessary, and there can be no fear that our pious monarchs, who have seen fit to make so many concessions to their subjects, would be angry with the Church if she were to reassert her rights in all their fulness. The Divine moral right, then, as to the election of the Pastors of the Church, enacts:—

I. That these elections be made freely by the Church, that is, by ecclesiastical authority. But is not this liberty enormously restricted and diminished when the right of nomination is ceded to the secular power? How can the Church assure herself that the worthiest man, and he in whom the people have most confidence, will be elected? What guarantee does or can the lay power give her? Any diminution of the Church's liberty in the choice of her Pastors, wounds the Church's Divine moral right; for Jesus Christ created her free and independent. So that in our time, when it is quite possible, it is convenient that her liberty be at once reaffirmed and reinstated in this particular.

II. That the Christian people should have a voice in the elections, that their testimony should be received; and that they should not be forced, even morally, to accept a Pastor in whom they have no confidence, and who may be unknown to them by look, by name, by works, even by repute. For our Lord says that the sheep know their shepherd (St. John x. 4). I do not say how this is to be carried out: that is a further question; what the best way is must be matter for consideration. But, meanwhile, it is clear that there can be no impossibility in finding it at a time when the people elect their parliamentary representatives without difficulty. All I seek to establish is, that such a limited share in Episcopal elections is of Divine right as well as of natural right; that is to say, that it proceeds from the nature of the institution of Pastors. St. Athanasius refers to Apostolic tradition when, in order to prove that Gregory had unduly invaded the Church of Alexandria, he says that the election was not conducted " *secundum verba Pauli* congregatis populis et spiritu ordinantium cum virtute Domini nostri Jesu Christi" (Ep. ad Ep. Orthod., §. 2); so that the opinion set forth by certain authors, founded on a passage of St. Jerome, alluding to the priests and omitting the people, that the first Bishops of Alexandria were appointed regardless of the people, will not bear investigation, as undoubtedly St. Athanasius must have known the traditions of his own Church better than any one else. Moreover, the people do not elect the Bishops, and St. Jerome is speaking solely and briefly of the *election*. It is enough that the people accept willingly, and recognize the election. Thus Alexander Natalis writes: "De traditione *Divina* et Apostolica observatione descendit, quod populus in electionibus sacris suffragetur suo testimonio, concedo; judicio, nego" (Diss. de jure Christianæ plebis; Thesaurus Theologicus Zachariæ xii. p. 614). But where there is a royal nomination, the people practically know nothing of the matter, and can take no share in it, without coming into collision with the supreme authority, and with the physical force of the lay rulers.

It is true that the Church ceded the right of nomination to the sovereigns; but only because she was constrained to do so by hard circumstances, in order to avoid still greater evils. When your life is in danger, you give up your purse readily. But it is none the less certain that theft and assault are prohibited by God's laws.

In a work lately published I have set forth at greater length what share in Episcopal elections belongs to the people; and how urgent the necessity is that the present exceptional form of such elections should be done away with, and the

legitimate Canonical practice be restored. I will therefore say no more here, than that I am, gratefully and respectfully,
Your humble servant,
A. ROSMINI.

LETTER II.

While kindly acknowledging my letter of June 8th, in which I declared the free election of Bishops to be of Divine right, inalienable, unalterable, you invite me to throw light upon the difficulties which present themselves to you as standing in the way of the practical restoration to the Church of this important right.

You think it unlikely that the sovereign will be ready voluntarily to renounce Episcopal nominations, and that it is a very arduous task to decide how to work for such an end without involving the evils of discord. Such difficulties would have been more serious formerly than now: for instance, in the last century. In our own times, it seems to me that they do not exist, or, at any rate, that they may be easily overcome, if the clergy desire it. There are no liberties belonging to the Church which may not be reasserted, if the clergy so will. Physical force must yield to moral force, and that which is just and reasonable is sure to find a suitable practical issue.

At present, I will only allude to your first difficulty. You fear that monarchs will refuse to cede voluntarily the usurped right of Episcopal nominations. I think that such resistance is chiefly caused by the thick veil of ignorance which has for long shrouded the whole subject of Episcopal elections. Let that veil be lifted up, and the light of truth will do the rest.

I believe it is enough to proclaim loudly, so that all,

clergy and laity, may hear, that the election of Bishops by the clergy and people is of Divine right, as I explained in my former letter; that the Church's liberties in general, and this liberty in particular, are of Divine right; and that if, after centuries of struggle in their defence, the Church gave up some part of them, it was in order to avoid still greater evils, in order to put a limit to the still greater usurpations which were threatened by the arrogance of the secular power, which had become absolute in the time of Francis, King of France. It will suffice to publish this fact on the housetops to make known why the restoration of freedom in elections is the first and foremost requirement of the Church at present; to make known to all men, specially to the laity, that this is the only way by which the clergy can be reformed and rendered equal to the exigencies of our day. Not that our existing clergy are deficient in teaching or practice. But both need enlargement. The Evangelical Word should shine with a brighter light in their mouths, in their lives, in the abundance of their good works. Such a revival of the spirit of the Church is desired and called for by all, save the devil and his angels. We must, then, set forth how it is to be attained; we must convince all men that the shortest, the only sure way, is to put an end to the Church's slavery as regards the election of her ministers, and to restore her full liberty.

When once our Christian princes are convinced that they inflict a grievous injury upon the Church of Christ (and it belongs to the clergy so to convince them) by retaining the nomination of Prelates in their own hands, instead of leaving it to the Church herself according to the natural order of things, conscience will make itself heard. And if we might fear that in some cases the appearance of greater temporal power might prevail over conscience, at least I cannot think this of Charles Albert. I believe in his pure intentions, in his piety, in his attachment to the Church and in the influence that the heroic sanctity, of which his ancestors gave him the example, and which is the brightest ornament of his family, must have upon him. I believe that God will bless him if he is a loving son to the Church, if he glories in restoring her freedom, if he makes himself the champion of her liberty. May he prove that God has chosen him as the restorer of justice, as the servant of His eternal Spouse! May he prove another Constantine, a new Charlemagne!

But, while I believe Charles Albert capable of a magnanimous and holy act of justice like the restoration of free action to the Church, whence he would derive imperishable glory, I also believe that this great good is to be largely promoted by the clergy, if they educate public opinion by teaching the people. Why are the clergy assailed by calumnies? Why, but because the Bishops are of royal nomination? The faithful receive them in their dioceses without any knowledge of them, without confidence in them; as, indeed, the diocesan clergy do likewise. A Prelate is thrust upon both priests and people, who must take him as he is. He may be most excellent, but he will have to contend with indifference and even aversion before his possible gifts and virtues can bear good fruit to his flock. Our seminaries are subjects of criticism. Give us Bishops nominated by the clergy and the people, and our seminaries will soon receive a new life. The people are not over respectful to their Pastor; the diocesan clergy themselves are wanting in union with him. But once let the Bishop be elected by the clergy, and accepted by the people, and all this will be set right. Men suspect the Bishops of being creatures of the Court, and consequently opposed to such reforms and liberties as appear to diminish the royal power. However false such a suspicion may be, it exists, and it does serious damage to the Church and to religion. But such a suspicion would be extinct as soon as there was no longer any ground for imagining the Bishop to be a favourite or pensioner of the prince who nominates him.

I could say much more, but that I wish to write briefly. There is not a single point of Church reform that can be demanded, which might not be satisfied through the free election of Bishops. Let the subject only be carefully and popularly treated by learned ecclesiastics; let them explain the highly important consequences of free elections, and we shall soon witness the power of an enlightened opinion urgently calling for this precious liberty. Who can doubt that it will be granted by our princes?

You fear that princes will hold fast that which by threatening worse evils they formerly wrested from the Church, under the idea of securing their own interests, and from their sense of the moral influence of the Bishops upon the people? I do not think that such a theory of increasing the prince's power by sacrificing the liberties of the Church, and of the people, will stand in our times. I believe our princes too wise to err so grossly in their calculations; they cannot be so blind after so many lessons.

Bishops nominated, as at present, by the sovereign, cannot have much influence with the people, especially with free peoples who are especially jealous for their newly acquired freedom. A sovereign cannot reckon much on the influence of Bishops, who, in the eyes of the people, are tainted with an original sin. But matters are yet worse if such Bishops have but little influence with the people on behalf of the monarch who promoted them, and whose partisans they are generally considered; and if they have not much on behalf of the faith, of morals, and of Religion. And can it be for the real interest of a sovereign that his people should be indifferent about religion, misbelievers, neither respecting nor hearkening to their Pastors? No, of a truth; it is contrary to the interests of all; it is thus that princes have been driven from their thrones, and trampled on by mobs. These excesses will occur again, or at least we may continually look for them until both princes and people return to their obedience to their mother the Church. And this will never be while the Bishops are nominated by the sovereign.

If justice is the only solid foundation of thrones, let princes begin by being at least just to the Church, if not generous,—to that Church which existed before them, and which will exist after them. Let them sincerely desire to have impartial, pacific, authoritative arbitrators between themselves and the people, men who are esteemed and loved by both sides. Such they will find in Bishops elected freely, without royal interference. Princes have nothing to fear if they seek only justice: they have much to fear if they seek absolute power. But there can be no greater gain for a great and just prince (as I write these words, I am thinking of Charles Albert) than to be surrounded by men who are the ministers of the God of peace and righteousness, and who will tell him the unvarnished truth. Thiers said of late but too truly to his French constituency, that princes have been ruined because they have grasped too much.

Three centuries have proved that sovereigns (and I include their governments) are not fit to appoint worthy men to the sees of the Church; and that therefore Religion is reduced to the present low ebb. When was the Church ever so barren in men illustrious for their sanctity, their teaching, their energy, their largeness of aim, as during these three centuries, in which the Church has groaned under these usurped elections? No, the system is not good for sovereigns, it is not good for the people, for the general well-being, for liberty, or for the temporal prosperity of the world.

Now that we dare speak freely, and proclaim aloud these facts, they may reach the ears of sovereigns. It may be that, hearing them, they will humbly say, "We have cast bonds around the Church, and God has punished us." It may be that in a quiet hour they will reflect upon the tremendous responsibility which they assume before Jesus Christ in undertaking the nomination of Bishops, when even such moderate authors as St. Alfonso Liguori could say that the sovereign who does not appoint the most worthy priests whom he can find is guilty of mortal sin. What prince can in all good faith affirm that he has always promoted the worthiest man he knew to any vacant see? Will his incapacity to judge be an excuse before our Lord Christ? Neither the sovereign, nor the secular power generally, knows or can know the Church's true needs. They cannot justly appreciate the sublime gifts of the true Pastor; and therefore they are unfit to recognize and select him from amid the multitude, even if human views and interests do not pervert their aim. Let each fulfil his own office : the laity can do their own part admirably, but not that which is peculiar to the Church.

In conclusion, the true interest of princes, both temporal and spiritual, a wide enlightened conception of their interest, urges them to restore to the Church her right of electing her Pastors. I hope they will listen to this advice while it is time. If they do not, it will be seen that the people, seeking their own interests for themselves, and better advised than their sovereigns, will endeavour to wrest power from the hands of the sovereigns and to resume the right of electing their Bishops. This right is as sacred to the people as to the clergy, as we have seen; and it is certainly the best guarantee which they can have of the liberties granted to them in a constitutional government. If at the present moment the Christian people seem to give but little heed to the importance of Episcopal elections, the day will come when they will be fully alive to it, and then at the latest hour they will assuredly recover their liberty.

I have the honour, etc.[1]

[1] It is to be noted that the Giornale Romano, from which P. Ventura quoted this letter in his brochure, "Sui Martiri di Vienna," omitted these last lines.

INDEX.

A

ACHILLAS, St., 54
Adalbert, Bishop, 217
Adon, Bishop, 156
Adrian I., Pope, 169, 177, 241
Adrian VI., Pope, 243
Africa, 82, 83
Agapetus, Pope, 142
Agde, Council of, 332
Aix-la-Chapelle, 177
Albinus, Bishop, 150
Alessandria, 241
Alessandro, Bishop Girolamo, xliii.
Alexander, St., 29, 32, 36, 195
Alexander III., Pope, 241
Alexandria, 36, 37, 40, 52-54, 83
Amastris, Church of, 85
Ambrose, St., 29, 224, 228, 313, 314, 335, 339
America, United States of, 121
Anastasius, Bishop, 139, 144
Anaunia, martyrs of, 84
Andrew, St., 69
Anselm, St., Archbishop, 178, 228, 235
Anselm, St., Bishop, 192, 193, 197, 235, 270
Antioch, 37, 83, 144
—— Council of, 112
Antoninus, Sub-deacon, 148, 188
Apollinaris, 83
Aqui, 150
Aquileia, 82, 83
Aquitaine, 150
Aschaffenburg, Concordat of, 240
Athanasius, St., 32, 141
Arles, Council of, 140
Aristion, 69

Arturicus, Bishop, 186
Aristotle, 9, 62
Astolfus, King of Lombardy, 103
Augustine, St., xliv., xxlv., 10, 82, 83, 88, 89, 173, 334-336
Aurelius, Bishop, 224, 335
Avignon, 167

B

BADIA, Master of Sacred Palace, xliii.
Bâle, 103
Barnabas, St., 134
Basil, St., 82
Basle, Council of, 167, 239
Beauvais, 157, 158, 160, 164
Bede, Venerable, 60
Benedict XII., 167
Benevento, Council of, 236
Berardi, 314, 315, 332
Bernard, St., 61, 235, 256, 257
Bernarius, 156
Bologna, Concordat of, 243
Bonaventura, St., 61
Boniface IX., 167
Bonosus, 82
Bourges, 167
Bruno, 217

C

CÆSAREA, 36
Calixtus II., Pope, 235, 237, 269, 278
Cambrai, 153, 166
Canons, The, of Antioch, 144
—— Châlons-sur-Saône, 149, 306
—— Clermont, 234
—— Constantinople, 153, 154

Canons, The, of Lateran Councils, 63, 172, 252
—— Lyons, 63
—— Meaux, 183
—— Nice, 143, 151
—— Nicea, 90
—— Nîmes, 234
—— Orléans, 145
—— Pope Gelasius, 332
—— Riez, 181
—— Thionville, 152
—— Tours, 234
Canossa, 209, 218, 219
Cantinus, Bishop, 175
Caraffa, Cardinal, xliii.
Carthage, 37, 79
—— Council of, 128
Cato, Bishop, 150
Cedrenus, 179
Celestine I., Pope, 144, 261
Chalcedon, Council of, 181, 182
Châlons-sur-Saône, Council of, 149, 307
Charlemagne, 169, 171, 176, 177, 241, 294, 341
Charles, St., 59
Charles V., Emperor, 243, 245
Charles the Bald, of France, 152, 156, 180, 183
Charles VII. of France, 167
Charles VIII. of France, 167
Chilperic, King, 150
Christian, King of Sweden, 113
Chrodegang, St., 59
Chrysologus, St. Peter, 29
Chrysostom, St. John, 37, 68, 82, 84, 179, 312, 337, 345
Cibrario, Del Economia del Medio Evo, 311
Clement, St., of Rome, 85
Clement, St., of Alexandria, 53, 57, 62, 70, 72, 73, 76
Clement V., 167
Clermont, 150, 175
—— Council of, 144, 145, 236
Clothaire, 11, 149, 150, 175
Clovis II., 149, 171
Cod. Theod., 313
Compiegne, 164
Concilia Antiqua Galliæ, 145
Consilium delectorum Cardinalium, xliii.

Constance, 103
—— Council of, 239
Constantine the Great, 141, 312
—— Pogonatus, 147
Constantinople, 83, 84, 103, 142, 312
—— Council of (A.D. 381), 102
—— Patriarchate of, 142, 180
—— Synod of, 142
Contarini, Cardinal, xliii.
Corinth, Church of, 85, 305
Cornelius, St., 188
Corpus Juris Canonici., 339
Cortesi, Abbot, xliii.
Crete, 85, 134
Cyprian, St., 79, 87–89, 128, 141, 188, 307, 329

D

Dagobert, 149
Dalmatia, 83, 148
Damasus, Bishop, 36
Demetrius, Bishop, 36
Denmark, 116
Didymus, 83
Dominicy, M. Antoine, 171
Diodorus, Bishop, 82
Dionysius, St., Bishop of Alexandria, 54
Dionysius, St., Bishop of Corinth, 85
Donnus, Pope, 103
Ducange, 103, 173
Dupin, M., 137, 138

E

Eadmer, Hist. Novorum, 124, 178, 226, 241
Edward III. of England, 239
Edenulf, Bishop, 166
Eleutherius, Pope, 35
Elmoldus, Chronic Slavorum, 186
Emerius, Bishop, 150
England, 50, 113, 116, 170, 243, 281
Epiphanius, Patriarch of Constantinople, 142
Eugenius IV., Pope, 240
Euphonius, 150
Eusebius, 34, 36, 53, 69, 70, 85
Evodius, 33

Index.

F

FERREOLUS, Bishop, 150
Fismes, Council of, 157, 163
Flavian, St., Bishop of Antioch, 37
Fleury, Histoire Ecclesiastique, 58–60, 64, 67, 71, 88, 89, 96, 101, 144, 154, 215
Flodoardus, Hist. Remensis, 184
Florinus, 34
Florus, Deacon of Lyons, 187, 188
France, 50, 145, 170, 171, 277, 284, 286, 311
Francis I. of France, 245
Frank, Chancellor, 174
Frankfort, Concordat of, 240
Frederic I. of Denmark, 129
Frederic II., Emperor of Germany, 120, 238
Frederic III., Emperor of Germany, 240
Fregoso, Federigo, Bishop of Salerno, xliii.
Freeman, Norman Conquest, 120

G

GALATIA, Church of, 305
Gazzaniga, 66
Gelasius II., Pope, 235, 237, 313, 332
Gerbertus, 180, 182
Germany, 50, 113, 116, 192, 196, 209, 210, 240
Gervasius, Hist., 178
Giberti, Bishop, Giovamatteo, xliii.
Godfrey, Cardinal, 278
Gratianus, 313–315, 327, 332, 340
Gregory II., Pope, 151
Gregory VII., 192–195, 198–200, 210, 212, 213, 216, 217, 233–236, 238, 243, 275, 295
Gregory IX., 120
Gregory the Great, St., 41, 46, 97, 148, 149, 329, 332
Gregory of Tours, St., 147, 150, 175
Gregory Nazianzen, St., 71, 83, 125
Gregory Thaumaturgus, St., 74

Grenoble, 156
Guastalla, Council of, 236
Guibert, Archbishop, 216
Gustavus Vasa, 129

H

HALLAM, Middle Ages,, 119
Haussonville, D', L'Eglise Romaine et le Premier Empire, xxvii.
Heliodorus, Bishop, 82
Henry I. of England, 227, 229, 241
Henry VIII. of England, 113, 129
Henry IV. of France, 277
Henry IV., Emperor, 194–196, 198, 209, 210, 213, 214, 216–218, 275
Henry V., 219, 237, 250, 252
Heraclas, St., 54
Hilary, Bishop, 326
Hildebrand. *See* Gregory VII.
Hincmar, Archbishop, 153, 157, 158, 161, 166, 180, 182, 184, 246
Hippo, 335, 336
Horace, 312
Hormisdas, Pope, 142
Hugo Flaviniacensis, 215
Hume, Hist. of England, 233
Hussey, Rise of Papal Power, 80

I

IGNATIUS, St., 24, 33, 36, 85
Ilerda, Council of, 182
Ilduin, Bishop, 153
Ingulphus, Abbot, 191
Innocent I., Pope, 262
Innocent II., Pope, 254, 255
Innocent III., Pope, 166, 172
Innocent VIII., Pope, 256
Irenæus, St., 33, 35, 307
Isidore of Pelusium, 325
Italy, 170
Ivo, St., of Chartres, 235, 247

J

JAMES, St., 69, 84
Jerome, St., 36, 52, 74, 82, 83, 84, 313
John, St., 69, 84

Jovinus, Priest, 82
Jovinus, 150
Judas Iscariot, 122
Jude, St., 84
Julianus Pomerius, de Vita Comtemplativâ, 317, 326, 328
Julian the Apostate, 213
Julius I., Pope, 261
Julius II., Pope, 122, 256
Julius III., Pope, 168
Justinian, Emperor, 142, 147, 307
John Zymisca, Emperor, 180

L

LAMBERTUS, Scafnaburgensis, 209
Lanfranc, Archbishop, 178
Langen, Vat. Dogm., 80
Lateran Councils, the, 63, 166, 172, 238, 254, 269, 323
Laudun, 166
Laurence, St., 32
Lausanne, 238
Lenfant Concile de Constance, 119
Leo the Isaurian, 151
Leo., St., Pope, 139, 144, 261, 262
Leo II., Pope, 103
Leo IV., Pope, 184
Leo X., Pope, 122, 243, 256
Leontius, Metropolitan, 150
Lombard, Peter, 61
Lombardy, 103
Lothaire, Emperor, 152, 153, 156
Louis the Pious, 177
Louis I. of France, 152
Louis II., 156
Louis III., 156, 161, 164, 165
Louis VII., 245, 256
Louis XI., 167, 245
Louis XIV., 294
Loyola, Ignatius, 105
Lupo di Ferrara, Abbot, 294
Lyons, Council of, 63, 239
Lyons, Martyrs of, 35

M

MACAIRE, Theol. Dog. Orth., 80
Macon, Council of, 308
Magnesia, Church of, 36

Marcellus, Bishop, 150
Marculfus, 175, 176, 180
Mark, St., School of, at Alexandria, 37, 52
Marianus Scotus, 194
Martin, St., 29
Matthew, St., 69
Maurice, Emperor, 41
Maximus, St., Bishop, 82
Meaux, Council of, 183
Meletius, St., 82
Melfi, Council, 236
Mennas, Patriarch, 142
Milan, 84
Mopsuestia, 82
Muratori, 102

N

NAPOLEON I., 256, 284
Natalis, Alexander, 146, 181, 183, 187, 243
Natalis, Bishop, 148
Narbonne, 139
Nepotian, 82
Neri, St. Philip, 24
New Rome. See Constantinople.
Nice, Councils of, 143, 151, 152
Nicea, Council of, 90
Nicetius, Count, 150
Nicholas I., Pope, 152, 153
Nicholas V., Pope, 240
Nîmes, Council of, 234

O

Odo, Bishop, 157
Odoacer, Bishop, 157, 158, 163, 164
Onesimus, Bishop, 36
Origen, 36, 40, 58, 74, 135, 137, 307
Orleans, Council of, 145, 147, 182, 332
Orosius, 83
Otho I., 190, 191, 341
Otho IV., 238

P

PALESTINE, 36
Pantænus, St., 33, 53, 74

Papias, St., 69
Paris, Councils of, 147, 149, 175, 182
—— National Council of, 162
Pascal II., Pope, 219, 224-227, 229, 230, 235, 236, 241, 247, 250, 252, 253, 269, 348
Paul, St., 84, 130, 134, 173, 211, 305, 306, 325, 344
Paul III., Pope, xlii.
Paulus Benriedensis, 198
Paulinus, Bishop, 326
Peter, St., 69, 84, 122, 173, 211, 305
Peter Damian, St., 235
Peter di Castra, 254, 256
Pisa, Council of, 103
Pius VII., Pope, 284
Philip, St., 69
Philip I. of France, 191, 192
Phillimore's International Law, 299
Philo of Alexandria, 312
Phocas, Emperor, 179, 180
Plato, 62
Polo, Cardinal, xxiii.
Polybius, Bishop, 36
Polycarp, St., 33
Polyeuctes, Patriarch, 180
Procleus, Bishop, 191

R

RABANUS, 60
Ravenna, 103
Rheims, 153, 163, 164
—— Council of, 237, 269
Richard I. of England, 179
Richelieu, Cardinal, 126, 284, 295
Riez, Council of, 181
Robert, King of France, 175
Robert of Bamberg, 219
Robertson, View of State of Europe, 233
Rome, 54, 102, 143
—— Councils of, 236
Roncaglia, Constantine, 150
Rudolf I., Emperor of Germany, 238
Rudolph of Suabia, 276
Rufinus, 82
Russia, 116
Rusticus of Narbonne, 139

S

SADOLETO, Cardinal, xliii.
Salona, 148
Sardica, Council of, 112
Seleucia, 82
Socrates, 82
Sorbonne, The, 277
Soterius, St., 85
Simplician, St., 84
Sirmondus, 145
Sixtus, St., 32
Spain, 83, 243, 332
Sweden, 113, 116, 281
Symmachus, Pope, 143

T

TARSUS, 82
Tertullian, 58, 306
Theoctista, 41
Theoctistus, Bishop, 36
Theodorus, Bishop, 82
Thessalonica, 139, 144
Thionville, Synod at, 152
Thomas, St., 69
Thomas Aquinas, St., 210
Timotheus, 33
Titus, Bishop of Crete, 33, 134
Toledo, Synod of, 262
Tommassinus, Vet. and Nov. Eccl. Discip., 185, 307
Tournely, 66
Tours, Council of, 234
Trent, 84
—— Council of, 99, 199
Tribur, 209
Troyes, Council of, 236
Type, the, 102

U

UDALRIC of Costreim, 219
Urban II., Pope, 235, 236
Uzès, see of, 150

V

VALENTIA, Council of, 182
Valerian, St., 83
Valerian, St., School of, 82
Valerius, Bishop of Carthage, 37
Venice, 107

Victor III., Pope, 235, 236
Vienne, 139, 156
Vigilius, St., Bishop, 84
Vitri, Jacopo di, 67

W

WALTER, Manual of Ecclesiastical Law, 315

William I., 178
William II., 124, 178
William of Malmesbury, 171, 250
Worms, 238

Z

ZACHARY, Pope, 294

INDEX OF TEXTS.

	PAGE
Genesis iii. 5	10
Judges vi. 16	15
xx. 1, 8	15
Psalm ii. 2	121
xxvii. 9	42
lxix. 2	43
lxxiii.	43
Proverbs iii. 1	62
Isaiah viii. 1	57
liii. 14	42
lviii. 14	43
Hosea iv. 8	327
Joel ii. 12	43
St. Matthew v. 13	168
vi. 24	173
vii. 6	72
viii. 20	324
x. 14	305
15	305
16	110, 290
xvi. 18	122
xviii. 19	13
xx. 25, 26	309
xxviii. 19	7
20	15, 134
St. Luke ix. 58	324
x. 5-7	304
xxii. 19	8
25, 26	309
St. John iii. 2-6	1
x. 11	279

	PAGE
St. John xvii. 11	25, 81
22	14
Acts iii. 6	325
32	312
iv. 35	311
v. 3, 4	305
vi. 2, 3	344
4	97
xiv. 23	134
xx. 35	334
Romans vii. 12	20
1 Corinthians iv. 4, 15	304
vi. 12	88, 130, 345
ix. 4	306
11	310
xi. 24, 25	8
xvi. 2	305
2, 4	345
Ephesians iv. 4	78
5, 6	79
1 Timothy i. 8	20
iii. 1	105
v. 17, 18	304
vi. 6-8	325
2 Timothy ii. 2	54
3, 4	317
4	173
iv. 3	xliv.
Titus i. 5	134
Hebrews ix. 6-10	14

A Selection of Works
IN
THEOLOGICAL LITERATURE
PUBLISHED BY
Messrs. LONGMANS, GREEN, & CO.
39 PATERNOSTER ROW, LONDON, E.C.

Abbey and Overton.—THE ENGLISH CHURCH IN THE EIGHTEENTH CENTURY. By CHARLES J. ABBEY, M.A., Rector of Checkendon, Reading, and JOHN H. OVERTON, M.A., Rector of Epworth ; Rural Dean of Isle of Axholme. *Crown 8vo. 7s. 6d.*

Adams.—SACRED ALLEGORIES. The Shadow of the Cross—The Distant Hills—The Old Man's Home—The King's Messengers. By the Rev. WILLIAM ADAMS, M.A. *Crown 8vo. 3s. 6d.*
  The Four Allegories may be had separately, with Illustrations. *16mo. 1s. each.*

Aids to the Inner Life.
  Edited by the Rev. W. H. HUTCHINGS, M.A., Rector of Kirkby Misperton, Yorkshire. *Five Vols. 32mo, cloth limp, 6d. each; or cloth extra, 1s. each.*
  With red borders, 2s. each. Sold separately.
  OF THE IMITATION OF CHRIST. By THOMAS À KEMPIS.
  THE CHRISTIAN YEAR.
  THE DEVOUT LIFE. By ST. FRANCIS DE SALES.
  THE HIDDEN LIFE OF THE SOUL.
  THE SPIRITUAL COMBAT. By LAURENCE SCUPOLI.

Allen.—THE CHURCH CATECHISM : its History and Contents. A Manual for Teachers and Students. By the Rev. A. J. C. ALLEN, M.A., formerly Principal of the Chester Diocesan Training College. *Crown 8vo. 3s. 6d.*

Barry.—SOME LIGHTS OF SCIENCE ON THE FAITH. Being the Bampton Lectures for 1892. By the Right Rev. ALFRED BARRY, D.D., Canon of Windsor, formerly Bishop of Sydney, Metropolitan of New South Wales, and Primate of Australia. *8vo. 12s. 6d.*

A CATALOGUE OF WORKS

Bathe.—Works by the Rev. ANTHONY BATHE, M.A.

A LENT WITH JESUS. A Plain Guide for Churchmen. Containing Readings for Lent and Easter Week, and on the Holy Eucharist. 32*mo*, 1*s.*; or *in paper cover*, 6*d.*

AN ADVENT WITH JESUS. 32*mo*, 1*s.*; or *in paper cover*, 6*d.*

WHAT I SHOULD BELIEVE. A Simple Manual of Self-Instruction for Church People. *Crown 8vo.* 3*s.* 6*d.*

Bickersteth.—YESTERDAY, TO-DAY, AND FOR EVER: a Poem in Twelve Books. By EDWARD HENRY BICKERSTETH, D.D., Bishop of Exeter. *One Shilling Edition*, 18*mo.* *With red borders*, 16*mo*, 2*s.* 6*d.*

The Crown 8vo Edition (5*s.*) *may still be had.*

Blunt.—Works by the Rev. JOHN HENRY BLUNT, D.D.

THE ANNOTATED BOOK OF COMMON PRAYER: Being an Historical, Ritual, and Theological Commentary on the Devotional System of the Church of England. 4*to.* 21*s.*

THE COMPENDIOUS EDITION OF THE ANNOTATED BOOK OF COMMON PRAYER: Forming a concise Commentary on the Devotional System of the Church of England. *Crown 8vo.* 10*s.* 6*d.*

DICTIONARY OF DOCTRINAL AND HISTORICAL THEOLOGY. By various Writers. *Imperial 8vo.* 21*s.*

DICTIONARY OF SECTS, HERESIES, ECCLESIASTICAL PARTIES AND SCHOOLS OF RELIGIOUS THOUGHT. By various Writers. *Imperial 8vo.* 21*s.*

THE BOOK OF CHURCH LAW. Being an Exposition of the Legal Rights and Duties of the Parochial Clergy and the Laity of the Church of England. Revised by Sir WALTER G. F. PHILLIMORE, Bart., D.C.L. *Crown 8vo.* 7*s.* 6*d.*

A COMPANION TO THE BIBLE: Being a Plain Commentary on Scripture History, to the end of the Apostolic Age. *Two vols. small 8vo. Sold separately.*

THE OLD TESTAMENT. 3*s.* 6*d.*   THE NEW TESTAMENT. 3*s.* 6*d.*

HOUSEHOLD THEOLOGY: a Handbook of Religious Information respecting the Holy Bible, the Prayer Book, the Church, etc. etc. *Paper cover*, 16*mo.* 1*s.* Also the Larger Edition, 3*s.* 6*d.*

Body.—Works by the Rev. GEORGE BODY, D.D., Canon of Durham.

THE LIFE OF LOVE: A Course of Lent Lectures. *Crown 8vo.* 4*s.* 6*d.*

THE SCHOOL OF CALVARY; or, Laws of Christian Life revealed from the Cross. *Small 8vo.* 3*s.* 6*d.*

THE LIFE OF JUSTIFICATION. 16*mo.* 2*s.* 6*d.*

THE LIFE OF TEMPTATION. 16*mo.* 2*s.* 6*d.*

Bonney.—CHRISTIAN DOCTRINES AND MODERN THOUGHT: being the Boyle Lectures for 1891. By the Rev. T. G. BONNEY, D.Sc., Hon. Canon of Manchester. *Crown 8vo.* 5*s.*

IN THEOLOGICAL LITERATURE. 3

Boultbee.—A COMMENTARY ON THE THIRTY-NINE ARTICLES OF THE CHURCH OF ENGLAND. By the Rev. T. P. BOULTBEE, formerly Principal of the London College of Divinity, St. John's Hall, Highbury. *Crown 8vo.* 6s.

Bright.—Works by WILLIAM BRIGHT, D.D., Canon of Christ Church Oxford.

MORALITY IN DOCTRINE. *Crown 8vo.* 7s. 6d.

LESSONS FROM THE LIVES OF THREE GREAT FATHERS: St. Athanasius, St. Chrysostom, and St. Augustine. *Crown 8vo.* 6s.

THE INCARNATION AS A MOTIVE POWER. *Crown 8vo.* 6s.

Bright and Medd.—LIBER PRECUM PUBLICARUM ECCLESIÆ ANGLICANÆ. A GULIELMO BRIGHT, S.T.P., et PETRO GOLDSMITH MEDD, A.M., Latine redditus. [In hac Editione continentur Versiones Latinæ—1. Libri Precum Publicarum Ecclesiæ Anglicanæ; 2. Liturgiæ Primæ Reformatæ; 3. Liturgiæ Scoticanæ; 4. Liturgiæ Americanæ.] *Small 8vo.* 7s. 6d.

Browne.—AN EXPOSITION OF THE THIRTY-NINE ARTICLES, Historical and Doctrinal. By E. H. BROWNE, D.D., formerly Bishop of Winchester. *8vo.* 16s.

Campion and Beamont.—THE PRAYER BOOK INTERLEAVED. With Historical Illustrations and Explanatory Notes arranged parallel to the Text. By W. M. CAMPION, D.D., and W. J. BEAMONT, M.A. *Small 8vo.* 7s. 6d.

Carter.—Works edited by the Rev. T. T. CARTER, M.A., Hon. Canon of Christ Church, Oxford.

THE TREASURY OF DEVOTION: a Manual of Prayer for General and Daily Use. Compiled by a Priest. 18mo. 2s. 6d.; *cloth limp,* 2s.; *or bound with the Book of Common Prayer,* 3s. 6d. *Large-Type Edition. Crown 8vo.* 3s. 6d.

THE WAY OF LIFE: A Book of Prayers and Instruction for the Young at School, with a Preparation for Confirmation. Compiled by a Priest. 18mo. 1s. 6d.

THE PATH OF HOLINESS: a First Book of Prayers, with the Service of the Holy Communion, for the Young. Compiled by a Priest. With Illustrations. 16mo. 1s. 6d.; *cloth limp,* 1s.

THE GUIDE TO HEAVEN: a Book of Prayers for every Want. (For the Working Classes.) Compiled by a Priest. 18mo. 1s. 6d.; *cloth limp,* 1s. *Large-Type Edition. Crown 8vo.* 1s. 6d.; *cloth limp,* 1s.

[continued.

Carter.—Works edited by the Rev. T. T. CARTER, M.A., Hon. Canon of Christ Church, Oxford—*continued.*
SELF-RENUNCIATION. 16mo. 2s. 6d.
THE STAR OF CHILDHOOD: a First Book of Prayers and Instruction for Children. Compiled by a Priest. With Illustrations. 16mo. 2s. 6d.
NICHOLAS FERRAR: his Household and his Friends. With Portrait engraved after a Picture by CORNELIUS JANSSEN at Magdalene College, Cambridge, *Crown 8vo.* 6s.

Carter.—MAXIMS AND GLEANINGS FROM THE WRITINGS OF T. T. CARTER, M.A. Selected and arranged for Daily Use. *Crown 16mo.* 1s.

Chandler.—THE SPIRIT OF MAN: An Essay in Christian Philosophy. By the Rev. A. CHANDLER, M.A., Rector of Poplar, E., *Crown 8vo.* 5s.

Conybeare and Howson.—THE LIFE AND EPISTLES OF ST. PAUL. By the Rev. W. J. CONYBEARE, M.A., and the Very Rev. J. S. HOWSON, D.D. With numerous Maps and Illustrations.
LIBRARY EDITION. *Two Vols.* 8vo. 21s.
STUDENT'S EDITION. *One Vol.* Crown 8vo. 6s.
POPULAR EDITION. *One Vol.* Crown 8vo. 3s. 6d.

Copleston.—BUDDHISM—PRIMITIVE AND PRESENT IN MAGADHA AND IN CEYLON. By REGINALD STEPHEN COPLESTON, D.D., Bishop of Colombo. 8vo. 16s.

Devotional Series, 16mo, Red Borders. *Each 2s. 6d.*
BICKERSTETH'S YESTERDAY, TO-DAY, AND FOR EVER.
CHILCOT'S TREATISE ON EVIL THOUGHTS.
THE CHRISTIAN YEAR.
FRANCIS DE SALES' (ST.) THE DEVOUT LIFE.
HERBERT'S POEMS AND PROVERBS.
KEMPIS' (À) OF THE IMITATION OF CHRIST.
WILSON'S THE LORD'S SUPPER. *Large type.*
*TAYLOR'S (JEREMY) HOLY LIVING.
* ——   ——   HOLY DYING.
* *These two in one Volume.* 5s.

Devotional Series, 18mo, without Red Borders. *Each* 1s.
BICKERSTETH'S YESTERDAY, TO-DAY, AND FOR EVER.
THE CHRISTIAN YEAR.
FRANCIS DE SALES' (ST.) THE DEVOUT LIFE.
HERBERT'S POEMS AND PROVERBS.
KEMPIS' (À) OF THE IMITATION OF CHRIST.
WILSON'S THE LORD'S SUPPER. *Large type.*
*TAYLOR'S (JEREMY) HOLY LIVING.
* ——   ——   HOLY DYING.
* *These two in one Volume.* 2s. 6d.

Edersheim.—Works by ALFRED EDERSHEIM, M.A., D.D., Ph.D., sometime Grinfield Lecturer on the Septuagint Oxford.

THE LIFE AND TIMES OF JESUS THE MESSIAH. *Two Vols.* 8vo. 24s.

JESUS THE MESSIAH : being an Abridged Edition of 'The Life and Times of Jesus the Messiah.' *Crown* 8vo. 7s. 6d.

PROPHECY AND HISTORY IN RELATION TO THE MESSIAH : The Warburton Lectures, 1880-1884. 8vo. 12s.

Ellicott.—Works by C. J. ELLICOTT, D.D., Bishop of Gloucester and Bristol.

A CRITICAL AND GRAMMATICAL COMMENTARY ON ST. PAUL'S EPISTLES. Greek Text, with a Critical and Grammatical Commentary, and a Revised English Translation. 8vo.

1 CORINTHIANS. 16s.	PHILIPPIANS, COLOSSIANS, AND
GALATIANS. 8s. 6d.	PHILEMON. 10s. 6d.
EPHESIANS. 8s. 6d.	THESSALONIANS. 7s. 6d.
PASTORAL EPISTLES. 10s. 6d.	

HISTORICAL LECTURES ON THE LIFE OF OUR LORD JESUS CHRIST. 8vo. 12s.

Epochs of Church History. Edited by MANDELL CREIGHTON, D.D., LL.D., Bishop of Peterborough. *Fcap.* 8vo. 2s. 6d. each.

THE ENGLISH CHURCH IN OTHER LANDS. By the Rev. H. W. TUCKER, M.A.

THE HISTORY OF THE REFORMATION IN ENGLAND. By the Rev. GEO. G. PERRY, M.A.

THE CHURCH OF THE EARLY FATHERS. By the Rev. ALFRED PLUMMER, D.D.

THE EVANGELICAL REVIVAL IN THE EIGHTEENTH CENTURY. By the Rev. J. H. OVERTON, M.A.

THE UNIVERSITY OF OXFORD. By the Hon. G. C. BRODRICK, D.C.L.

THE UNIVERSITY OF CAMBRIDGE. By J. BASS MULLINGER, M.A.

THE ENGLISH CHURCH IN THE MIDDLE AGES. By the Rev. W. HUNT, M.A.

THE CHURCH AND THE EASTERN EMPIRE. By the Rev. H. F. TOZER, M.A.

THE CHURCH AND THE ROMAN EMPIRE. By the Rev. A. CARR.

THE CHURCH AND THE PURITANS, 1570-1660. By HENRY OFFLEY WAKEMAN, M.A.

HILDEBRAND AND HIS TIMES. By the Rev. W. R. W. STEPHENS, M.A.

THE POPES AND THE HOHENSTAUFEN. By UGO BALZANI.

THE COUNTER-REFORMATION. By ADOLPHUS WILLIAM WARD, Litt. D.

WYCLIFFE AND MOVEMENTS FOR REFORM. By REGINALD L. POOLE, M.A.

THE ARIAN CONTROVERSY. By H. M. GWATKIN, M.A.

Fosbery.—Works edited by the Rev. THOMAS VINCENT FOSBERY, M.A., sometime Vicar of St. Giles's, Reading.
VOICES OF COMFORT. *Cheap Edition. Small 8vo.* 3s. 6d.
The Larger Edition (7s. 6d.) *may still be had.*
HYMNS AND POEMS FOR THE SICK AND SUFFERING. In connection with the Service for the Visitation of the Sick. Selected from Various Authors. *Small 8vo.* 3s. 6d.

Garland.—THE PRACTICAL TEACHING OF THE APOCALYPSE. By the Rev. G. V. GARLAND, M.A. 8vo. 16s.

Gore.—Works by the Rev. CHARLES GORE, M.A., Principal of the Pusey House ; Fellow of Trinity College, Oxford.
THE MINISTRY OF THE CHRISTIAN CHURCH. 8vo. 10s. 6d.
ROMAN CATHOLIC CLAIMS. *Crown 8vo.* 3s. 6d.

Goulburn.—Works by EDWARD MEYRICK GOULBURN, D.D., D.C.L., sometime Dean of Norwich.
THOUGHTS ON PERSONAL RELIGION. *Small 8vo,* 6s. 6d. ; *Cheap Edition,* 3s. 6d. ; *Presentation Edition,* 2 *vols. small 8vo,* 10s. 6d.
THE PURSUIT OF HOLINESS : a Sequel to ' Thoughts on Personal Religion.' *Small 8vo.* 5s. *Cheap Edition,* 3s. 6d.
THE CHILD SAMUEL : a Practical and Devotional Commentary on the Birth and Childhood of the Prophet Samuel, as recorded in 1 Sam. i., ii. 1-27, iii. *Small 8vo.* 2s. 6d.
THE GOSPEL OF THE CHILDHOOD : a Practical and Devotional Commentary on the Single Incident of our Blessed Lord's Childhood (St. Luke ii. 41 to the end.) *Crown 8vo.* 2s. 6d.
THE COLLECTS OF THE DAY: an Exposition, Critical and Devotional, of the Collects appointed at the Communion. With Preliminary Essays on their Structure, Sources, etc. 2 *vols. Crown 8vo.* 8s. *each.*
THOUGHTS UPON THE LITURGICAL GOSPELS for the Sundays, one for each day in the year. With an Introduction on their Origin, History, the Modifications made in them by the Reformers and by the Revisers of the Prayer Book. 2 *vols. Crown 8vo.* 16s.
MEDITATIONS UPON THE LITURGICAL GOSPELS for the Minor Festivals of Christ, the two first Week-days of the Easter and Whitsun Festivals, and the Red-letter Saints' Days. *Crown 8vo.* 8s. 6d.
FAMILY PRAYERS compiled from various sources (chiefly from Bishop Hamilton's Manual), and arranged on the Liturgical Principle. *Crown 8vo.* 3s. 6d. *Cheap Edition.* 16mo. 1s.

Harrison.—Works by the Rev. ALEXANDER J. HARRISON, B.D., Lecturer of the Christian Evidence Society.
PROBLEMS OF CHRISTIANITY AND SCEPTICISM ; Lessons from Twenty Years' Experience in the Field of Christian Evidence. *Crown 8vo.* 7s. 6d.
THE CHURCH IN RELATION TO SCEPTICS : a Conversational Guide to Evidential Work. *Crown 8vo.* 7s. 6d.

IN THEOLOGICAL LITERATURE. 7

Holland.—Works by the Rev. HENRY SCOTT HOLLAND, M.A., Canon and Precentor of St. Paul's.

PLEAS AND CLAIMS FOR CHRIST. *Crown 8vo. 7s. 6d.*

CREED AND CHARACTER: Sermons. *Crown 8vo. 3s. 6d.*

ON BEHALF OF BELIEF. Sermons preached in St. Paul's Cathedral. *Crown 8vo. 3s. 6d.*

CHRIST OR ECCLESIASTES. Sermons preached in St. Paul's Cathedral. *Crown 8vo. 3s. 6d.*

LOGIC AND LIFE, with other Sermons. *Crown 8vo. 3s. 6d.*

Hopkins.—CHRIST THE CONSOLER. A Book of Comfort for the Sick. By ELLICE HOPKINS. *Small 8vo. 2s. 6d.*

Howard.—THE SCHISM BETWEEN THE ORIENTAL AND WESTERN CHURCHES. With special reference to the addition of the *Filioque* to the Creed. By the Rev. G. B. HOWARD, B.A., sometime Scholar of St. John's College, Cambridge. *Crown 8vo. 3s. 6d.*

Ingram.—HAPPINESS IN THE SPIRITUAL LIFE; or, 'The Secret of the Lord.' A Series of Practical Considerations. By W. CLAVELL INGRAM, D.D., Dean of Peterborough. *Crown 8vo. 7s. 6d.*

INHERITANCE OF THE SAINTS; or, Thoughts on the Communion of Saints and the Life of the World to come. Collected chiefly from English Writers by L. P. With a Preface by the Rev. HENRY SCOTT HOLLAND, M.A. *Crown 8vo. 7s. 6d.*

Jameson.—Works by Mrs. JAMESON.

SACRED AND LEGENDARY ART, containing Legends of the Angels and Archangels, the Evangelists, the Apostles. With 19 etchings and 187 Woodcuts. *Two Vols. Cloth, gilt top, 20s. net.*

LEGENDS OF THE MONASTIC ORDERS, as represented in the Fine Arts. With 11 etchings and 88 Woodcuts. *One Vol. Cloth, gilt top, 10s. net.*

LEGENDS OF THE MADONNA, OR BLESSED VIRGIN MARY. With 27 Etchings and 165 Woodcuts. *One Vol. Cloth, gilt top, 10s. net.*

THE HISTORY OF OUR LORD, as exemplified in Works of Art, Commenced by the late Mrs. JAMESON; continued and completed by LADY EASTLAKE. With 31 Etchings and 281 Woodcuts. *Two Vols. 8vo. 20s. net.*

Jennings.—ECCLESIA ANGLICANA. A History of the Church of Christ in England from the Earliest to the Present Times. By the Rev. ARTHUR CHARLES JENNINGS, M.A. *Crown 8vo. 7s. 6d.*

Jukes.—Works by ANDREW JUKES.
THE NEW MAN AND THE ETERNAL LIFE. Notes on the Reiterated Amens of the Son of God. *Crown 8vo.* 6s.
THE NAMES OF GOD IN HOLY SCRIPTURE: a Revelation of His Nature and Relationships. *Crown 8vo.* 4s. 6d.
THE TYPES OF GENESIS. *Crown 8vo.* 7s. 6d.
THE SECOND DEATH AND THE RESTITUTION OF ALL THINGS. *Crown 8vo.* 3s. 6d.
THE MYSTERY OF THE KINGDOM. *Crown 8vo.* 2s. 6d.

Keble.—MAXIMS AND GLEANINGS FROM THE WRITINGS OF JOHN KEBLE, M.A. Selected and Arranged for Daily Use. By C. M. S. *Crown 16mo.* 1s.
SELECTIONS FROM THE WRITINGS OF JOHN KEBLE, M.A. *Crown 8vo.* 3s. 6d.

King.—DR. LIDDON'S TOUR IN EGYPT AND PALESTINE IN 1886. Being Letters descriptive of the Tour, written by his Sister, Mrs. KING. *Crown 8vo.* 5s.

Knowling.—THE WITNESS OF THE EPISTLES: a Study in Modern Criticism. By the Rev. R. J. KNOWLING, M.A., Vice-Principal of King's College, London. *8vo.* 15s.

Knox Little.—Works by W. J. KNOX LITTLE, M.A., Canon Residentiary of Worcester, and Vicar of Hoar Cross.
SKETCHES IN SUNSHINE AND STORM: a Collection of Miscellaneous Essays and Notes of Travel. *Crown 8vo.* 7s. 6d.
THE CHRISTIAN HOME. *Crown 8vo.* 6s. 6d.
THE HOPES AND DECISIONS OF THE PASSION OF OUR MOST HOLY REDEEMER. *Crown 8vo.* 3s. 6d.
CHARACTERISTICS AND MOTIVES OF THE CHRISTIAN LIFE. Ten Sermons preached in Manchester Cathedral, in Lent and Advent. *Crown 8vo.* 3s. 6d.
SERMONS PREACHED FOR THE MOST PART IN MANCHESTER. *Crown 8vo.* 3s. 6d.
THE MYSTERY OF THE PASSION OF OUR MOST HOLY REDEEMER. *Crown 8vo.* 3s. 6d.
THE WITNESS OF THE PASSION OF OUR MOST HOLY REDEEMER. *Crown 8vo.* 3s. 6d.
THE LIGHT OF LIFE. Sermons preached on Various Occasions. *Crown 8vo.* 3s. 6d.
SUNLIGHT AND SHADOW IN THE CHRISTIAN LIFE. Sermons preached for the most part in America. *Crown 8vo.* 3s. 6d.

IN THEOLOGICAL LITERATURE. 9

Lear.—Works by, and Edited by, H. L. SIDNEY LEAR.

FOR DAYS AND YEARS. A Book containing a Text, Short Reading, and Hymn for Every Day in the Church's Year. 16mo. 2s. 6d. *Also a Cheap Edition*, 32mo. 1s.; *or cloth gilt*, 1s. 6d.

FIVE MINUTES. Daily Readings of Poetry. 16mo. 3s. 6d. *Also a Cheap Edition*. 32mo. 1s.; *or cloth gilt*, 1s. 6d.

WEARINESS. A Book for the Languid and Lonely. *Large Type. Small 8vo.* 5s.

THE LIGHT OF THE CONSCIENCE. 16mo. 2s. 6d. 32mo. 1s.; *cloth limp*, 6d.

CHRISTIAN BIOGRAPHIES. *Nine Vols. Crown 8vo.* 3s. 6d. *each*.

MADAME LOUISE DE FRANCE, Daughter of Louis XV., known also as the Mother Térèse de St. Augustin.

A DOMINICAN ARTIST: a Sketch of the Life of the Rev. Père Besson, of the Order of St. Dominic.

HENRI PERREYVE. By A. GRATRY.

ST. FRANCIS DE SALES, Bishop and Prince of Geneva.

THE REVIVAL OF PRIESTLY LIFE IN THE SEVENTEENTH CENTURY IN FRANCE.

A CHRISTIAN PAINTER OF THE NINETEENTH CENTURY.

BOSSUET AND HIS CONTEMPORARIES.

FÉNELON, ARCHBISHOP OF CAMBRAI.

HENRI DOMINIQUE LACORDAIRE.

DEVOTIONAL WORKS. Edited by H. L. SIDNEY LEAR. *New and Uniform Editions. Nine Vols.* 16mo. 2s. 6d. *each*.

FÉNELON'S SPIRITUAL LETTERS TO MEN.

FÉNELON'S SPIRITUAL LETTERS TO WOMEN.

A SELECTION FROM THE SPIRITUAL LETTERS OF ST. FRANCIS DE SALES.

THE SPIRIT OF ST. FRANCIS DE SALES.

THE HIDDEN LIFE OF THE SOUL.

THE LIGHT OF THE CONSCIENCE.

SELF-RENUNCIATION. From the French.

ST. FRANCES DE SALES' OF THE LOVE OF GOD.

SELECTIONS FROM PASCAL'S THOUGHTS.

Library of Spiritual Works for English Catholics. *Original Edition. With Red Borders. Small 8vo.* 5s. *each. New and Cheaper Editions.* 16mo. 2s. 6d. *each.*

OF THE IMITATION OF CHRIST.

THE SPIRITUAL COMBAT. By LAURENCE SCUPOLI.

THE DEVOUT LIFE. By ST. FRANCIS DE SALES.

OF THE LOVE OF GOD. By ST. FRANCIS DE SALES.

THE CONFESSIONS OF ST. AUGUSTINE. *In Ten Books.*

THE CHRISTIAN YEAR. 5s. *Edition only.*

A CATALOGUE OF WORKS

Liddon.—Works by HENRY PARRY LIDDON, D.D., D.C.L., LL.D., late Canon Residentiary and Chancellor of St. Paul's.

ESSAYS AND ADDRESSES: Lectures on Buddhism—Lectures on the Life of St. Paul—Papers on Dante. *Crown 8vo.* 5s.

THE EPISTLE TO THE ROMANS. 8vo. [*In the press.*

SERMONS ON OLD TESTAMENT SUBJECTS. *Crown 8vo.* 5s.

SERMONS ON SOME WORDS OF CHRIST. *Crown 8vo.* 5s.

THE DIVINITY OF OUR LORD AND SAVIOUR JESUS CHRIST. Being the Bampton Lectures for 1866. *Crown 8vo.* 5s.

ADVENT IN ST. PAUL'S. Sermons bearing chiefly on the Two Comings of our Lord. *Two Vols. Crown 8vo. 3s. 6d. each. Cheap Edition in one Volume. Crown 8vo.* 5s.

CHRISTMASTIDE IN ST. PAUL'S. Sermons bearing chiefly on the Birth of our Lord and the End of the Year. *Crown 8vo.* 5s.

PASSIONTIDE SERMONS. *Crown 8vo.* 5s.

EASTER IN ST. PAUL'S. Sermons bearing chiefly on the Resurrection of our Lord. *Two Vols. Crown 8vo. 3s. 6d. each. Cheap Edition in one Volume. Crown 8vo.* 5s.

SERMONS PREACHED BEFORE THE UNIVERSITY OF OXFORD. *Two Vols. Crown 8vo. 3s. 6d. each. Cheap Edition in one Volume. Crown 8vo.* 5s.

THE MAGNIFICAT. Sermons in St. Paul's. *Crown 8vo.* 2s. 6d.

SOME ELEMENTS OF RELIGION. Lent Lectures. *Small 8vo.* 2s. 6d.; *or in paper cover,* 1s. 6d.
The Crown 8vo Edition (5s.) may still be had.

SELECTIONS FROM THE WRITINGS OF H. P. LIDDON, D.D. *Crown 8vo.* 3s. 6d.

MAXIMS AND GLEANINGS FROM THE WRITINGS OF H. P. LIDDON, D.D. Selected and arranged by C. M. S. *Crown 16mo.* 1s.

DR. LIDDON'S TOUR IN EGYPT AND PALESTINE IN 1886. Being Letters descriptive of the Tour, written by his Sister, Mrs. KING. *Crown 8vo.* 5s.

Luckock.—Works by HERBERT MORTIMER LUCKOCK, D.D., Dean of Lichfield.

AFTER DEATH. An Examination of the Testimony of Primitive Times respecting the State of the Faithful Dead, and their Relationship to the Living. *Crown 8vo.* 6s.

[*continued.*

Luckock.—Works by HERBERT MORTIMER LUCKOCK, D.D., Dean of Lichfield—*continued.*

THE INTERMEDIATE STATE BETWEEN DEATH AND JUDGMENT. Being a Sequel to *After Death. Crown 8vo. 6s.*

FOOTPRINTS OF THE SON OF MAN, as traced by St. Mark. Being Eighty Portions for Private Study, Family Reading, and Instructions in Church. *Two Vols. Crown 8vo. 12s. Cheap Edition in one Vol. Crown 8vo. 5s.*

THE DIVINE LITURGY. Being the Order for Holy Communion, Historically, Doctrinally, and Devotionally set forth, in Fifty Portions. *Crown 8vo. 6s.*

STUDIES IN THE HISTORY OF THE BOOK OF COMMON PRAYER. The Anglican Reform—The Puritan Innovations—The Elizabethan Reaction—The Caroline Settlement. With Appendices. *Crown 8vo. 6s.*

THE BISHOPS IN THE TOWER. A Record of Stirring Events affecting the Church and Nonconformists from the Restoration to the Revolution. *Crown 8vo. 6s.*

LYRA GERMANICA. Hymns translated from the German by CATHERINE WINKWORTH. *Small 8vo. 5s.*

MacColl.—CHRISTIANITY IN RELATION TO SCIENCE AND MORALS. By the Rev. MALCOLM MACCOLL, M.A., Canon Residentiary of Ripon. *Crown 8vo. 6s.*

Mason.—Works by A. J. MASON, D.D., Canon of Truro, formerly Fellow of Trinity College, Cambridge.

THE FAITH OF THE GOSPEL. A Manual of Christian Doctrine. *Crown 8vo. 3s. 6d. Also a Large-Paper Edition for Marginal Notes. 4to. 12s. 6d.*

THE RELATION OF CONFIRMATION TO BAPTISM. As taught in Holy Scripture and the Fathers. *Crown 8vo. 7s. 6d.*

Mercier.—OUR MOTHER CHURCH: Being Simple Talk on High Topics. By Mrs. JEROME MERCIER. *Small 8vo. 3s. 6d.*

Molesworth.—STORIES OF THE SAINTS FOR CHILDREN: The Black Letter Saints. By Mrs. MOLESWORTH, Author of 'The Palace in the Garden,' etc. etc. With Illustrations. *Royal 16mo. 5s.*

Mozley.—Works by J. B. MOZLEY, D.D., late Canon of Christ Church, and Regius Professor of Divinity at Oxford.

ESSAYS, HISTORICAL AND THEOLOGICAL. *Two Vols.* 8*vo.* 24*s.*

EIGHT LECTURES ON MIRACLES. Being the Bampton Lectures for 1865. *Crown* 8*vo.* 7*s.* 6*d.*

RULING IDEAS IN EARLY AGES AND THEIR RELATION TO OLD TESTAMENT FAITH. Lectures delivered to Graduates of the University of Oxford. 8*vo.* 10*s.* 6*d.*

SERMONS PREACHED BEFORE THE UNIVERSITY OF OXFORD, and on Various Occasions. *Crown* 8*vo.* 7*s.* 6*d.*

SERMONS, PAROCHIAL AND OCCASIONAL. *Crown* 8*vo.* 7*s.* 6*d.*

Mozley.—Works by the Rev. T. MOZLEY, M.A., Author of 'Reminiscences of Oriel College and the Oxford Movement.'

THE CREED OR A PHILOSOPHY. *Crown* 8*vo.* 7*s.* 6*d.*

THE WORD. *Crown* 8*vo.* 7*s.* 6*d.*

THE SON. *Crown* 8*vo.* 7*s.* 6*d.*

LETTERS FROM ROME ON THE OCCASION OF THE ŒCUMENICAL COUNCIL 1869-1870. *Two Vols.* Cr. 8*vo.* 18*s.*

Newbolt.—Works by the Rev. W. C. E. NEWBOLT, M.A., Canon and Chancellor of St. Paul's.

THE FRUIT OF THE SPIRIT. Being Ten Addresses bearing on the Spiritual Life. *Crown* 8*vo.* 2*s.* 6*d.*

THE MAN OF GOD. Being Six Addresses delivered during Lent at the Primary Ordination of the Right Rev. the Lord Alwyne Compton, D.D., Bishop of Ely. *Small* 8*vo.* 1*s.* 6*d.*

THE PRAYER BOOK : Its Voice and Teaching. Being Spiritual Addresses bearing on the Book of Common Prayer. *Crown* 8*vo.* 2*s.* 6*d.*

Newnham.—THE ALL-FATHER : Sermons preached in a Village Church. By the Rev. H. P. NEWNHAM. With Preface by EDNA LYALL. *Crown* 8*vo.* 4*s.* 6*d.*

Newnham.—ALRESFORD ESSAYS FOR THE TIMES. By Rev. W. O. NEWNHAM, M.A., sometime Rector of Alresford. CONTENTS :—Bible Story of Creation—Bible Story of Eden—Bible Story of the Deluge—After Death—Miracles : A Conversation—Eternal Punishment—The Resurrection of the Body. *Crown* 8*vo.* 6*s.*

IN THEOLOGICAL LITERATURE. 13

Newman.—Works by JOHN HENRY NEWMAN, B.D., sometime Vicar of St. Mary's, Oxford.

PAROCHIAL AND PLAIN SERMONS. *Eight Vols. Cabinet Edition. Crown 8vo. 5s. each. Popular Edition. 3s. 6d. each.*

SELECTION, ADAPTED TO THE SEASONS OF THE ECCLESIASTICAL YEAR, from the 'Parochial and Plain Sermons.' *Cabinet Edition. Crown 8vo. 5s. Popular Edition. 3s. 6d.*

FIFTEEN SERMONS PREACHED BEFORE THE UNIVERSITY OF OXFORD. *Cabinet Edition. Crown 8vo. 5s. Popular Edition. 3s. 6d.*

SERMONS BEARING UPON SUBJECTS OF THE DAY. *Cabinet Edition. Crown 8vo. 5s. Popular Edition. Crown 8vo. 3s. 6d.*

LECTURES ON THE DOCTRINE OF JUSTIFICATION. *Cabinet Edition. Crown 8vo. 5s. Popular Edition. 3s. 6d.*

⁎⁎ *For other Works by Cardinal Newman, see Messrs. Longmans & Co.'s Catalogue of Works in General Literature.*

Osborne.—Works by EDWARD OSBORNE, Mission Priest of the Society of St. John the Evangelist, Cowley, Oxford.

THE CHILDREN'S SAVIOUR. Instructions to Children on the Life of our Lord and Saviour Jesus Christ. *Illustrated. 16mo. 2s. 6d.*

THE SAVIOUR-KING. Instructions to Children on Old Testament Types and Illustrations of the Life of Christ. *Illustrated. 16mo. 2s. 6d.*

THE CHILDREN'S FAITH. Instructions to Children on the Apostles' Creed. *Illustrated. 16mo. 2s. 6d.*

Oxenden.—Works by the Right Rev. ASHTON OXENDEN, formerly Bishop of Montreal.

PLAIN SERMONS. *Crown 8vo.*

THE HISTORY OF MY LIFE : An Autobiography. *Crown 8vo. 5s.*

PEACE AND ITS HINDRANCES. *Crown 8vo. 1s. ; sewed, 2s., cloth.*

THE PATHWAY OF SAFETY ; or, Counsel to the Awakened. *Fcap. 8vo, large type. 2s. 6d. Cheap Edition. Small type, limp. 1s.*

THE EARNEST COMMUNICANT. *New Red Rubric Edition. 32mo, cloth. 2s. Common Edition. 32mo. 1s.*

OUR CHURCH AND HER SERVICES. *Fcap. 8vo. 2s. 6d.*

[continued

Oxenden.—Works by the Right Rev. ASHTON OXENDEN, formerly Bishop of Montreal—*continued.*
FAMILY PRAYERS FOR FOUR WEEKS. First Series. *Fcap.* 8*vo.* 2*s.* 6*d.* Second Series. *Fcap.* 8*vo.* 2*s.* 6*d.*
  LARGE TYPE EDITION. Two Series in one Volume. *Crown* 8*vo.* 6*s.*
COTTAGE SERMONS; or, Plain Words to the Poor. *Fcap.* 8*vo.* 2*s.* 6*d.*
THOUGHTS FOR HOLY WEEK. 16*mo, cloth.* 1*s.* 6*d.*
DECISION. 18*mo.* 1*s.* 6*d.*
THE HOME BEYOND; or, A Happy Old Age. *Fcap.* 8*vo.* 1*s.* 6*d.*
THE LABOURING MAN'S BOOK. 18*mo, large type, cloth.* 1*s.* 6*d.*

Paget.—Works by FRANCIS PAGET, D.D., Dean of Christ Church, Oxford.
THE SPIRIT OF DISCIPLINE: Sermons. *Crown* 8*vo.* 6*s.* 6*d.*
FACULTIES AND DIFFICULTIES FOR BELIEF AND DISBELIEF. *Crown* 8*vo.* 6*s.* 6*d.*
THE HALLOWING OF WORK. Addresses given at Eton, January 16-18, 1888. *Small* 8*vo.* 2*s.*

PRACTICAL REFLECTIONS. By a CLERGYMAN. With Prefaces by H. P. LIDDON, D.D., D.C.L., and the Bishop of Lincoln. *Crown* 8*vo.*

THE HOLY GOSPELS. 4*s.* 6*d.*	THE PSALMS. 5*s.*
ACTS TO REVELATION. 6*s.*	THE BOOK OF GENESIS. 4*s.* 6*d.*

PRIEST (THE) TO THE ALTAR; or, Aids to the Devout Celebration of Holy Communion, chiefly after the Ancient English Use of Sarum. *Royal* 8*vo.* 12*s.*

Pusey.—Works by the Rev. E. B. PUSEY, D.D.
PRIVATE PRAYERS. With Preface by H. P. LIDDON, D.D. 32*mo.* 1*s.*
PRAYERS FOR A YOUNG SCHOOLBOY. With a Preface by H. P. LIDDON, D.D. 24*mo.* 1*s.*
SELECTIONS FROM THE WRITINGS OF EDWARD BOUVERIE PUSEY, D.D. *Crown* 8*vo.* 3*s.* 6*d.*
MAXIMS AND GLEANINGS FROM THE WRITINGS OF EDWARD BOUVERIE PUSEY, D.D. Selected and Arranged for Daily Use. By C. M. S. *Crown* 16*mo.* 1*s.*

Reynolds.—THE NATURAL HISTORY OF IMMORTALITY. By the Rev. J. W. REYNOLDS, M.A., Prebendary of St. Paul's. *Crown* 8*vo.* 7*s.* 6*d.*

IN THEOLOGICAL LITERATURE. 15

Sanday.—THE ORACLES OF GOD : Nine Lectures on the Nature and Extent of Biblical Inspiration and the Special Significance of the Old Testament Scriptures at the Present Time. By W. SANDAY, M.A., D.D., LL.D., Dean Ireland's Professor of Exegesis and Fellow of Exeter College. *Crown 8vo. 4s.*

Seebohm.—THE OXFORD REFORMERS—JOHN COLET, ERASMUS, AND THOMAS MORE : A History of their Fellow-Work. By FREDERIC SEEBOHM. *8vo. 14s.*

Stanton.—THE PLACE OF AUTHORITY IN MATTERS OF RELIGIOUS BELIEF. By VINCENT HENRY STANTON, D.D., Fellow of Trinity Coll., Ely Prof. of Divinity, Cambridge. *Cr. 8vo. 6s.*

Stephen.—ESSAYS IN ECCLESIASTICAL BIOGRAPHY. By the Right Hon. Sir J. STEPHEN. *Crown 8vo. 7s. 6d.*

Swayne.—THE BLESSED DEAD IN PARADISE. Four All Saints' Day Sermons, preached in Salisbury Cathedral. By R. G. SWAYNE, M.A. *Crown 8vo. 3s. 6d.*

Tweddell.—THE SOUL IN CONFLICT. A Practical Examination of some Difficulties and Duties of the Spiritual Life. By MARSHALL TWEDDELL, M.A., Vicar of St. Saviour, Paddington. *Crown 8vo. 6s.*

Twells.—COLLOQUIES ON PREACHING. By HENRY TWELLS, M.A., Honorary Canon of Peterborough. *Crown 8vo. 2s. 6d.*

Welldon. — THE FUTURE AND THE PAST. Sermons preached to Harrow Boys. By the Rev. J. E. C. WELLDON, M.A., Head Master of Harrow School. *Crown 8vo. 7s. 6d.*

Williams.—Works by the Rev. ISAAC WILLIAMS, B.D.

A DEVOTIONAL COMMENTARY ON THE GOSPEL NARRATIVE. *Eight Vols. Crown 8vo. 5s. each. Sold separately.*

THOUGHTS ON THE STUDY OF THE HOLY GOSPELS.
A HARMONY OF THE FOUR GOSPELS.
OUR LORD'S NATIVITY.
OUR LORD'S MINISTRY (Second Year).
OUR LORD'S MINISTRY (Third Year).
THE HOLY WEEK.
OUR LORD'S PASSION.
OUR LORD'S RESURRECTION.

FEMALE CHARACTERS OF HOLY SCRIPTURE. A Series of Sermons. *Crown 8vo. 5s.*

THE CHARACTERS OF THE OLD TESTAMENT. *Crown 8vo. 5s.*

THE APOCALYPSE. With Notes and Reflections. *Crown 8vo. 5s.*

SERMONS ON THE EPISTLES AND GOSPELS FOR THE SUNDAYS AND HOLY DAYS. *Two Vols. Crown 8vo. 5s. each.*

[continued.

16 A CATALOGUE OF WORKS

Williams.—Works by the Rev. ISAAC WILLIAMS, B.D.—*continued*.
PLAIN SERMONS ON CATECHISM. *Two Vols. Cr. 8vo. 5s. each.*
SELECTIONS FROM ISAAC WILLIAMS' WRITINGS. *Cr. 8vo. 3s. 6d.*
THE AUTOBIOGRAPHY OF ISAAC WILLIAMS, B.D., Author of several of the 'Tracts for the Times.' Edited by the Venerable Sir GEORGE PREVOST, as throwing further light on the history of the Oxford Movement. *Crown 8vo. 5s.*

Woodford.—Works by J. R. WOODFORD, D.D., Bishop of Ely.
THE GREAT COMMISSION. Addresses on the Ordinal. Edited, with an Introduction, by H. M. LUCKOCK, D.D. *Crown 8vo. 5s.*
SERMONS ON OLD AND NEW TESTAMENT SUBJECTS. Edited by H. M. LUCKOCK, D.D. *Two Vols. Crown 8vo. 5s. each.*

Woodruff.—THE CHILDREN'S YEAR. Verses for the Sundays and Holy Days throughout the Year. By C. H. WOODRUFF, B.C.L. With an Introduction by the Lord Bishop of SOUTHWELL. *Fcap. 8vo. 3s. 6d.*

Wordsworth.
For List of Works by the late Christopher Wordsworth, D.D., Bishop of Lincoln, see Messrs. Longmans & Co.'s Catalogue of Theological Works, 32 pp. Sent post free on application.

Wordsworth.—Works by ELIZABETH WORDSWORTH, Principal of Lady Margaret Hall, Oxford.
ILLUSTRATIONS OF THE CREED. *Crown 8vo. 5s.*
THE DECALOGUE. *Crown 8vo. 4s. 6d.*
ST. CHRISTOPHER AND OTHER POEMS. *Crown 8vo. 6s.*

Wordsworth.—Works by CHARLES WORDSWORTH, D.D., D.C.L., Lord Bishop of St. Andrews, and Fellow of Winchester College.
ANNALS OF MY EARLY LIFE, 1806-1846. *8vo. 15s.*
PRIMARY WITNESS TO THE TRUTH OF THE GOSPEL, to which is added a Charge on Modern Teaching on the Canon of the Old Testament. *Crown 8vo. 7s. 6d.*

Younghusband.—Works by FRANCES YOUNGHUSBAND.
THE STORY OF OUR LORD, told in Simple Language for Children. With 25 Illustrations from Pictures by the Old Masters, *Crown 8vo. 2s. 6d.*
THE STORY OF GENESIS, told in Simple Language for Children. *Crown 8vo. 2s. 6d.*
THE STORY OF THE EXODUS, told in Simple Language for Children. With Map and 29 Illustrations. *Crown 8vo. 2s. 6d.*

Printed by T. and A. CONSTABLE, Printers to Her Majesty,
at the Edinburgh University Press.

10,000/3/93.

www.ingramcontent.com/pod-product-compliance
Lightning Source LLC
Chambersburg PA
CBHW020739020526
44115CB00030B/595